DIAGNOSING LEARNING DISABILITIES

WILMA JO BUSH
West Texas State University

KENNETH W. WAUGH
West Texas State University

DIAGNOSING LEARNING DISABILITIES

Second Edition

CHARLES E. MERRILL PUBLISHING COMPANY
Columbus, Ohio   *A Bell & Howell Company*

THE SLOW LEARNER SERIES
Newell C. Kephart, Founding Editor

Published by
Charles E. Merrill Publishing Company
A Bell & Howell Company
Columbus, Ohio 43216

This book was set in Times Roman.
The production editor was Joanne Morelli Harris.
The cover was designed by Will Chenoweth.

International Standard Book Number: 0-675-08612-4

Library of Congress Catalog Card Number: 73-36030

2 3 4 5 6 7 8 9 10 — 80 79 78 77 76

Printed in the United States of America

Preface

All educators share a common problem: how to make teacher-learner efforts most productive. When students have learning disabilities, the challenge of effective instruction becomes critical. Procedures adequate for the normal student may prove inadequate for the handicapped student. If teacher-learner productivity is to be enhanced, a diagnosis must provide cues for appropriate instruction and remediation. Differential diagnosis with appropriate prescriptive teaching is the key to unlocking a reservoir of intellectual ability.

Diagnosing Learning Disabilities is written for people, whatever their professional orientation, who want to help youngsters with learning problems. Further, it is written for those who see the improved teaching-learning environment as an important vehicle to aiding the emotionally disturbed. Knowledge and understanding of learning disorders is vital to school counselors, psychologists, supervisors, principals, and various special service personnel if the school is to carry out its primary function: helping people achieve to the maximum of their ability, congruent with good mental health.

Formulating new ways of looking at relevant data and of relating it to appropriate teaching methods is the basis for improving the instructional program and for reducing the emotional problems of the child with learning and behavioral handicaps. This book in its initial publication and in its revision is directed at facilitating the consultant's work in bringing about behavior changes in such children. It has been designed to

(1) Help identify the major learning disorders in terms of behaviors
(2) Show how to use data in making a diagnosis for remediation
(3) Improve communication between consultant and teacher regarding the student's learning and emotional difficulties
(4) Make use of case studies to show how to translate diagnostic information into effective components of the teaching-learning process

The case studies, grouped according to grade levels, identify various types and combinations of types of learning handicaps. This identification helps consultants select valuable data for making an educational diagnosis and provides a check on their own interpretation of the data. The teacher should consider each of these studies carefully in order to gain insight into the various possibilities of instruction and remediation leading to prescriptive teaching and to a more appropriate learning environment.

Graduate and undergraduate classes in education and psychology will find this text a handy source in the study of behavior, learning disorders, teaching, and psychometrics. For the consultant, *Diagnosing Learning Disabilities* will prove to be neither theoretical nor abstract. But it will serve as a working tool for making more meaningful evaluations that may contribute to the improvement of learning and the reduction of anxiety and frustration.

We salute all those consultants striving to produce appropriate evaluations of the educationally handicapped student and to communicate these evaluations to the teacher. We also salute those teachers who have worked so diligently and patiently with learning-disabled children and have made special efforts to understand them and their problems. We hope the information contained herein will be of value to both teachers and consultants as they work to better the lives of these children.

WILMA JO BUSH

KENNETH W. WAUGH

Acknowledgements

In the past decade there has been a surge of requests from teachers, parents, and students to provide the kind of diagnosis that would aid in prescribing appropriate techniques for remediation of academic problems. As the demands grew, it became evident that there was a need to train personnel in this service. Our first attempt to do so occurred when we enrolled Bill Auvenshine, Joseph Teeters, and Joy Wieland in a course at West Texas State University. It was they who demonstrated the practicability of the experimental program that motivated us to begin the preparation of the first manuscript. We wish to again acknowledge the support and help of other counseling students who offered their encouragement. They are Daniel Collins, Margaret Davis, Cassandra Deavers, Alyce McClain, Ural Stone, Tyne Sturdevant, Elizabeth Wilson, William Burcham, Charles Detten, Pat Groom, Jean Harris, Lorian Hart, Nathan Lockmiller, Barbara Meador, Saundra Meek, Harriet Nichols, George Rhodes, Mary Smith, and Mary Young. We thank Daniel Collins for his initial work on the Stanford Binet graphs and Gerald Garst for his work on the Stanford Binet Analysis sheet.

We are indebted to Marjorie Rives and again to Gerald Garst for their adaptations of tally sheets to be used with the Meeker (1969) Structure of Intellect Codes for the Stanford Binet, WISC, ITPA, Slosson, and the Detroit Test of Learning Aptitudes. We thank Joy Porterfield for her evaluation of the approach used in the first edition and for her suggestions that make the second edition a more useful publication; and we thank Charles Turner for his valuable information and consultation on criterion referenced testing. We thank Mr. Don Partridge and Dr. Jim George of the Texas Education Agency for making available the research data and publication of Project Child and for their willingness to permit the reproduction of screening instruments developed in the project. We also thank Mrs. Patsy Acker from the Texas Education Agency for securing data from the other various state agencies in the nation.

Avaril Wedemeyer provided challenges, expert critique and motivation professionally, and loving, delightful relationships socially — so to her we say thanks. We also are indebted to her for her organization of the S.O.I., which is included in the Appendix. We thank our colleagues, who were most helpful and thoughtful during the preparation of the first manuscript, and we are also most appreciative of our president, Dr. Lloyd I. Watkins, for his leadership and encouragement. To Marilyn Ray, Gloria Thomas, Gloria Clyburn, Beverly Koenig, Sharon Owen, Kay Cochran and Betty Vaughn, who provided clerical help; to Dwight W. Huber, who read the manuscript in its initial stages; to Bob Haimes for his assistance in referencing and organization of the manuscript; and to Deborah Clark, Deborah Grantham and Stephanie Kordas for checking the revised manuscript, we share a debt of gratitude. Then to Jeanie, Mike, Celinda, Patti and Sam and to Guy and Jo Betsy our most special thanks for their patience and moral support.

Contents

Case Studies

Introduction

The role of the school consultant is expanding at a fastmoving pace in our changing world.* New demands are being made, and often school consultants are confronted with new ideas and terminology not included in their preparatory course work. They must also deal with parents and teachers who expect not only diagnosis but also remediation. Because of these trends this book will be useful to those who do not have time to go back to school and also to those participating in college training programs.

In most college programs in the past the student was trained to identify and understand such categorical terms as cerebral palsy, emotional disturbance, mental subnormality, or juvenile delinquency. The new emphasis appears to be an educational attempt to view the child through another perspective (category) — *learning disability.* It is inadequate today to report to a teacher, a parent, or a principal that a child has an emotional problem or a certain level of intellectual development. That this diagnosis is gross has already been recognized by most educated laypeople and professional people. Therefore, in order for consultants to fulfill their role in the light of the new emphasis, they must arm themselves with a new understanding of learning disorders. This will enhance

---

*The consultant referred to in this handbook is *any person* responsible for help in the diagnosis and remedial planning of academic problems of students enrolled in school. This could be the psychologist, the counselor, the principal, the supervisor, or any other person so qualified.

total knowledge and afford skills that will accentuate a sense of self-actualization or self-fulfillment — that feeling of having contributed something worthwhile to the child and to the school. Demands from confused or unhappy parents and teachers seem to suggest that consultants can attain this self-actualization if they are able not only to diagnose beyond gross measures but also to recommend some remediation techniques for specific problem areas. Fortunately there have been new tests devised to help in this diagnosis, and there are many remediation techniques beyond the experimental stage that can be recommended in most cases.

This handbook is designed to introduce the reader to the following: (1) a variety of behaviors typical of the deficiencies found in children with learning problems; (2) informal and clinical tests and diagnostic procedures; (3) legal and ethical aspects of reporting; (4) task analysis; (5) criteria-referenced tests; and (6) possible means of remediation. The purpose is to identify classifications and terminology of the learning process, to offer a means of interpreting test data as it relates to the learning process, and to provide sources for the collection of data and remediation materials.

It is assumed that readers will have a sincere interest in the specifics of learning disabilities and that they will be realistic enough not to assume that every case attempted will terminate in a cure. It is hoped that they will be imbued with the philosophy that each discovery will enable them to go even further in achieving their goals. Considering the existing problem, the test battery used, the rapport established with the teacher, and the ability to make a differential diagnosis, it is expected that readers will be provided with the tools and motivation to effect a workable solution. In conclusion, it is hoped that consultants will have a ready adviser in this text — one that will help to answer questions pertinent to their present problems.

chapter 1

Identification and Classification

After you have studied this chapter, you should be able to

1. Understand the term *learning disability.*
2. Identify common terms used to designate the problems of learning disability.
3. Identify authorities and their emphasis in the field of learning disabilities.
4. Discuss the relationships among the different classifications.
5. Find direction for diagnosis and planning of remediations.

INTRODUCTION

There have always been children who by nature of their abilities and disabilities cannot be placed in discrete categories, such as "blind," "deaf," "intellectually retarded," "emotionally disturbed," or "phys- ically handicapped." They are children who are sighted yet do not "correctly" interpret visual stimuli. They may be children who hear yet fail to discriminate specific sounds, sound blends, or even words. They may have normal intelligence yet be retarded in the achievement of basic skills.

There are many statements that seek to describe this relatively new concept, which is labeled *learning disabilities.* State agencies tend to be

3

more specific in their definitions than do individual authorities. To highlight thoughts concerning learning disabilities and to illustrate the various levels of specificity of content, the following sampling of definitions from both individual theorists and state agencies are presented.

Children listed under the caption of specific learning disabilities are children who cannot be grouped under the traditional categories of exceptional children, but who show significant retardation in learning to talk, or who do not develop normal visual or auditory perception, or who have great difficulty in learning to read, to spell, to write, or to make arithmetic calculations. [Kirk, 1971, p. 42]

[Learning disability is a] behavioral deficit almost always associated with academic performance and that can be remediated by precise individual instruction programming. [Haring, 1974, p. 226]

Language and/or Learning Disabled children are children who are so deficient in the acquisition of language and/or learning skills including, but not limited to, the ability to reason, think, speak, read, write, spell, or to make mathematical calculations, as identified by educational and/or psychological and/or medical diagnosis that they must be provided special services for educational progress. The term, "language and/or learning disabled children" shall also apply to children diagnosed as having specific developmental dyslexia. [Texas Education Agency, 1973, p. 4]

Learning disabled students are those children who have a disorder in one or more of the basic psychological processes involved in understanding or in using language, spoken or written, which disorder may manifest itself in imperfect ability to listen, think, speak, read, write, spell, or do mathematical calculations. Such disorders include such conditions as perceptual handicaps, brain injury, minimal brain dysfunction, dyslexia, and developmental aphasia. Such term does not include children who have learning problems which are primarily the result of visual, hearing, or motor handicaps, or mental retardation, or emotional disturbance, or of environmental disadvantage. [Pennsylvania Department of Education, 1972, pp. 3, 8–12]

In this text a *learning disability* will be defined as a disturbance in the perceptual, conceptual, memory, and/or expressive processes of learning, interfering with the interchange of communication. Though such disturbances in learning may be found at any level of intelligence, "learning disability" as a category is accepted as being limited to the intellectually normal and intellectually bright and gifted. The learning-disabled child has erratic functioning in his mental or physical processes, which intrudes upon the normal learning pathways, causing a slower processing in some specific perceptual-motor or language task(s). Generally these problems are first noted when the child is engaged in the basic school subjects reading, writing, arithmetic, and spelling.

A learning disability is not confined to one level of intelligence, nor is it necessarily confined to a general global deficiency in functioning. In the United States most public school agencies classify learning disabilities ranging from the dull-normal to the above-normal levels of intellectual functioning. Generally, for the purposes of identifying children with handicaps to learning, the conditions of retardation and sensory deprivation (blindness or deafness) take priority over learning disabilities. This is true even when there is erratic achievement by the retarded child or where perceptual deficiencies exist along with the sensory deprivation. Thus learning disability differs from sensory deprivation; in learning disabilities a specific learning pathway is not completely blocked. With the learning-disabled child, learning may occur through the affected channel(s), although the learning is partially impeded, delayed, or occurs only with much difficulty.

The person responsible for identifying a learning-disabled child for the purpose of placing the child in an approved program needs administrative guidelines. Many states have such guidelines, and the diagnostician should follow the procedures outlined for placement. The following guidelines from the states of North Carolina, Ohio, and Texas are somewhat representative:

North Carolina (1973, p. 29)
1. Diagnosis of a learning disability shall be made by a multidisciplinary team composed of at least a teacher with background in prescriptive remediation techniques and/or a principal, a school or clinical psychologist, and an attending physician (preferably a pediatric neurologist or a pediatrician). It is recommended that a child have a complete neurological evaluation.

2. A child to be enrolled should have an intelligence quotient of 90 or above as determined by an individual psychological examination administered by a qualified psychologist. [Occasionally, a child with a borderline I.Q. (70–90) and a learning disability may be placed in the program if he would not profit from any other available program.]

Ohio (1973, pp. 24–25)
1. Any child who meets the following requirements shall be eligible for and may be placed in a special education unit for children with learning and/or *behavioral disabilities:*

(a) Is of legal school age.
(b) Functions within the normal range of intelligence, or above (attained I.Q. above 80), as determined through a multi-factored assessment procedure administered by a qualified psychologist.
(c) Cannot meet the academic and social behavioral expectations of the regular instructional program because of a significant performance deficit in one or more of the basic educational areas as determined through an educational assessment that includes standardized test data and classroom observational data.
(d) Does not have severe visual, hearing, or motor involvements.

2. All children being considered for initial placement shall be given a complete examination including a neurological examination by a licensed physician.

3. Medical consultation shall be encouraged on a continuing basis — especially when school authorities feel that there has been a change in a child's behavior or educational function, or when new symptoms are detected.

Texas (1973, p. 11)
4. Language and/or learning disabilities
Written report of assessment showing total intellectual functioning not more than two standard deviation units below norm

A written report of assessment revealing evidence of a deficit or deficits in one or more of the basic psychological learning processes of auditory, visual, or haptic processing, intersensory integration and/or concept formation

A written report of educational assessment substantiating a discrepancy between age level expectancy and current educational performance. This criterion may not necessarily apply to pupils ages 3 through 5 years of age

Documented evidence must be offered to indicate that the child's learning style deviates so markedly from the norm of his age group that he requires special education intervention

Physician's written report of general medical evaluation.

Although guidelines like the above provide some direction for assessment, they fail to provide a completely definitive structure, as explained here.

1. Which intelligence test will be used to show no more than two standard deviation units below the norm? The Slosson, which

has a standard deviation of 25 points, would allow a learning-disabled person to be categorized at the borderline level of moderate retardation (trainable). If the WISC or Stanford Binet tests are used, there is a more realistic lower limit to to identify the learning disabled, since the standard deviation is 15 points. For such assessment the authors recommend the WISC and the Stanford Binet in conjunction with the Meeker-SOI analysis of learning abilities (Meeker, 1969).

2. The guidelines are not specific regarding which tests to use nor how much of a deficiency a child must have to meet the criteria. (See Chapter 6 for recommended tests to use.)

3. There are a number of formulas to determine significant discrepancies between achievement and age-level expectancy. Although each begins with a mental age, the obtained mental age may not be valid. Special care must be taken to establish a valid mental age. Kaluger and Kolson (1969) offer a learning expectancy level formula that is easy to follow and is described in the Appendix.

4. How is the learning style of the child to be determined? Tests that have visual and auditory channel subtests could be used, but they would not provide a complete pattern of styles of learning. Screening instruments, such as Mill's test or Boder's classification (see Chapter 3), help identify different styles of learning. Also, the *Illinois Test of Psycholinguistic Abilities* and the *Detroit Test of Learning Aptitudes* distinguish possible learning styles. Other well-known tests can aid in this task, but a single test will not likely provide enough information to determine learning styles in many cases.

NEED FOR CLASSIFICATIONS

Learning disability is a relatively new concept and pioneer authorities such as Cruickshank, Clements, Kephart, Kirk, James McCarthy, Myklebust, Frostig, Jeanne McCarthy, Johnson, and others have made invaluable contributions to our knowledge in theory and practice. Since the refining of the total concept is apparently not complete, the first step toward a diagnostic procedure is to understand the terminology provided by those who have laid the groundwork.

A large number of descriptive terms identified with learning problems have withstood the test of research and use. To aid in diagnostic procedure, a select group of classifications by various authorities will be given here. Most tests do not measure one specific function, but rather they overlap from one area of assessment to another. Diagnosticians must be able to identify the different components related to the learning process in order to more readily identify the malfunctioning components of learning from the variety of responses made by children. The following classifications include the earlier identifying terms, followed by selections from current authorities in special education.

EARLIER IDENTIFYING TERMS

The earliest identification of problems in learning appears in the writings of medical doctors prior to 1800. Thompson (1966) identifies some terminology used by these early writers, including terms like *loss of reading, apoplexy, verbal amnesia,* and *perseveration of writing.* After 1800 writers like Broca, a French surgeon and anatomist, focused attention on speech disorders, using the term *motor aphasia.* The terms *word blindness* and *word deafness* were used by Kussmaul in 1877, and the term *sensory aphasia* was used by a German neuropathologist, Wernicke, in 1874.

By 1950 the term *dyslexia* was being used by neurologists who had followed Orton's theories of lateral dominance (Thompson, 1966). Since dyslexia was confined to the reading problem, this term could not encompass the other problems in learning. Other terms became popular among authorities, and the classifications seen in the following table are among the earliest used to identify perceptual or learning problems:

Group I	*Group II*
Aphasia	Dysphasia
Alexia	Dyslexia
Acalculia	Dyscalculia
Apraxia	Dyspraxia
Agraphia	Dysgraphia

The words in the first group have as a prefix the letter *a,* which means *without* in its earliest origin. The terms have the following meanings:

Aphasia — without the capacity to interpret and express language
Alexia — without the capacity to read or interpret letters of words
Acalculia — without the capacity to understand and interpret numbers and engage in problem solving dealing with numbers
Apraxia — without the capacity to make movement

as in *inner-being awareness*. The importance of this awareness is that it is the first step in learning directions of right, left, up, down, before, behind, etc. The human body is anatomically and neurologically designed to be bilaterally symmetrical. There are two relatively independent systems, one for the right and one for the left. "All the nerve systems, for example, innervating the left side of the body are kept distinct, pass up through the spinal cord, cross in the brain stem, and enter the right hemisphere of the cortex" (Kephart, 1971, p. 86). If these two systems are functioning adequately, the basis for learning *where one is in time and space* is intact, and there is no problem in this area.

Directionality problem. This is the inability to project directional concepts into external space whether up, down, in front of, in back of, right, or left. Movement patterns experienced are not directed to objects and/or individuals. Such a problem makes it difficult for children to relate to fixed objects in a room or to materials on their desks. It can also affect the child's ability to follow directions. If the teacher tells the child to start reading at the top of the page or on the left side of the page, the child is unable to comply. The child hears the directions and understand the words the teacher is using but lacks a basic reference point from which to proceed and complete the task.

Body-image problem. Body-image problems result from the lack of a point of reference around which relative impressions can be organized. When there is a poor body image, objects and persons cannot be referred to one's body, and thus cannot be oriented in space with reference to it. The importance of a sound body image is that it provides a reference point from which to estimate direction and amplitude of movement. Those who have written on concepts of the body image are L. Bender, 1956; M. B. Bender, 1952; Fisher and Cleveland, 1958; Goldstein, 1939; Kolb, 1959; and Schilder, 1935.

Discussion

There is a distinct relationship among the motor problems of posture, laterality, directionality, and body image. When children do not experience a sound motor base, it is very likely they will have difficulty with fine motor tasks such as writing, drawing, keeping up with the place in reading, catching a ball, picking up a book, or innervating movement from the teacher's directions. The difficulty experienced will depend on the degree of the impairment, compensatory factors (not easily identified), and the teacher's awareness of the problem.

Figure-ground relationship problems. Figure-ground relationship disturbance is the inability to discriminate foreground stimulus from background stimulus or background stimulus from foreground stimulus. This causes letters in words and words in sentences to become fused or separated in erratic ways. In faulty auditory figure-ground relationships, sounds may not be heard from their points of origin, or they may not be discriminated properly, causing a person to separate words and syllables incorrectly. The phonemes and morphemes become less meaningful, or stated another way, the grouping of sounds within the spoken sentence become like nonsense syllables. Kephart has cited an auditory figure-ground problem situation of a child who heard "I pledge allegiance to the flag" and interpreted it as "Yipes led alley chintz tooth lag." An example of a visual figure-ground problem is that of a child who sees "Tim batted the ball" and interprets it as "Timbat tedtheball."

Form perception problems. Form perception disturbance is the inability to perceive objects, sounds, texture, odors, and taste correctly and in a manner common to the mode of perception utilized. Veridical discrimination and interpretation are involved. A child may see all the points around a square (that is, each side) but may not perceive the sides arranged in such a manner that four 90-degree angles are fitted into the organization of the lines. This child sees the four sides but may not see any angles. People with a "sound-form perceptual" problem may not perceive the sound form of words in the same manner as they are perceived by people who have no auditory perceptual problems. A child may perceive a door as being slanted rather than upright or a banana as having a rough texture rather than a smooth one. In the case of form perception problems, the form of the stimulus is always perceived incorrectly.

Space discrimination problems. Space discrimination problems deal with the location of objects in space. The child who has difficulty perceiving spatial relations will have difficulty dealing with grouping phenomena in arithmetic and forming abstract concepts. This child will have difficulty making associations of events seen or heard. Vision is considered to be one of the most efficient senses to indicate the relationship of objects in space (Kephart, 1971); but sound, smell, taste, and vibrations are also indicators. Those who have written about the importance of space discrimination in the learning process are Strauss and Lehtinen (1947); Stern (1949); Piaget and Inhelder (1956); Vinacke (1952); Welch (1947); and Barsch (1965 and 1967).

Time-dimension problems. Time-dimension problems deal with inability to perceive the meanings of time as related to tomorrow, yesterday, last week, next month, and "pretty soon." Children with this problem do not have the temporal dimension to help them locate events in terms of the future or the past. The child may not be able to skip, jump rope, or even jump in a simple pattern without getting one foot out of step. Kephart relates this problem to reading: "Many children read along, moving from one fixation to another until, at a given fixation, they do not pick up the clue or clues vital to the recognition of the word. At this point their eyes glue to the page" (1971, p. 179). The temporal activity of the visual process is disrupted. This type of performance is typical of the child with a reading problem. In order to develop fluency in reading it is necessary for a child to develop temporal-spatial skills.

Discussion

The problems in figure-ground relationship, form perception, space discrimination, and temporal dimension are closely related and may affect each other. For example, figure-ground problems could create problems in form perception, space discrimination, and time discrimination. Further, there is a relationship between perception and muscle tension. Kephart (1972) explains that hypokinetic and hyperkinetic states become the origin for the discrimination of foreground and background. The theory is that hyperkinetic conditions in the body in the early stages of development cause children to feel more foreground (become aware of more foreground), and this influences the sensations of seeing or hearing. The figure stands out unrealistically against a background and catches the attention without reference to background visual or auditory stimuli.

The hypokinetic condition in the child (lack of muscle tonus) is said to cause awareness of less foreground. The child is therefore perceptually fixated on background without reference to the foreground.

BARSCH CATEGORIES

Barsch (1967), another writer who espouses motor theories, does not identify specific perceptual motor functions, but like Kephart, he identifies functions that he relates to learning and establishes these as components of movement efficiency. He identifies the following components of movement efficiency:

Muscular strength
Dynamic balance
Body awareness
Spatial awareness
Temporal awareness

Muscular strength problems. If there is a breakdown in the muscular strength of a person, the first dimension of movement efficiency is disturbed. The thrust-counterthrust operation in a moving body is disrupted, and the person does not have control. The implications for academic learning are specifically noted in both fine motor coordination tasks and gross motor coordination tasks. For example, with a fine motor task such as *holding a pencil,* the grasp may be insufficient to propel the pencil back and forth.

Dynamic balance problems. Balance problems relate to the state of instability resulting from failure to establish an equal distribution of weight on each side of the vertical axis. Lowman and Young indicate that when the body segments are aligned in a state of equilibrium with a minimum amount of energy and a minimum amount of fatigue upon any particular muscle or muscle group, a person can be described as being *in balance* (Barsch, 1967). The importance of body balance in the learning process appears to be related to the proper development of physical growth, which in turn contributes to the body self-image each person holds.

Body awareness problems. Body awareness problems include the inability to have a coordinated and coherent understanding of one's own body image. A child with this problem does not realize that there is meaning to the relationship of the several parts of the body. Body awareness is associated with the lack of foundation needed for the development of number concepts, the building of a system of spatial relationships, and finally the act of reading.

Spatial awareness problems. A person with this problem is unable to physically relate to objects and other people. The problem appears to be related to laterality and right and left orientation, and spatial awareness is believed to be a part of the foundation for the learning process.

Temporal awareness problems. A child with a temporal awareness problem will have difficulty understanding time concepts and will be unable to accelerate or decelerate his/her own actions according to the demands of the environment. This specifically may result in problems of punctuality, tardiness, "saving for the future," and travel time from place to place (Barsch, 1967). A student with temporal awareness problems will have difficulty completing work on a time schedule and learning time concepts.

FROSTIG VISUAL-PERCEPTUAL CATEGORIES

Among the first to identify categories of visual perception was Frostig (1966). Her classification includes the following categories:

Eye-hand coordination
Figure-ground
Form constancy
Position in space
Spatial relations

Eye-hand coordination dysfunction. This is the inability to accurately reproduce visual symbols through the media of writing, drawing, and printing.

Figure-ground perception dysfunction. This is the inability to identify relevant visual stimuli from distracting backgrounds. The ability is needed in such activities as using a dictionary, finding specific items in a table of contents or an index, reading the printed word in a paragraph or sentence, and solving word problems in arithmetic.

Form constancy dysfunction. This is the inability to identify forms, regardless of differences in size, color, position, or angle of viewing. This skill is needed in the recognition of a word, regardless of whether it is in a different print or in any unfamiliar context.

Position in space dysfunction. This causes an inability to recognize the formation and directionality of figures and characters. This ability is needed in reading and writing skills, for example, to distinguish *3* from *E* and *was* from *saw.*

Spatial relationship dysfunction. This is the inability to perceive positional relationships between various objects or points of reference, as in the order of letters in a word or of digits in a number. This skill is needed in reading and in computation.

(The Frostig visual-perception categories cannot be purely separated from the language categories which follow, but they are included with the perceptual-motor classification because they show greater similarity to that area.)

AYRES CATEGORIES

Jean Ayres's (1975) approach to the study of learning disabilities includes five perceptual-motor classifications, which provide a base from which to examine problems in children. She calls these the *sensory integrative dysfunctions,* and they include

Generalized dysfunctions
Postural and bilateral integrative deficit
Apraxia
Problems in the left cerebral hemisphere
Problems in the right cerebral hemisphere

Generalized dysfunction. These are "across the board" dysfunctions involving sensory integrative deficiencies in most sensory channels and not falling into a recognizable pattern.

Postural and bilateral integrative dysfunction. This is a disorder of the vestibular system that results in inadequate interhemisphere communication and a subsequent poor lateralization of language in the hemispheres, as shown on dichotic listening tests.

Apraxia. Apraxia is a disorder of motor planning resulting from poor sensory integrative processes. The tactile and vestibular systems are usually involved; kinesthesia occurs occasionally.

Problems in the left cerebral hemisphere. These cause problems in verbal learning and sometimes poor auditory perception.

Problems in the right cerebral hemisphere. These are harder to ascertain and the symptoms are more varied than in the left hemisphere. One symptom is the tendency to disregard the left side of self and space. The interference with academic work often is not severe until about the third grade.

CRATTY CATEGORIES

Another leader in the field of perceptual-motor education is Cratty, whose classifications show similarity to those of Kephart and Barsch. His pragmatic approach regarding activity has grown out of his research with handicapped children. He considers the following sequence to be of importance in planning a program of motor abilities (Cratty, 1967).

Perceptions of the body and its position in space
Balance
Locomotion
Agility
Strength, endurance, flexibility
Catching and throwing
Moving and thinking

Cratty relates his sequences, most of which have been described under some of the previous classifications, to the social and emotional aspects of development. He also theorizes that figure recognition, serial memory ability, and similar perceptual attributes may be enhanced by the proper kinds of motor tasks (Cratty, 1968, p. 205). He says that intellectually applied motor tasks aid in formation of basic perceptions necessary to reading and writing. Motor tasks help people to think in a more organized fashion and improve their general self concept (Cratty, 1969, p. 87).

LANGUAGE CLASSIFICATIONS

INTRODUCTION

Language function encompasses many aspects of learning, and because of its relationship to the basic skills taught in public schools, an examination of the components within the language structure is necessary to provide the consultant with insight for planning remediation. One source of these language functions has unquestionably been in the writings of special education personnel who have worked with the deaf, the speech handicapped, and the mentally retarded. A sampling of such classifications follows.

JOHNSON AND MYKLEBUST CATEGORIES

Johnson and Myklebust (1967) were among the first to delineate typologies that described language disabilities. The categories they identify are listed as behavioral classifications related to brain functions. They include (1) five functions of the learning process — sensation, perception, imagery, conceptualization, and symbolization; and (2) three language processes — inner language, receptive language, and expressive language.* There can be an inter-relationship between the two groups, for example, the receptive language process may be disturbed at the perceptual level or at the conceptual level. Also, any sensory deficiency may create a problem in both inner and receptive language, or imagery and/or symbolization processes may create problems in the area of expressive language. A description of each of the categories follows.

---

*The authors have grouped the categories identified by Johnson and Myklebust into learning processes and language processes.

*Sensation dysfunction.** Deficiencies in the senses result in deafness, blindness, tactile and kinesthetic impairments, gustatory (taste) impairments, and olfactory (smell) impairments. Impairment in the senses of sight, hearing, and tactile and kinesthetic impairments restrict a person's ability to perform academic tasks.

Perceptual dysfunction. This is a dysfunction in the reaction to patterns of stimuli, whether it be auditory, visual, tactile-kinesthetic, olfactory, or gustatory. Young (1964) says in Johnson and Myklebust (1967, p. 33) that the neurological deficiency may consist of inadequate converting of sensations into electrical impulses. When this occurs, the child may not be able to discriminate among letters or among sounds; or he may not be able to perceive differences in texture, taste, or smell. The function of perception is considered to be the second in the hierarchial steps in learning and "by reciprocation disturbs all the levels of experience that fall above it" (Johnson & Myklebust, 1967, p. 33).

Imagery dysfunction. A misinterpretation of presented stimuli after the stimuli has been perceived is classified as an imagery dysfunction. It is related to memory in that there may be faulty memory of the event, object, or sound. In addition it could be related to a difficulty in the sequencing of events or the order and arrangement of things.

Symbolization dysfunction. This is the verbal or nonverbal misrepresentation of the *meaning* of objects, places, things, sounds, and events. It is identified by the failure to learn "to estimate and recall time, size, distance, volume, shape, height, speed and other qualitative aspects of experience" (Johnson & Myklebust, 1967, p. 35).

Conceptualization dysfunction. A conceptualization dysfunction is the inability to make associations and discriminations and/or to see the relationship between the two. Children may readily perceive objects and events, either auditorially or visually, but they may not be able to abstract ideas or associate similarities or differences among them.

Inner language dysfunction. This dysfunction is the inability to transform experiences into symbols, and it may be either verbal or nonverbal in nature. Inner language is generally defined as the language with which one thinks. Johnson and Myklebust (1967) refer to this as the *native tongue,* or the language that a child learns first. Vygotsky (1962) speaks

---

*Although this is included in typologies of learning disabilities most writers classify sensation deficiencies as blindness and deafness and therefore do not treat it as a learning disability category.

of it as inner speech or thought connected with words. The inability to develop inner language makes it very difficult for children to perceive, comprehend, or acquire meaning, and therefore the task of remediation is made more difficult. The prognosis is generally poor where there is inner language difficulty caused by brain pathology.

Receptive language dysfunction. An impairment in a person's ability to comprehend the spoken or the written word or to comprehend what he feels, smells, or tastes is referred to as a receptive language dysfunction. A child who does not understand sights and sounds has a problem with auditory or visual reception. There is a dependency on memory, for in order to comprehend, one must remember certain subsidiary facts.

Expressive language dysfunction. This is a dysfunction in the verbal or manual expressive actions of children. There is an impairment of output, since the person experiences an inability to generate the appropriate flow of words that an idea has stimulated. The person may also be unable to use appropriate gestures to express ideas.

BATEMAN CATEGORIES

Bateman (1964) delineates three major subcategories of learning disabilities: (1) dyslexia, or reading disability; (2) verbal communication disorders, or difficulties with the comprehension or expression of spoken language; and (3) visual-motor integration problems. These are not positioned in a hierarchial arrangement but seem to focus on (1) a major academic problem; (2) language problems generally; and (3) motor problems as they interact with the visual sense. Although these are not as detailed as the other categories listed, they provide an overview and suggest broad areas specifically pertinent to learning problems.

KIRK AND MCCARTHY CATEGORIES

One of the most widely used classifications describing language functions is that from the *Illinois Test of Psycholinguistic Abilities,* commonly known as the ITPA subtests (Kirk, McCarthy & Kirk, 1968). These subtest titles are direct derivatives of the Osgood model, known as the Semantic Differential (Osgood, 1954). The 12 subtests follow:

Auditory Reception
Visual Reception

Auditory Association
Visual Association
Verbal Expression
Manual Expression
Grammatic Closure
Visual Closure
Auditory Sequencing Memory
Visual Sequencing Memory
Auditory Closure
Sound Blending

When these subtests show significantly different low scores, it is said that a significant problem exists. For example, a significantly different low score in auditory reception reflects a critical or significant problem in auditory reception for the participant taking the test. In this manner these problems can be identified as dysfunctions.

Auditory reception dysfunction — dysfunction in the ability to comprehend the spoken word
Visual reception dysfunction — dysfunction in the ability to comprehend pictures and written designs and/or words
Auditory association dysfunction — impairment in the ability to relate auditory symbols in a meaningful way
Visual association dysfunction — impairment in the ability to relate visual symbols in the form of pictures in a meaningful way
Verbal expression dysfunction — inability to satisfactorily express ideas through spoken words
Manual expression dysfunction — inability to satisfactorily express ideas through gestures
Grammatic closure dysfunction — disability in the use of proper grammar
Visual closure dysfunction — disability in the perceptual interpretation of any visual object when only a part of it is shown
Auditory memory dysfunction — inability to satisfactorily repeat a sequence of auditory symbols heard just prior to the expected response
Visual memory dysfunction — inability to satisfactorily reproduce a sequence of visual symbols seen just prior to the expected response
Auditory closure dysfunction — dysfunction of perceptual interpretation of any word or group of letters when only portions of it are heard
Sound blending dysfunction — dysfunction in determining the correct blends of sounds heard

An important feature of this classification is that each function can be studied from three dimensions. It can be studied (1) from specific levels, such as representative and automatic; (2) different channels, such as visual or auditory; and (3) from input and output. The three dimensions add the possibility of greater understanding of the problem. In many cases children may be impaired in *both* visual and auditory channels, and the true differentiating difference lies in whether the function is *representational* or *automatic*. The importance of such information necessitates that remediation be planned to deal with aspects of time and speed of presentation and with making the material more meaningful, and not with sensory channels alone.

CHALFANT AND SCHEFFELIN CATEGORIES

The structure reported by Chalfant and Scheffelin (1969) organizes language function into three major categories:

Dysfunctions in the analysis of sensory information
Dysfunctions in the synthesis of sensory information and
Dysfunctions in symbolic operations.

Dysfunctions in the analysis of sensory information. This includes auditory, visual, and haptic processing. Auditory processing dysfunction causes difficulty in (1) identifying the source of sounds; (2) the discrimination between sounds or words; (3) discrimination of pitch, rhythm, and melody; (4) discriminating significant from insignificant stimuli; and (5) combining speech sounds into words and/or understanding the meaning of environmental sounds in general. Visual processing dysfunction causes difficulty in (1) visually examining the individual details of an object; (2) determining the dominant visual cues; (3) integrating individual visual stimuli into simultaneous groups and obtaining meaning; (4) classifying objects into visual categories; and (5) making comparisons of the visual hypothesis with the actual object as it is perceived. Haptic processing dysfunction causes difficulty in obtaining information from the cutaneous and kinesthetic systems, as they operate independently and simultaneously.

Dysfunction in the synthesis of sensory information. This second category includes both multiple stimulus integration and short-term memory. Multiple stimulus integration dysfunctions cause difficulty in the synthesis of multiple stimuli presented to the same sensory modality or different sensory modalities. Short-term memory dysfunctions involve difficulty in the storage and retrieval of inputs, whether verbal or nonverbal.

Dysfunctions in symbolic operations. The third category of Chalfant and Scheffelin organizes symbolic operations into four language areas —

auditory language, decoding written language, encoding written language, and quantitative language.

Auditory language is the language or auditory-vocal communication system common to a community's speech patterns. There are many dialects among minority groups and subcultures that are different enough from the usual speech pattern to create atypical syntax in sentence structure and to give different meanings to words. Some states do not allow children to be placed in special education programs if the only deficiencies identified are directly attributable to a different cultural life-style. If an auditory language problem is caused by poor auditory perception, then the child would be eligible for special services because of a perceptual problem. The consultant should understand the language patterns of the community and be able to distinguish between any atypical language pattern and a learning disability.

The act of expressing speech and language vocally is called auditory expressive language. Johnson and Myklebust (1967) point out that many deficiencies may combine to cause disorders in auditory expressive language. The three kinds of disorders they identify are as follows:

1. Inability to remember or retrieve words for spontaneous usage
2. Failure to voluntarily initiate movements of the articulators — this is an aspect of apraxia in the absence of paralysis
3. Failure to organize words in their proper word order (syntax), failure to use the correct verb tense, and other grammatical errors

Decoding written language is related to the act of reading and spelling. Glass (1971) states that one can read only if one is able to (1) decode the written word; (2) obtain meanings of prescribed dimensions from the decoded words; and (3) react to and utilize these meanings for personal growth. He further states that decoding is easier than learning to read. If one is decoding the word *cow,* only one correct response is expected — a response that does not allow for uniqueness and/or creativity. In contrast to decoding, reading depends upon decoding the words and also attaching meaning to the words being read. Whether one interprets *decoding* as being the act of decoding sounds or the more involved act of reading, what is important is that the decoding of written language is considered by many to be the most common and most insidious of all learning defects (Jastak, 1965). The consultant must understand the dynamics of the total reading process to be able to perform an analysis of the poor reader's responses.

Encoding written language is the act of expression in drawing or writing. Some children fail in this task because they say they can think of nothing to write about, while others have difficulty because they cannot produce written symbols. If children have difficulty in expressing language vocally or in perceiving the written word, they will likely have difficulty in expressing themselves through writing. Myklebust suggests that the assessment of writing skills should include: (1) developmental deviations; (2) psychomotor aspects, such as paralytic disorders, ataxia, and apraxia; (3) visual processes; (4) auditory processes, including dysnomia, syntactical aphasia, receptive aphasia, reauditorization of letters, auditory sequencing, syllabication, and auditory blending; (5) a discrepancy between spoken and written language; (6) reading disability; (7) speech handicaps; (8) deafness; (9) cultural deprivation; and (10) instructional factors (Myklebust, 1965, p. 13).

Quantitative language represents the more abstract language of numerical concepts. Children who have difficulty in this area may exhibit difficulty with time, number concepts, and logical thinking. They may or may not have reading disabilities. Some of the quantitative language behavior problems are as follows:

1. Lack of understanding of verbal concepts such as "up — down," "before — behind," "near — far," "over — under," "high — low," "front — back," and "in — out" — a prerequisite to such understanding is theorized to involve cognizance of body image and one's position in space
2. Failure to understand size relationship such as "little," "big," "long," "more than," and "less than" — form perception is related to this problem
3. Inability to perceive relative distances between numbers (spatial relationships), or space discrimination problems, as discussed by Strauss and Lehtinen (1947) — essential for numerical operations on an abstract level
4. Directional confusion, which can result in writing *17* as *71* or can result in improper sequencing steps in adding, subtracting, multiplying, and dividing
5. Inability to comprehend group sets as used in modern math

MCCARTHY (JEANNE MCRAE) CATEGORIES

Another classification as a structure for examining learning disabilities is the one suggested by Jeanne McRae McCarthy (1974). She theorizes that teachers should possess competency in and an understanding of six processing functions and their relationships to achievement and social and emotional problems. These processing functions are as follows:

Cognitive processing
Sensory-motor processing
Visual processing
Auditory processing
Memory processing
Intersensory and intrasensory integrative processing

In addition, teachers must be able to relate these skills to the following areas:

Academic achievement
Social functions
Emotional functions

The emphasis on teacher competency provides a challenge to teacher-training programs, which too often assume that only language-disability and learning-ability children possess these problems in processing. If a teacher does not have these skills, many problems may not be recognized. This structure should result in teachers who are not constrained to a rigid outward view; that is, one without reference to internal personal learning problems. The teacher who possesses skills in these six processing functions and understands how they relate to the areas of academic achievement, social functions, and emotional functions will be more adept in the management of learning disabilities.

The following descriptions show each process differentiated in regard to dysfunctions.

Cognitive processing problems. The term *cognitive* is derived from the Latin verb, *cognoscere,* which means "to know." Processing is the dynamics of an action, and when the two words are paired (cognitive processing), the meaning becomes the "dynamics of knowing." The term *cognition* includes both judgment and awareness; when people have a problem in judgment and awareness, they have difficulty in the activity of analysis integration and synthesis of visual and auditory information. In analysis there is difficulty in perceiving the component parts of a whole. In integration of information there is trouble coordinating mental processes. In synthesis there is difficulty combining elements into a recognizable whole.

Sensory-motor processing problems. A sensory-motor problem is a dysfunction in the processing of kinesthetic and tactile information. People with this problem may experience difficulty with any of the following:

Body image
Body orientation

Body movement
Haptic processing

Visual processing problems. This condition is a central dysfunction in which the subject can see but experiences difficulty in the following:

Examining individual details of a picture or an object
Designating the dominant visual cues
Obtaining meaning from a visual object
Classifying visual objects into a particular category
Associating pictorial events into a meaningful visual pattern

Auditory processing problems. When the auditory processing operation is disturbed, a person may experience difficulty in the following:

Recognizing the source of the projection of sound
Discriminating among phonemes and graphemes
Determining sounds as either figure foreground or figure background
Blending speech sounds into words
Perceiving pitch, rhythm, and melody
Discriminating environmental sounds

Memory processing problems. The function of memory has long been considered a major factor affecting learning-disabled children. It is important to emphasize that through factor analysis, Guilford (1965) found no general memory factor — only a number of special memory functions. Children with memory problems may have difficulty in the following:

Remembering what has just been read
Remembering words they had recognized readily on a prior day
Sequencing directions properly
Remembering music, sound blends, pictorial events
Remembering specific content but not other content
Remembering steps in calculating

Intrasensory and intersensory integrative processing problems. Intrasensory integration refers to the processing of multiple stimuli that are being received through the same modality, such as the hearing channel. Intersensory integration refers to the processing of multiple stimuli that are being transmitted through different modalities, such as visual and auditory modalities. Examples of these follow:

Intrasensory—associating the rhythm of a tune with a title of the tune
Intersensory—associating the sound of a word with the written (or visual) word

Achievement problems. Although signs of a learning disability may be evident long before children start school, they then become more obvious. In school children compete with peers, and failure to maintain an expected achievement rate is soon noted. Desire to learn and motivation through competition help nondisabled children to progress normally. But since a belief that there is a chance of success is rare with learning-disabled children, they generally soon lose the motivation of competition. These children must have a structure that allows for success in some task. The teacher and consultant must understand this and provide the child with an academic program structured to include meaningful achievements.

Social behavior problems. Learning problems are often associated with social behavior problems. It is sometimes a social problem that provokes initial recommendations for evaluation. Learning-disabled children who experience hypertension or hypotension, perceptual difficulties, and poor motor coordination tend to develop inappropriate social patterns. They may move away from their peer group, or they may move toward their group in an unacceptable manner, causing them to be rejected. Learning-disabled children may also become defiant of authority and the law. Many of these people will need group and/or individual counseling therapy. The teacher and the diagnostician should recognize this need.

Emotional development problems. Emotional development problems are also common among persons with learning disabilities. It is often the overlying emotional problem that causes social behavior problems. However, some emotionally disturbed people do not exhibit inappropriate social behavior. Some have fears and anxieties that interfere with learning processes but not with peer relationships. Individual therapy and group therapy should be provided in these cases.

It is imperative that those whose learning disabilities have been compounded with problems of emotional and social disturbances have the opportunity to learn to adjust to each other and to accept themselves as worthwhile individuals. Consultants have a moral responsibility to see that these children have the opportunity to develop a wholesome self-image and become able to adjust to their environment.

KASS CATEGORIES

Kass (Wissink, Kass; & Ferrell, 1975) lists five processes from which to proceed to determine efficient and economical means for identifying learning disabilities. Her list is as follows:

Sensory orientation
Memory
Reception
Expression
Interpretation

Sensory orientation — physiological and functional readiness to respond
Memory — function by which experience is stored and recalled for awareness or response
Reception — acquisition of personal meaning from external or internal stimuli
Expression — communication of meaning
Integration — coordination of the separate components from the above processes into internal representations. To pursue the problem of identification further, these five processes were differentiated into forty disability components. These are listed in the section "Components of the Learning Process."

Discussion

The language categories listed up to this point reveal similarity of thought regarding many of the characteristic behaviors attributed to the source of learning problems. For example, such terms as *memory, reception,* and *expression* are commonly cited and are considered to be important in the process of learning. When failure is reported, an examination of these functions (and others) is generally made. The theorists do contribute individual and descriptive definitions, which provide a broader and more in depth view of the same terms.

The following two sets of categories afford a different position from which to identify factors also related to the learning process. One can see in these different vantage points for diagnostic purposes.

MEEKER CATEGORIES (1974)

Most texts in psychology offer descriptions of the Guilford Structure of Intellect, commonly called SOI. The construct is a factor-analyzed system of three-dimensional functions, each of which can be isolated as separate intellectual entities. There are 120 factors in the original construct. The three-dimensional structure of the SOI is shown in Appendix I.

Meeker (1969, 1971, 1973, 1974) applied the Guilford constructs to develop templates for translating tests (such as the Stanford Binet,

WISC, WPSSI, WISC-R, WAIS, *Illinois Test of Psycholinguistic Abilities,* Slosson, and *Detroit Test of Learning Aptitude*) into SOI profiles of individual learning patterns. These profiles allow teachers to identify learning patterns as they relate to achievement. The learning patterns can be derived from a small grouping of factors that have been identified with reading and math. Meeker reports that the following factors are critical for reading:

For Reading Skills

CFU-A	Cognition of figural units	— auditory
MFU-A	Memory for figural units	— auditory
EFU-A	Evaluation of figural units	— auditory
CFU-V	Cognition of figural units	— visual
MFU-V	Memory for figural units	— visual
EFU-V	Evaluation of figural units	— visual

For Advanced Reading

CMR	Cognition of semantic relations
EMR	Evaluation of semantic relations
NMR	Convergent production of semantic relations

Meeker also reports that the following factors are important for math:

For Remediation in Math

EFU	Evaluation of figural units
EFC	Evaluation of figural classes
EFR	Evaluation of figural relations
CSR	Cognition of symbolic relations
CSS	Cognition of symbolic systems
CSI	Cognition of symbolic implications
CMU	Cognition of semantics units
CMS	Cognition of semantics systems

For Higher Math

NSR	Convergent production of symbolic relations
NSS	Convergent production of symbolic systems
NSI	Convergent production of symbolic implications

The various categories described by other investigators fall discretely into the Meeker SOI profile. Decoding skills, regardless of mode, are

cognition abilities. Encoding skills similarly are encompassed within convergent and divergent production. Association skills are memory skills.
Meeker's conceptual model dictates changing at least one generally
accepted basic assumption. She states that intelligence can be developed;
that it is not a static, unchanging entity over which no one has control.
Ball (1971) has also shown similar findings.

Chapter 3 includes several examples from the SOI abilities workbooks.
The workbooks give definite tasks to train any learning function as
shown in the SOI construct. The Appendix includes profiles for use in
the diagnostic procedure. This is a new approach and has been highly
successful.

BLOOM, LIGHTBOWN, AND HOOD CATEGORIES

Bloom, Lightbown, and Hood (1975) provide a new set of categories
that deal with early language development. The reader is referred to
Chapter 4 for these categories and their descriptions. They are placed
with the functions of task analysis because they form a different analytical
dimension than the ones included in this chapter.

COMPONENTS OF THE LEARNING PROCESS

The preceding classifications include most terms associated with learning disabilities. The following lists of components of the learning process
include some terms not previously covered. They are considered to be
important additions, whether as subcategories or as separate entities. The
first group is suggested by the authors. The second group, from Wissink,
Kass, and Ferrell (1975), lists 40 component disabilities and the process
with which each is identified. (See Kass categories.) These 40 components were chosen from a group of 110 "symptoms" of learning disabilities, and they have been refined to reduce the overlap among the factors.
The purpose was to follow a Bayesian approach to the screening of learning disabilities.* By special permission the components have been re-
aligned according to processes. The originally reported data presents the
components in order of their median specialist estimates, likelihood ratios,
and diagnosticity values.

The authors suggest both groups as possible terms to be understood
by the potential teacher and diagnostician. It is recommended that those

---

*See Wissink, Kass, and Ferrell, 1975, p. 158 for an explanation of the Bayesian
approach to screening.

who diagnose and plan remediation have a thorough understanding of all the components related to the act of learning. Such knowledge is the base position from which to begin evaluation.

GROUP I

TABLE 1.   Components of the learning process.*

Attention span
Auditory association (auditory-vocal)
Auditory closure
Auditory discrimination
Auditory reception (decoding)
Auditory sequencing memory (auditory-vocal)
Balance
Color discrimination and color constancy
Conceptual thinking
Convergence
Depth perception
Directionality
Eye movement
Eye-hand coordination
Figure-ground relationship
Fine motor development
Form perception
Freedom from destractibility
Grammar closure (auditory-vocal automatic)
Laterality
Left to right progression
Manual expression (motor encoding)
Meaningful memory
Perceptual organization
Perceptual speed
Perseveration
Form discrimination and form constancy
Sound blending
Spatial orientation
Temporal-spatial relationships
Verbal expression (vocal encoding)
Visual association (visual-motor)
Visual attention span
Visual classification and grouping
Visual closure
Visual discrimination
Visual reception (decoding)
Visual sequencing memory (visual-motor)

*Adapted by K. Waugh, 1971.

GROUP II

TABLE 2.   Learning component disabilities classified according to processes identified by Kass.*

Component Disability	Process
Attention	Sensory orientation
Auditory-visual coordination	Sensory orientation
Hyperexcitability	Sensory orientation
Auditory-visual-haptic-coordination	Sensory orientation
Perseveration	Sensory orientation
Auditory discrimination	Sensory orientation
Visual discrimination	Sensory orientation
Temporal	Sensory orientation
Maturational lag	Sensory orientation
Auditory-haptic coordination	Sensory orientation
Visual-haptic coordination	Sensory orientation
Visual pursuit	Sensory orientation
Spatial	Sensory orientation
Body balance	Sensory orientation
Kinesthetic discrimination	Sensory orientation
Hypoexcitability	Sensory orientation
Tactile discrimination	Sensory orientation
Auditory direction	Sensory orientation
Rehearsal	Memory
Auditory short-term memory span	Memory
Long-term memory	Memory
Visual short-term memory span	Memory
Reading comprehension	Reception
Mathematical comprehension	Reception
Listening comprehension	Reception
Auditory closure	Reception
Social comprehension	Reception
Visual figure-ground	Reception
Visual closure	Reception
Writing	Expression
Quantitative	Expression
Oral expression	Expression
Affect	Expression
Body language	Expression
Auditory speed of perception	Integration
Visualization	Integration

*Adapted from J. F. Wissink, C. Kass, and W. R. Ferrell, "A Bayesian Approach to the Identification of Children with Learning Disabilities," *Journal of Learning Disabilities* 8 (1975): 3, p. 163.   Reprinted by permission of Professional Press, Inc.

Component Disability	*Process*
Sound blending	Integration
Monitoring	Integration
Visual speed of perception	Integration
Prediction	Integration

SUMMARY

This chapter has provided definitions of learning disabilities and guide-lines for placing children in language-disability and learning-disability programs. Because state educational agencies are concerned with the problems of placement and identification, the definitions of these agencies are more specific than those of individual authorities.

Researchers and writers have provided classification categories that provide a base for explaining reasons for academic failures and for establishing directions for remediation. The two major classifications identified are perceptual-motor and language. Although there is a common thread in the two classifications, they have different theoretical bases, and therefore they warrant separate classifications for examination. The perceptual-motor classifications discussed are those of Kephart, Barsch, Ayres, Cratty, and Frostig. The language classifications are those of Kirk and James McCarthy, Myklebust and Johnson, Bateman, Jeanne McCarthy, Chalfort and Scheffelin, Kass, and Meeker.

A summary of components of the learning process and a structure of the language functions have been included to aid the diagnostician in identifying all the areas that may need to be evaluated in the process of diagnosis and planning for remediation.

chapter 2

Etiology

After you have studied this chapter, you should be able to

1. Understand the causes of learning problems.
2. Trace these causes to prior sources.
3. See the need to understand the behavior of children at a level practical for educational planning.
4. Understand the purpose of diagnosis.
5. Relate diagnosis to styles of learning.

CAUSES

The following questions are often asked by parents: "Why did this happen to my child?" "What did we do wrong?" "Are we to blame?" They must be met by intelligent and logical answers. The competent consultant must understand cause-behavior relationships and interpret this information from an educator's standpoint. These skills are developed through training in counseling and familiarity with the possible sources of learning problems.

Kephart (1967) groups the causes of learning problems in three major categories — brain injury, emotional disturbance, and experience. He explains that brain injury means destruction of nerve tissue, as in a lesion.

Encephalitis, meningitis, and toxic conditions, such as lead poisoning, are sources of brain injury that produce symptoms of learning disability similar to those found in the destruction of nerve tissue. Any of these conditions could result in an interference with the cerebral functions required for the normal learning process in children and youth. Some children may have minimal brain dysfunction at birth or at a very early age, and then through disuse of some functions the minimal brain dysfunction may become a major problem. For example, a child may have sporadic hearing loss at an early age and may prefer the visual mode for direction and communication, and through disuse of the hearing mode a more critical problem in auditory perception results (Jeanne McCarthy, 1975).

The kind of emotional disturbance that causes learning problems is likely to be a prolonged emotional trauma in which there is an interference with functional relationships within the nervous system. Behavior in such cases is similar to that in cases of brain injury, including interference with learning. However, not all children who undergo emotional trauma incur interference with learning. There may be fear, anxiety, rebellious behavior, or lack of motivation, but when there is adequate psychotherapy the learning function generally is not disturbed.*

"Experience" as a cause of learning disabilities includes factors like developmental lag and lack of environmental experiences. Some children deprived of proper stimulation have never had the opportunity to handle tools (or toys), which could facilitate the proper manipulation skills for handling pencils and crayons. Also they may have been deprived of auditory experiences, and thus do not have the tools (words) to use in logic and reasoning.† Likewise, lack of exposure to visual aids, such as picture books, deprives the child of an experience common to most preschoolers. This kind of deprivation is not confined to any socioeconomic group, and it can be found in any stratum of society. This is also true of maturational lag, first introduced by Schilder (Bender, 1969). Bender explains maturational lag, stating "it is based on a concept of functional areas of the brain and of personality which mature according to a recognized pattern longitudinal wise. A maturational lag signifies a slow differentiation in this pattern. It does not indicate a structural defect, deficiency, or loss. There is not necessarily a limitation in the potentialities and, on

---

*Some children who have endured emotional trauma may excel because of their problems. An example is a person who achieves excellent grades, reasoning this to be the quickest escape from an undesirable environment.

†A child whose mother while talking over the telephone says, "Shut up!" has a deprived experience when compared to a child whose mother under the same circumstances says, "Frances, would you please be quiet while Mother is talking. I need to hear what Aunt Mary is saying."

variable levels, maturation may tend to accelerate but often unevenly" (1958, pp. 160-61). Though Kephart (1967) does not mention maturational lag, he adds to this concept, stating that the development of one stage is essential to the development of the next stage. This is true in physical maturation and in reading readiness or academic skills. It is implied that if normal maturation is disrupted at any stage, and it is not corrected or aided before the next normal stage of development, the learning process will be affected. The degree of interference will depend upon the severity of the disruption.

Haring reports the work of Reitan and Boll (1972) to substantiate this concept. The Reitan research has shown "that in the absence of actual structural damage, academic or perceptual deficits may be related to a lag in development of normal organization of brain-behavior relationships" (Haring, 1974, p. 226). The genetic factor, which is not emphasized by Kirk or Kephart, is given considerable attention by Bannatyne (1968) and Critchley (1964). Should the genetic factor be a source of learning problems, the overt results probably would be similar to the effects of brain injury or of developmental lag; i.e., a malfunction in the learning process.

General malnutrition and biochemical changes are now being researched to determine their effects on hyperactivity, distractibility, and learning. Grady (1974) states that there is a positive relationship between dyslexia and lactose intolerance. The theory is that many young children among various races do not possess the enzymes to digest lactose. Special diets are proving effective in many cases (Grady, 1974). This is different from theories calling for use of megavitamins as a therapeutic agent for children with learning problems.

It is helpful in most cases *to understand the reasons behind learning* problems, although Skinner (1938) suggests that we should work with behavior rather than with causes. Effective means of help may be overlooked if consultants believe that home and physical conditions are beyond their jurisdiction. The research of the behaviorists and field psychologists shows that behavior can be changed when the school or the therapy is structured to meet specific needs.

CAUSE AS A FACTOR OF TIME AND SEQUENCE

The major causes for learning problems discussed in the preceding section of this chapter may be considered in terms of a sequence of stages that culminate in a condition producing failure in learning. Causes, thus, may be projected in a broader perspective when a graphic view, Figure 1, shows the possibility of an original source and a variety of ensuing problems. In this sense, causes can be considered as a factor of *time,* that is, having an original source creating a physiological condition which in turn creates problems in the processing of information. These processing problems may then result in a particular style of learning, which if not nurtured by the teacher, may finally cause failure or underachievement.

If one should ask about the cause of the failure, the consultant can present these interrelated forces to provide this broader perspective. The inquiring agent can understand at which level or stage special attention should be provided. Such a scheme highlights the level (I and II) at which the medical profession should be involved, the level (III) at which the diagnostician and/or psychologist should be involved, and the level (IV) at which the teacher should be involved.

Figure 1 traces the progression of learning disabilities, classified in four levels, from cause to result. Level I shows the original cause, either congenital or acquired after birth. Secondary results (level II) may be brain injury, chemical imbalance, emotional blocking, maturational lag, or deprivation of experience, leading to the third level in this hierarchy, where there is difficulty in perception, difficulty in concept formation,

FIGURE I. A hierarchy of causes for learning problems

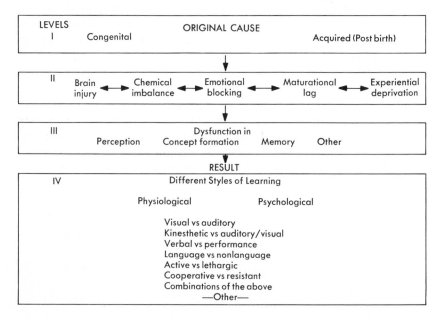

deficiency of memory and other processes, and/or semantic aspects. The result is a preferred or "forced" style of learning (level IV). All causes may be dual or multifaceted. For example, a person might have both brain injury and chemical imbalance, which could lead to perceptual *and* memory deficiencies or any other combination. The use of the term *congenital* does not completely exclude genetics as a cause. But since there would be a dubious relationship between a genetic factor and brain injury, the term congenital is used in this time-cause concept.

The original causes, whether acquired before or after birth, provide a basis for understanding *why* a child might have learning problems. However, since this level is either medical and/or biological or sociological, it does not provide the practical information needed for working with school-related tasks. For educational and psychological planning in diagnosis and remediation, different styles of learning, level IV, should be the focus of treatment.

It is a common practice, however, to examine causes of learning problems at level III. Once sensory deprivations (blindness or deafness) and mental retardation are *ruled out,* examinations of processes like perception, conception, and memory are made. The recognition of these problems, which include all sensory *deficits*—visual, auditory, haptic (both kinesthetic and tactile), olfactory, and gustatory—as interferences in the learning process is relatively new. The study of perception, concept formation, and memory, however, have long been important in psychological research. Although the Gestalt psychologists have reported volumes of information on visual perception, little has been reported on the other sensory areas and their relationships to learning. In the past the isolated writings regarding auditory deficiencies have been directed specifically to some classifications of auditory aphasia.

The fourth level, different styles of learning, represents a relatively new but very important dimension to the etiology of learning problems. There are many children who employ specific styles of learning that they have inadvertently acquired because of a unique combination of deficiencies and strengths in their learning and behavior skills. For example, if a child is a visual learner because of an auditory deficiency and he is being trained in the classroom by a program devoid of pictorial stimuli, he may not be learning as rapidly as he could. Thus it can be said that the wrong style of presentation becomes the *current* cause for slowness or failure.

It is at this fourth level that both the diagnostician and the teacher should consider the need to make a *task and behavior analysis of the child.* McCarthy (Jeanne) (1974) has stated that diagnosis is primarily for the purpose of effecting a match between the cognitive styles of learning and the cognitive demands of the task. The authors support this thesis and suggest that it should be the principle around which all diagnosis is organized. This requires that special emphasis be given to different styles of learning to help identify the cause of the difficulty and also to provide direction for individual instruction (see Chapter 4).

STYLES OF LEARNING

Different styles of learning are classified under the two major areas — physiological and psychological. Both are pertinent to the proper approach to remediation. It is recognized that some styles of learning may be both physiologically and psychologically induced. If the perceptual problem has its source in emotional trauma, emphasis in the remediation should include psychotherapeutic intervention, as in play therapy, counseling, drama, music and art therapy, and behavioral management. If the source of the perceptual problem is a physiological dysfunction caused by brain injury or maturational lag, the intervention techniques should emphasize an elaboration of sensory stimulation. In either case there might be an overlapping of overt behaviors; i.e., if there are emotionally based interferences with learning, perceptual deficiencies might result (as in a student's unconsciously not responding adequately to the spoken voice or to the written symbols). Conversely, if there are perceptually based interferences, the child may experience emotional reactions from failure and will not relate satisfactorily with peers or with authority figures.

Different styles of learning are difficult to isolate within any one person. It is, however, possible to categorize broad bases of visual and auditory styles (Border, 1973; Myklebust, 1967; Kirk & James McCarthy, 1968). The Wechsler Intelligence Scales delineate verbal vs. performance functions. The *California Test of Mental Maturity* delineates language vs. nonlanguage functions, and there are tests to delineate kinesthetic vs. auditory/visual skills in learning to read, for example, Mills' *Learning Methods Test,* (1965). Psychologically based styles may be categorized as cooperative vs. resistant or active vs. lethargic. It is practical, however, to examine each style from its possible source. Teachers aware of physiological differences will recognize a need to examine their classroom activities in regard to stamina or strength required by the child. If psychological causes are the main source and children are experiencing morbid fear and/or anxiety, teachers must avoid confronting them with certain content related to their fears.

It is believed that there are no limits to the different styles of learning, (Guilford, 1959). Meeker (1973), for instance, cites examples of convergent thinkers and divergent thinkers according to the structure of intellect. The divergent thinker must have a structure that allows for creativity of expression, while the convergent thinker is better satisfied learning in a structure that is methodical and consistent according to form. The master teacher-remediator of the future will be expected to become an expert in task analysis to compare different styles of learning with demands of the task.

SUMMARY

Traditional theories of causes of learning disorders include brain injury, emotional disturbance, maturational lag, and lack of experience. Brain injury is identified as destruction of nerve tissue, and emotional disturbance is identified as that which stems from critical trauma endured so long that it causes an interference with learning. Experiential cause relates to the poverty of experiences which, if not lacking, would otherwise facilitate learning. Maturational lag is the slowness of growth pattern transitions in the process of physiological development. A new interest and direction is to examine malnutrition and bio-chemical changes as causes for hyperactivity, distractibility and learning. There is a hierarchy of causes of learning problems. Three levels of which were identified with different professionals primarily or exclusively involved in the diagnosis of learning disabilities at each level. Learning disabilities result in the adoption of different styles of learning. These must be identified, and instruction must be adapted to the particular style of learning.

chapter 3

Teacher Assessment

After you have studied this chapter, you should be able to

1. Identify common procedures to follow in recognizing academic problems — visual, auditory and kinesthetic problems, and social behavior problems.

2. Choose from among a variety of sources the screening instruments that aid in identifying specific learning disorders.

3. Understand the procedure to follow in screening children to determine who might have learning disorders.

4. Establish normative data for a school population.

INTRODUCTION

Diagnosis of learning and/or behavior problems has been the responsibility of clinical experts, psychologists, and counselors. Today, however, a new type of qualified professional is available to many schools — the educational diagnostician. Educational diagnosticians are refining their knowledge and skill in terms of differential diagnosis. There is also a move to prepare teachers to handle a part of this duty. Checklists covering the varieties of observable behavior in children with learning problems are now available for teachers. Even as early as 1957 Slingerland had a checklist survey for language disabilities. More recently Giles;

Meier, Cazier, and Giles; Goodman and Hammill; Mann; and Meeker have authored screening instruments designed specifically for student evaluation by teachers.* In 1966 Clements identified the characteristics of the minimally brain injured (see Appendix N), which provided some clues in determining channels of learning as well as perception, discrimination, conceptual, motor and academic problems.

Teacher observation and clinical testing together provide a thorough evaluation, but to complete the total picture, medical and social knowledge about a child should also be added. It is expected that the consultant will make proper referrals to secure this additional data.

This chapter covers the informal techniques available to the teacher and the consultant and the teamwork needed for diagnostic purposes preparatory to remediation planning. The information presented in this section can be used by any person who works directly with the child. If the teacher is not aware of the possibility of teacher assessment, the consultant should make these informal techniques known so that information will be gathered from both the classroom and the clinical settings. The optimum in educational diagnosis will be possible with such teamwork.

NEED FOR TEACHER ASSESSMENT

There is a scarcity of diagnosticians, which often causes diagnosis to take an inordinate amount of time. Some teachers have reported that three to six months have elapsed before children are evaluated and/or reports are returned. This leaves teachers with pressures very difficult to handle. Daily they are reminded that certain children are not *keeping up,* but demands from the rest of the children take normal priority.

A teacher may be very alert and may have had courses in assessment and evaluation, but this training may not have been designed to detect specific problems. When such is the case, the teacher may examine possible learning modes through less formal procedures. Through various checklists and daily planned observation, teachers may be able to determine whether a child is a visual, auditory, or kinesthetic learner (or any combination of the three). This will facilitate the remediation planning when no other data is available.

The administration of any assessment tool should be preceded by careful study and practice. However, there are some tests that do not require formal training. These tests require only qualified training in the

---

*Screening instruments and teacher checklists are listed in the Appendix.

general use of instruments used in the classroom and careful adherence to standardized procedure.

Although there are many dimensions to intellectual function (Guilford, 1959); (Osgood, 1954), teachers may make an evaluation with materials designed specifically for one dimension, such as visual training, auditory training, or kinesthetic training. They may then add other dimensions to this design, such as specific content (words and knowledge meaningful to child) determined from a daily observation.

INDIVIDUAL ASSESSMENT INSTRUMENTS

CREATIVE CLASSROOM OBSERVATION

The standard procedure of observation reported by Prescott (1957) has had years of success. If sensory dimensions are added to Prescott's time-sampling technique, the teacher can consider, for instance, whether content and/or energy depletion could be influential factors along with visual or auditory perceptual problems. Figure 2 suggests the procedure to follow. A similar checklist of behaviors common to learning-disability problems should be completed daily for each child who is failing and

FIGURE 2. Teacher observation talley sheet

Weekly Teacher Observation
Talley Sheet

	Mon.	Tues.	Wed.	Thurs.	Fri.
8–9 Class Behavior*					
9–10 Class Behavior*					
10–12 Class Behavior*					
12–1 Class Behavior*					
1–2 Class Behavior*					
2–3 Class Behavior*					
3–4 Class Behavior*					

*See code

FIGURE 2. (cont.)   Code for behavior

Child Behavior	*Code*		*Observed Behavior*
	O-X	1.	Oral expression problems,
	sow		stumbles on words
	wos		Words out of sequence
			Poverty of expression
	poe		(Can't tell story from pictures)
	art		Articulation problem
	W-X	2.	Written expression problems
	poe		Poverty of expression
	uwa		Unfinished written assignments
	eo		Erases often
	C-M	3.	Gross motor expression problems
	cig		cannot imitate in gestures
	A-P	4.	Auditory perception problems
	ar		Asks to repeat
	lop		Looks at other's papers
	dnl		Does not listen
			or
	occ		Observes closely for clues
	V-P	5.	Visual perception problems
	cr		Cannot read well
	sow		Stumbles on words
	bro		Bumps into room objects
	bpe		Books placed on edges
	Mot	6.	Motor problems
	aw		Awkward walk
	b		Balance
	csl		Can't stay in line
	cwl		Can't write within lines
	ppg		Poor pencil grasp

Teacher Behavior	T-GD	1.	Giving directions
Prior to Overt	T-WD	2.	Writing directions on board
Actions of Child	T-AQ	3.	Asking questions
	T-R	4.	Reprimanding

shows need for individual diagnosis. At the end of a week a talley should be made, including such things as the times of day the child appeared most disturbed, the classes in which the problem behaviors occurred, the conditions surrounding the problem, and the teacher's behavior just

prior to each atypical performance. If teachers use this anecdotal observation procedure and some of the following assessments described, they
should have selective information from which individualized planning
can be pursued. This procedure also serves as a way of getting a base
line (number of observations in a specified time) for use with operant
conditioning techniques.

It is expected that the teacher will become creative in the use of any
observation sheet and devise other codes of reporting. O-X (oral expression) and W-X (written expression) are easy codes to remember. The
subcodes might be more difficult to remember, and the teacher might
prefer to write the description of the entire behavior observed. Consistency of reporting is of much greater importance than use of a specified
code. Coding devices make tallying the number of times certain behaviors
occur easier, and for this reason the teacher may wish to code the behavior only after a complete week of observation. It is important to
emphasize that the *situation surrounding the eventful behavior* must also
be recorded and this, of course, includes the teacher's actions at the time.

There are many checklists available for individual observation. One
developed by Serio (1970), "Know The Child to Teach The Child," is
suggested for the teacher who wants only one very broad instrument.
Some teachers may want to use only parts of it to report certain academic
and social behaviors, while others may find it helpful in reporting and
counseling parents. The checklist is in the Appendix.

TEACHING-TESTING TECHNIQUES AND
SCREENING INSTRUMENTS

There are many good teacher-oriented assessment instruments that
may be used in addition to the daily observation. Only a few of these are
described here. Others are listed in Appendix C.

INSTRUMENTS RELATED TO MODAL LEARNING

The Learning Methods Test

The *Learning Methods Test* (Mills, 1964) is a test to aid the remedial
reading teacher in determining *the student's ability to learn new words
under different teaching procedures.* Basically it is a series of lessons with
tests that measure immediate and delayed learning so that the appro-
priateness of the various teaching methods can be identified. The test
and the teaching steps have been standardized in order that direct com-

parisons may be made with some degree of reliability. The *Learning Methods Test* (LMT) should help teachers answer such questions as

1. How many words can the child learn in a 15-minute lesson?
2. How well does the child retain these words?
3. By what method does the child apparently learn most easily?
4. Does the child retain things learned by any one method more easily than things learned by other methods? (Mills, 1964).

There is no pure approach to the teaching of word recognition. All words have visual, phonic, and kinesthetic elements, which cannot be completely divorced from one another. Mills defines the phonic method as one in which emphasis is given to the auditory characteristics of the word, and this emphasis becomes the differential between the various methods.

The four learning (or teaching) methods used in the LMT are

1. *Visual method.* The child is taught recognition of words by stressing exclusively the visual appearance and other visual clues and associations of the words.
2. *Phonic or auditory method.* Word recognition is taught by the sound qualities of words.
3. *Kinesthetic or tracing method.* The child learns to recognize words by tracing, writing, and other kinesthetic procedures, as outlined by Fernald.
4. *Combination method.* Word recognition is taught by giving equal stress to the visual, auditory, and kinesthetic approaches. [Mills, 1964]

The test materials contain picture-word cards and test record forms. There are four sets of picture-word cards. The sets include primer-grade (blue), first-grade (peach), second-grade (green), and third-grade (pink) level words. The cards are 2 x 4 inches and are designed in the manner of Dolch's picture-word cards, as suggested by Gates (1935), except that a colored card is used in order to prevent transparency, and the LMT picture-word cards are graded.

The words chosen for each grade level are selected from the *Author's Word List for the Primary Grades* (Krantz, 1945), a list drawn from a compilation of frequencies of word use in 84 preprimers, 69 primers, 85 second readers, and 47 third readers in use in 104 representative school systems. Only nouns that can be pictorially represented and possess the more common sound qualities are included. There are 46 word cards for the primer level, 120 cards for the first-grade level, 114 for the second-grade level, and 130 picture-word cards for the third-grade level.

A test record form is necessary to record the forty words selected for the four methods, to record pertinent data about the student, to record the results of the immediate recall test after each fifteen minute lesson, and to record the results of the delayed recall tests. A completed sample record form is shown in Table 3. [Mills, 1964, p. 28]

TABLE 3.   Learning methods test record form

Child's name   Jack Smith   Date   April 2, 1955   Grade   3
Sex   M   Age   9-3   I.Q.   96   Name of Intelligence Test   WISC
Level of Word Cards Used: Primer ____   1st _X_   2nd ___   3rd ___

Set I Phonic method			Set II Kinesthetic method		
	Immediate	*Delayed*		*Immediate*	*Delayed*
1. nose			1. dress		
2. park			2. animals		
3. glass			3. fish		
4. hair			4. mouth		
5. circus			5. people		
6. candy			6. hay		
7. book			7. bowl		
8. letter			8. corn		
9. basket			9. sled		
10. arm			10. woman		
Totals	8	6	Totals	9	9

Set III Visual method			Set IV Combination method		
1. yard			1. street		
2. river			2. train		
3. string			3. robin		
4. wagon			4. game		
5. face			5. car		
6. cap			6. meat		
7. nest			7. plant		
8. butter			8. lion		
9. pony			9. horse		
10. city			10. room		
Totals	5	5	Totals	6	6

*From Robert E. Mills, Manual of Directions for the Learning Methods Test, 1955. p. 30.

The sample test record form of Jack Smith, an imaginary third-grade student, reveals that Jack makes a score of 9 in the kinesthetic method; thus he will learn more comfortably when the kinesthetic method is used.

The manual of directions for this test is easy to follow and the explanations for determining the significance of the scores on the immediate and delayed learning is adequate. This manual has additional features which the interested teacher will find of benefit. It has good coverage of the four methods of teaching and includes research findings on each method.

Test for Three Types of Learners

Baster has designed a test to determine whether a person is a visual learner, an audio learner, or a kinesthetic learner. It is a test that can be administered in about fifteen minutes and should not be given to more than 13 students at one time because of the difficulty of observing more than that number at once. Three reactions should be observed by the teacher, each related to a specific area of learning. There are three simple presentations. In one the teacher writes a list of words on the board and the students reproduce them from memory after they have been erased. In the second presentation the teacher dictates the list orally and has the students repeat it. In the third presentation the students write down words that are dictated orally. They are then rewritten by copying and then from memory. The instructions for interpretations are easy, and the teacher can quickly determine a mode for planning remediation for a child.

Vads

Elizabeth Koppitz has designed a test dealing only with digit span, as on the Stanford Binet and the Wechsler scales. The uniqueness of her test lies in the variety of presentations and responses required. The following four learning modes are measured:

Aural intake
Visual intake
Oral expression
Written expression

In the aural-oral test the teacher dictates a list of digits, and the child repeats the same digits in the same order. In the visual-oral test the teacher shows a series of digits on a stimulus card to a child and asks the child to say as many as possible in the same order after the card has been removed. The child writes the series of digits heard in the aural-written test and writes the series of digits seen in the visual written test.

This short test has been normed to identify learning problems among those with I.Q.'s from 70 to 89 and a group with I.Q.'s of 90 and above. It is an easy test to give and should be a very good supplement to any battery of tests.

A Diagnostic Screening Procedure Based on Styles of Learning
Boder Reading and Spelling Patterns*

This screening procedure (Boder, 1969) is based on reading and spelling patterns. Boder has categorized three different kinds of problems seen in the daily work of children with academic problems. Group I is by far the largest of the three groups, and it includes dysphonetic problems, which indicate dysfunction in the auditory channel. Children in this group read globally, responding to whole words as gestalten or configurations. Lacking phonetic skills, they are unable to decipher words that are not yet in their sight vocabulary, and they consistently spell nonphonetically. Their most striking errors are "semantic-substitution errors" — words that are related conceptually but not phonetically are confused so that these children might substitute *funny* for *laugh, human* for *person, quack* for *duck,* or the name of their own city for the word *city.*

In Group II are dyseidetic problems. Children with these problems reflect a deficiency in the function of the visual channel. Their reading-spelling pattern shows an inability to perceive whole words as configurations. When reading, these children sound out every word as if it had never been seen before. They spell phonetically, and the words are intelligible. Examples of spellings are: *sed* for *said, litl* for *little, lisn* for *listen, sos* for *sauce,* and *onkle* for *uncle.*

Group III includes dysphonetic and dyseidetic problems. These indicate patterns of deficiencies in both the visual and the auditory channels. Children with this problem spell nonphonetically, as in Group I, but their spelling is even more bizarre, and they neither perceive configurations nor are able to sound out words. The prognosis for this group is guarded and if there has not been intensive training at early grade levels, children with these problems remain nonreaders, even at the high school level.

---

*This test also may be used to identify modal learning styles.

Boder's reading and spelling patterns provide the following diagnostic screening format of learning disability children:

1. The visual learner (auditory deficit or dysphonetic)

Sees	Says
laugh	funny
person	human
ask	answer
duck	quack
train	airplane
city	hometown
father	daddy
home	house

   (a)   Spells nonphonetically
   (b)   Misspellings unintelligible
   (c)   Is dependent on words learned by sight

2. The auditory learner (visual deficit or dyseidetic)

Spells		
said	as	sed
little		letl
listen		lisn
sauce		sos
right		rit
business		bisnis
uncle		onkle or uncal

   (a)   Reads phonetically
   (b)   Sounds out each word as if seen for the first time
   (c)   Does not recognize words by sight

3. The learner with both auditory and visual deficits, dysphonetic and dyseidetic

Spells*		
pamaset	for	picture
pamlhe		front
pame		court
came		frame
phasene		scene
bamthe		person

   (a)   Spelling is nonphonetic — usually an unintelligble jumble
   (b)   Remains nonreader even at high school level.

---

*Examples from author's files

SCREENING INSTRUMENTS

THE INDIVIDUAL LEARNING DISABILITIES CLASSROOM SCREENING
INSTRUMENT (ILDCSI) — ELEMENTARY LEVEL

The Individual Learning Disabilities Classroom Screening Instrument
(ILDCSI) by Meier, Cazier, and Giles (Appendix C) is composed of two
major areas of measurement based on "pupil productions" and "behavioral indices."* The section of pupil productions consists of three pages
of tasks which the children are to perform. These include writing their
names, copying a sentence, spelling a group of words, and drawing a
person. On the behavioral indices section the teacher rates a child's behavior compared to behaviors typical of children with visual, auditory,
speech, or emotional problems. Code sheets representing different disability categories provide quick information concerning the child's behavior responses. The following categories are rated:

1. High-risk Disability Case
2. Auditory Perception Disability
3. Neurological Involvement
4. Visual Acuity Disability
5. Visual Perception Disability
6. Spatial Orientation Disability
7. Sequential Memory (Visual and/or Auditory) Disability
8. Social-Emotional Involvement

In addition to screening for learning disabilities, this test includes suggestions for remediation for each disability category. It is a very simple
tool to use for measurement of the specific weaknesses in children which
interfere with reading, writing, spelling, and problem solving.

THE INDIVIDUAL LEARNING DISABILITIES CLASSROOM SCREENING
INSTRUMENTS (ILDCSI)—PRESCHOOL AND KINDERGARTEN LEVEL,
AND ADOLESCENT LEVEL

Giles has developed two additional individual learning disabilities
classroom screening instruments to aid in the screening of learning dis-

---

*Beatty (1975) shows that the number of items necessary to locate common
factors can be reduced from the 80 items on the test to 48 items. This substantially
decreases testing and scoring time.

abilities for ages prior to school and for grades covering upper elementary, junior high, and senior high. The format is the same as described by the ILDCSI, which provides screening techniques for visual, auditory, motor, verbal, and integrational disorders. While the primary/kindergarten (P/K) level instrument provides screening for social-emotional problems, the adolescent level instrument screens for emotional disturbances and social maladjustments separately. An additional feature of the adolescent level instrument is that it screens for vocational attributes, thus providing information which should be of specific interest to those teachers and consultants involved in career development and vocational counseling.

SCREENING FOR LANGUAGE AND/OR
ADJUSTMENT BEHAVIORS

THE MEEKER-CROMWELL EVALUATION OF PERSONALITY

The Meeker-Cromwell Evaluation Scale of Behavior offers a different approach to individual assessment of children with difficult language or personality development. The scale provides a rating on both a normal (N) scale and a defective (D) scale. Children are rated on both scales, since they show a combination of normal and interrupted growth characteristics. The scales range from age one through adolescence. A section of the instrument is shown in Figures 3 and 4.

Meeker indicates there is a correlation between language development and personality growth. She states that often it is the lack of language which forces abnormal growth. An assessment as provided by the Meeker-Cromwell scale helps the teacher to begin a program for the child at the earliest levels of development.

FIGURE 3.   Example, normal developmental progression

MEEKER-CROMWELL EVALUATION OF
PERSONALITY DEVELOPMENT

Name _____Age _____Grade _____School _____

Date _____Clinician _____I.Q. Score _____Test _____

The numbers 1 to 5 represent the degree to which the characteristics are descriptive of the subject. Circle the number most nearly descriptive. The bases for making the judgment are:

(1) Not at all descriptive
(2) Descriptive to a slight degree
(3) Descriptive to a considerable degree
(4) Descriptive to a large degree
(5) Descriptive to a very large degree

1.0 N BASIC BOUNDARY OF SELF-DEVELOPMENT
(Normal)

Rating Scale

1.1 N   Shows developing of thought processes 1 2 3 4 5

1.2 N   Makes boundary differentiation of the self from others .. 1 2 3 4 5

1.3 N   Realizes the basic elements of good and bad 1 2 3 4 5

2.0 N INTACT HEDONISM
(Normal)

2.1 N   Behavior is oriented toward immediate gratification 1 2 3 4 5
2.2 N   Actions seem to be impulsive 1 2 3 4 5
2.3 N   Makes self-restrictions on the basis of avoidance learning
         rather than on satisfaction of acting properly 1 2 3 4 5
2.4 N   Reacts to failure or pressure with decreased effort 1 2 3 4 5
2.5 N   Reacts to failure or pressure with withdrawal 1 2 3 4 5
2.6 N   Conceptualizes performance in terms of success of the
         final product 1 2 3 4 5
2.7 N   Sees his role in controlling the outcome of events 1 2 3 4 5
2.8 N   Understands personal responsibility and control on
         limited basis 1 2 3 4 5
2.9 N   Understands personal responsibility and control when
         pointed out by others 1 2 3 4 5

**FIGURE 4.   Example, developmental progression in
the mentally defective**

MEEKER-CROMWELL EVALUATION OF
PERSONALITY DEVELOPMENT

Name _____Age _____Grade _____School _____

Date _____Clinician _____I.Q. Score _____Test _____

The numbers 1 to 5 represent the degree to which the characteristics to be rated are descriptive of the subject. Circle the number most nearly descriptive. The bases for making the judgment are

(1) Not at all descriptive
(2) Descriptive to a slight degree
(3) Descriptive to a considerable degree
(4) Descriptive to a large degree
(5) Descriptive to a very large degree

1.0 D BASIC BOUNDARY OF SELF-DEVELOPMENT
(Defective)

Rating Scale

1.1 D Poor reality contact, vocal encoding
    1.101 D Bizarre behavior or mannerisms 1 2 3 4 5
    1.102 D Idiosyncratic speech 1 2 3 4 5
    1.103 D Language predominantly gutteral 1 2 3 4 5
    1.104 D Language predominantly fantasy 1 2 3 4 5
    1.105 D Speech fragmentation 1 2 3 4 5
    1.106 D No speech 1 2 3 4 5
    1.107 D Auditory or vocal self-stimulation 1 2 3 4 5
    1.108 D Echolalia 1 2 3 4 5
    1.109 D Perseveration of sounds 1 2 3 4 5
1.2 D Deficient relations with people or objects
    1.201 D No organized avoidance-approach response 1 2 3 4 5
    1.202 D Unable to relate adequately one object
           to another 1 2 3 4 5
    1.203 D Unable to see relationships between
           self and people 1 2 3 4 5
    1.204 D Unable to see relationships between objects 1 2 3 4 5
    1.205 D Unable to see relationships between
           people and objects 1 2 3 4 5
1.3 D Poor body identification
    1.301 D No signs of body admiration,
           grooming or pride 1 2 3 4 5
    1.302 D No self-consciousness 1 2 3 4 5
    1.303 D Apparent disregard for the body itself 1 2 3 4 5

2.0 D INTACT HEDONISM
(Defective)

2.1 D Regression to any level of above fragmentation of
basic boundaries 1 2 3 4 5

PROCEDURE FOR SCREENING EMOTIONAL PROBLEMS

This text is concerned with the assessment and diagnosis of learning problems and gives only minimum references to any other handicapping condition. There are, however, other categories of disabilities that overlap with learning disabilities, compounding the problem and making remediation more difficult. One of these is emotional disturbance, which often results from learning problems in combination with evironmental problems.

Schoolrooms for the emotionally disturbed have been established throughout the nation. Many of the children in these programs are known to experience perceptual problems, and they need individualized instructions. Some learning-disabled children are known to have emotional problems, and they also need management programs and individualized prescriptions for instruction.

The responsibility of diagnosis of emotional disturbances is rightly the domain of the psychologist or psychiatrist; but the responsibility for instructing the emotionally disturbed falls to the teacher. Because of the complexity of the overlapping conditions of emotional disturbance, teachers need guidelines to help them know when to refer a child to a psychologist or psychiatrist.

The following list of characteristics can serve as a guide to help identify children who may need psychological help.

1. Withdrawal and isolation
2. Frequent irritability without cause
3. Inability to tolerate low-level frustration
4. Explosive anger or temper tantrums
5. Excessive concern and worry when not warranted
6. Fear of any kind when not warranted
7. Constant predictable distractability
8. Physiological symptoms with no *apparent* cause such as headaches, excessive sweating, excessive fatigue, stomach aches, nausea, unidentifiable pain

9. Nail biting, stuttering, frequent urination, tics, obesity, sleepiness
10. Inability to accept direction or authority
11. Poor self-evaluation when unrealistic
12. Emotional reactions (lability) inappropriate to stimulus or response
13. Depression, sadness, inability to smile or laugh
14. Excessive fear of failure

Jones (1974) provides another set of behaviors to look for in very young children for signs of maladjustment. These are as follows:

1. The child may be uneasy about entering any new situation or trying any new activity.
2. The child may not move easily from one activity to another or may choose the same activity day after day until he feels sure enough of himself to try something else.
3. The child may avoid any activity which requires close contact.
4. The child may stay away from other children or relate only to one friend.
5. The child may force himself on other children.
6. The child is likely to talk only to his teacher or to talk very little.
7. The child may refuse to share objects in the room and may demand much of the teacher's time.
8. The child may be extremely shy or may lash out at the teacher and other children.
9. The child may behave in such a way as to indicate that things are not going well, giving way to crying or anger.
10. The child generally does not appear to be happy.
11. The child is seldom enthusiastic or begins things on his own.
12. The child hesitates to do anything without first asking permission.
13. The child almost always does exactly what he is told, acting almost like a robot.

When any behavior interferes with appropriate classroom behavior or limits learning, a conference with the child's parents should be held to be sure this behavior is typical and has existed over a long period of time. The questionable behavior may be the result of a normal crisis, and the child's coping may be only temporarily stressed. If the behavior has existed over a prolonged period of time, referral should be made as soon as possible.

SCREENING FOR ACHIEVEMENT RELATED TASKS

SPELLING AND READING INSTRUMENTS

The Zevely Survey of Spelling Skills.

The Zevely Survey of Spelling Skills (Experimental Edition) is designed to be used by the classroom teacher or by a specialist in learning disabilities. It gives insights into the child's abilities in visual memory, letter memory, sequencing, and configuration.

Textbook Screening

Something often overlooked is the facility of the textbook in screening for levels of achievement in children. The teacher may choose a reading, an arithmetic, or spelling text and readily determine at which grade level the child functions with ease. The teacher may then use this information as an aid in planning remediation.

The International Reading Association suggests the following formula as a guideline criteria for three levels of reading (Wilbur, 1975).

Independent level	99% word recognition (in context)
	90% comprehension
Instructional level	95% word recognition (in context)
	75% comprehension
Frustration level	90% or less word recognition (in context)
	50% or less comprehension

Cloze Technique

Bormuth suggests a simple technique for determining readability. The teacher selects a passage of 250 words of continuous writing in which every fifth word is omitted (clozed); in its place there should be a blank line. The blank lines should be of uniform length. All students in the class can be given the same passage at the same time; there is no time limit.

There will be 50 clozures in the 250-word passage, since every fifth word is deleted. Each correct response counts for two percentage points.

To be correct the student must supply the exact word that was deleted. No credit for synonyms is allowed.

An independent level of reading is indicated when a student is 58%– 100% correct. The instructional level is indicated if a student is 44%– 57% correct; a frustrational level is indicated if the student is 43% or below. In addition to being a good testing technique for readability, this is also a good instrument for teaching comprehension skills.

GROUP SCREENING TECHNIQUES

Time and cost pressures have created a great need for upgrading the efficiency with which learning problems are diagnosed. This has led to use of group tests, which as a whole are far below the optimum level. The Texas Education Agency has sponsored research seeking simple, effective means of identifying children with language difficulties. This research shows that two assessments, the LD/Screen-Syllabication and the LD/Screen-Pupil Behavior, were successful in identifying the severe language problems of 6% to 7% of the tested school population for grades three and four and 3% of the tested school population for grade five (Project CHILD, Texas Education Agency, 1974). Comparison of these percentages with other research suggests that they are acceptable (Mykelbust & Boshes, 1969; Kirk, 1972, p. 45), but each school district using these tests must construct its own set of norms.

Some school districts would consider this an advantage in order to reflect the subcultural differences within a community, which itself is culturally distinct compared to the nation's norms. It seems axiomatic that children will compete more willingly and effectively if they are challenged by their own level expectancies within their own culture.

The two screening instruments, the LD/Screen-Syllabication and the Pupil Behavior Rating Scale, are to be used together. Scores from forms A and B of the syllabication test are to be combined, providing a total score for this instrument.

A grid is made from the local norms, and each child's score can be found in the grid, readily identifying whether or not he/she falls in the critical zone that suggests a language disorder.

Some children's scores may be found to show high syllabication skills and low ranking behavior, or vice-versa. These children cannot be identified on the basis of the research as language-problem children, and additional examination is necessary for appropriate identification of their problems.

The description of the two tests, the directions for administering and scoring them, and the instructions on how to prepare the norms are presented as follows: *†

A. LD/Screen-Syllabication
1. No time limit (average student takes 3–6 minutes)
2. Teacher administered
3. Teacher scored
4. Teacher identified (lower 15% of population by using Mean and Standard Deviation Form — Tables 4 and 5)

B. LD/Screen-Pupil Behavior
1. No time limit
2. Teacher rates each child individually (average time for rating each child is 5–7 minutes)
3. Teacher scored
4. Teacher identified (lower 15% of population by using Mean and Standard Deviation Form — Tables 6 and 7)
(Caution: Do no more than seven screenings at one sitting. After a certain number, teacher tends to lump all children into average category.)

COMPUTATION MODELS

Models for computing mean and standard deviation (Tables 4, 5, 6, and 7 show 100 subjects for ease of computation)

A. Computation of LD/Screen-Syllabication
1. Add correct scores of LD/Screen-Syllabication
2. Compute mean for LD/Screen-Syllabication (see Table 4)
3. Compute standard deviation of LD/Screen-Syllabication (See Table 5)
4. Subtract standard deviation from mean to obtain one standard deviation below mean
5. All scores falling below one standard deviation are identified on X axis of grid (Table 8)

---

*Reprinted by permission of Don Partridge, Texas Education Agency, Austin, Texas and Dr. Jim George, Education Service Center, Region X, Richardson, Texas.

†Sources for technical questions: Dr. Billie Grisham, East Texas State University, Commerce, Texas; Dr. Frank Jackson and Dr. Norman McDaniel, Dallas ISD, Dallas, Texas.

B. Computation of LD/Screen-Pupil Behavior
   1. Compute mean for LD/Screen-Pupil Behavior (see Table 6)
   2. Compute standard deviation for LD/Screen-Pupil Behavior (see Table 7)
   3. Subtract standard deviation from mean to obtain one standard deviation below mean.
   4. All scores falling below one standard deviation are identified on Y axis of grid (Table 8)

GRID EXPLANATIONS

(See Table 8)
1. Scores from LD/Screen-Pupil Behavior are on Y axis.
2. Scores from LD/Screen-Syllabication are on X axis.
3. Scores that fall in (1) category represent students who score one standard deviation below the mean on both LD/Screen-Syllabication and LD/Screen-Pupil Behavior. These children, who are considered the most severe in the language-disabled area, constitute between 6% and 7% of the school population for grades three and four and 3% of the school population for grade five.

LIMITATIONS

A. Tests have only been validated for third-, fourth-, and fifth-grade children.
B. Each school district must construct its own set of norms.
C. District size or composition (ethnic groups) of district could cause significant differences.
D. Administrators should be aware that this system is not 100% effective, but is to be viewed as a gross screening to identify children needing further attention.

TABLE 4. LD/screen-syllabication (mean)

Step 1.

	Names	Form "A"		Form "B"		Scores
1.	Joe	12	+	13	=	25
2.	Jack	12	+	12	=	24
3.	Betty	15	+	12	=	27
100.	Bill	8	+	11	=	19
				Sum of scores		2187

Step 2. $2187 \div 100 = 21.87$ mean

TABLE 5.   LD/screen-syllabication (standard deviation)

Step 1.

	Names	Scores
1.	Joe	25
2.	Jack	24
3.	Betty	27
100.	Bill	19
		2187

Step 2.   Square each score then add again.

Scores
25^2
24^2
27^2
19^2
49,611

Step 3.   Square the total of step 1 and divide by 100.

$$\frac{2187^2}{100} = \frac{4,782,696}{100} = 48,829$$

Step 4.   Subtract step 3 from step 2.

49,611   (Step 2)
− 48,829   (Step 3)
782

Step 5.   Divide step 4 by 99 or $(N - 1)$.

$$782 \div 99 = 18$$

Step 6.   Find the square root of step 5.

$$\sqrt{18} = 4.24 \quad \text{standard deviation}$$

Step 7.   Subtract the standard deviation from the mean.

21.87
− 4.24
17.63   one standard deviation below mean

TABLE 6.   LD/screen-pupil behavior (mean)

Step 1.

	Names	Scores
1.	Joe	58
2.	Jack	49
3.	Betty	53
100.	Bill	47
	Total	5257

Step 2. $5257 \div 100 = 52.57$ mean

TABLE 7.   LD/screen-pupil behavior (standard deviation)

Step 1.

	Names	Scores
1.	Joe	58
2.	Jack	49
3.	Betty	53
100.	Bill	47
		5257

Step 2.   Square each score then add again.

Scores

$$28^2$$
$$49^2$$
$$53^2$$
$$47^2$$
$$285{,}072$$

Step 3.   Square the total of step 1 and divide by 100.

$$\frac{5257^2}{100} = \frac{27{,}636{,}049}{100} = 276{,}360$$

Step 4.   Subtract step 3 from step 2.

285,072	(Step 2)
− 276,360	(Step 3)
8712	

Table 7. (cont.)

Step 5.   Divide step 4 by 99 or $(N - 1)$.

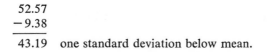

$$99 \overline{\smash{\big)}\ 8712} = 88$$

Step 6.   Find square root of step 5.

$$\sqrt{88} = 9.38 \quad \text{standard deviation}$$

Step 7.   Subtract standard deviation from mean.

$$\begin{array}{r} 52.57 \\ -9.38 \\ \hline 43.19 \end{array} \quad \text{one standard deviation below mean.}$$

TABLE 8. Grid for identification of language disabled children

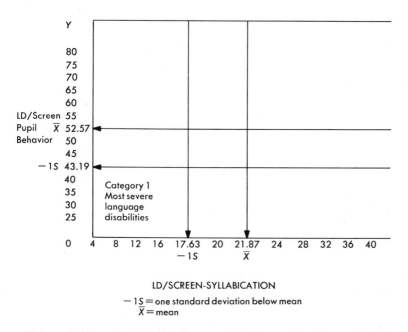

LD/SCREEN-SYLLABICATION

$-1\underline{S}$ = one standard deviation below mean
$\overline{X}$ = mean

Note   In this example, any child who scores 43 or below on the LD/Screen-Pupil Behavior and who scores 17 or below on the LD/Screen-Syllabication will fall into the most severe language disability category (1) .

FIGURE 5. LD/screen-syllabication teacher instructions

Form A

1. Pass out Form A.
2. Have the student record name, date and teacher's name in the appropriate spaces.
3. Read directions orally.
4. Do examples A, B, and C on the chalkboard with children.
5. No time limit.
6. Collect test sheets.

LD/SCREEN-SYLLABICATION

Form A

Name _____Teacher's name _____

Date _____

I. Directions

Look at each word. Count the number of parts (syllables) that you hear in that word.

Blacken the circle in front of the number you counted.

EXAMPLE

A. Until	O 1	O 2	O 3
B. Bat	O 1	O 2	O 3
C. Company	O 1	O 2	O 3
1. Ball	O 1	O 2	O 3
2. Bicycle	O 1	O 2	O 3
3. Tower	O 1	O 2	O 3
4. Course	O 1	O 2	O 3
5. Lemonade	O 1	O 2	O 3
6. Eleven	O 1	O 2	O 3
7. Angry	O 1	O 2	O 3
8. Long	O 1	O 2	O 3
9. Danger	O 1	O 2	O 5
10. Banana	O 1	O 2	O 3
11. Eight	O 1	O 2	O 3

FIGURE 5.   (cont.)

12. Another	O 1	O 2	O 3
13. Fence	O 1	O 2	O 3
14. Happy	O 1	O 2	O 3
15. Finger	O 1	O 2	O 3
16. Terrible	O 1	O 2	O 3
17. Able	O 1	O 2	O 3
18. Sweet	O 1	O 2	O 3
19. Yesterday	O 1	O 2	O 3
20. Lesson	O 1	O 2	O 3

FIGURE 6.   LD/screen-syllabication teacher instructions

Form B

1. Pass out Form B.
2. Have the student record name, date, and teacher's name in appropriate spaces.
3. Read directions orally.
4. Do examples A and B on the chalkboard with children.
5. No time limit.
6. Collect test sheets.

LD/SCREEN-SYLLABICATION

Form B

Name _____Teacher's name _____

Date _____

II.   Directions

Look at the first word in each row. Then find the word that is correctly separated into parts (syllables) and blacken the circle in front of it.

EXAMPLE

A. TODAY	O Tod-ay	O To-day	O To-da-y
B. DISCOVER	O Di-sco-ver	O Disc-over	O Dis-cov-er
1. BIRTHDAY	O Birth-day	O Bir-thd-ay	O Bi-rth-day
2. PICNIC	O Pic-ni-c	O Picn-ic	O Pic-nic

FIGURE 6.   (cont.)

3. PENNY	⭘ Penn-y	⭘ Pen-ny	⭘ P-enn-y
4. WOMAN	⭘ Wo-man	⭘ Wom-an	⭘ W-om-an
5. PENCIL	⭘ Penc-il	⭘ Pen-ci-l	⭘ Pen-cil
6. EMPTY	⭘ Em-pt-y	⭘ Emp-ty	⭘ E-mp-ty
7. TOGETHER	⭘ To-geth-er	⭘ Tog-eth-er	⭘ T-og-ether
8. MAGIC	⭘ Ma-gic	⭘ M-ag-ic	⭘ Mag-ic
9. ANIMAL	⭘ An-i-mal	⭘ Ani-ma-l	⭘ A-nim-al
10. BEAUTIFUL	⭘ B-eaut-i-ful	⭘ Beau-ti-ful	⭘ Bea-uti-ful
11. ELEPHANT	⭘ Ele-pha-nt	⭘ El-eph-ant	⭘ El-e-phant
12. FARTHER	⭘ Far-ther	⭘ F-ar-ther	⭘ Fa-rth-er
13. TOMORROW	⭘ Tom-o-rrow	⭘ Tom-orr-ow	⭘ To-mor-row
14. REMEMBER	⭘ Rem-ember	⭘ Re-mem-ber	⭘ R-emem-ber
15. TELEPHONE	⭘ Te-le-phone	⭘ T-elep-hone	⭘ Tel-e-phone
16. WONDERFUL	⭘ Wo-nde-rful	⭘ Won-der-ful	⭘ Wond-erful
17. PRINCESS	⭘ Prin-cess	⭘ P-ri-ncess	⭘ Pr-in-cess
18. SECRET	⭘ Se-c-ret	⭘ Se-cret	⭘ S-ecr-et
19. ADVENTURE	⭘ Adv-ent-ure	⭘ Ad-ven-ture	⭘ Adve-nture
20. DELICIOUS	⭘ D-elic-ious	⭘ Deli-cious	⭘ De-li-cious

FIGURE 7.   Project child LD/screen-pupil behavior

To the teacher

The purpose of the LD/Screen-Pupil Behavior is to identify children who have deficits in learning.

Adequate opportunity for observation of the student should be a prerequisite for using the checklist. Care and consideration should be given to each item as it relates to the child being evaluated.

A rating of 1, 2, or 3 should be given on each item by circling the appropriate number. Upon completion of the checklist, the circled numbers should be added and the total should be recorded where rating score is indicated.

PROJECT CHILD

LD/SCREEN-PUPIL BEHAVIOR

Name _____ Date _____

School _____ Rating score _____

FIGURE 7. (cont.)

Rating

GENERAL INTELLIGENCE APPEARS TO BE

Below average   1
Average   2
Above average   3

SPEECH IS CHARACTERIZED BY ARTICULATION PROBLEMS, UN-USUAL TONAL QUALITY, CLUTTERING, OR VOLUME CHANGES

Frequently   1
Occasionally   2
Rarely   3

ACTUAL SCHOOL ACHIEVEMENT IN COMPARISON WITH ABILITY TO LEARN APPEARS TO BE

Significantly below expectations   1
Average for abilities   2
Superior to what might be expected for one of his abilities   3

ABILITY IN ARITHMETIC MAY BEST BE DESCRIBED AS

Below average for age and/or grade placement   1
Average for age and/or grade placement   2
Above average for age and/or grade placement   3

HAS DIFFICULTY REMEMBERING AND FOLLOWING INSTRUC-TIONS GIVEN VERBALLY

Frequently   1
Occasionally   2
Rarely   3

HANDWRITING MAY BEST BE DESCRIBED AS

Below average for age and/or grade placement   1
Average for age and/or grade placement   2
Above average for age and/or grade placement   3

ABILITY TO DEVELOP A CONCEPT OF TIME — INCLUDING TELL-ING TIME AND THE AWARENESS OF THE PASSAGE OF TIME

Significantly inadequate   1
Adequate   2
Superior   3

FIGURE 7. (cont.)

Rating

MOTOR COORDINATION CAN BEST BE DESCRIBED AS

Clumsy, awkward	1
Average for age	2
Superior for age	3

WORD RECOGNITION IN READING MAY BEST BE DESCRIBED AS

Below average for age and/or grade placement	1
Average for age and/or grade placement	2
Above average for age and/or grade placement	3

HAS DIFFICULTY RECALLING WORDS AND EXPRESSING IDEAS VERBALLY

Frequently	1
Occasionally	2
Rarely	3

SPELLING SKILLS MAY BEST BE DESCRIBED AS

Below average for age and/or grade placement	1
Average for age and/or grade placement	2
Above average for age and/or grade placement	3

EXHIBITS VERY LIMITED ATTENTION SPAN BEING UNABLE TO ATTEND TO A TASK FOR A REASONABLE LENGTH OF TIME

Frequently	1
Occasionally	2
Rarely	3

TENDS TO BE WITHDRAWN, AVOIDING PEOPLE, NEW SITUATIONS, CONFLICT, OR DIFFICULT TASKS

Frequently	1
Occasionally	2
Rarely	3

REVERSES LETTERS, WORDS, OR NUMBERS IN ARITHMETIC, READING, WRITING, AND/OR SPELLING, SUCH AS *d* FOR *b, n* FOR *u, was* FOR *saw, 14* FOR *41*

Frequently	1
Occasionally	2
Rarely	3

FIGURE 7. (cont.)

Rating

APPEARS TO BE HYPERACTIVE, i.e. GETTING OUT OF HIS SEAT, TALKING TO OTHER CHILDREN, SHARPENING PENCIL, GOING TO RESTROOM, SHUFFLING FEET, TAPPING HIS PENCIL EXCESSIVELY

Frequently	1
Occasionally	2
Rarely	3

APPEARS TO BE UNABLE TO KEEP HIS ATTENTION ON THE MAJOR ISSUE WHILE IGNORING BACKGROUND NOISES AND ACTIVITIES

Frequently	1
Occasionally	2
Rarely	3

FAILS TO REMEMBER SEQUENCES SUCH AS THE ORDER OF LETTERS IN WORDS, NUMBERS IN SEQUENCE, EVENTS IN SEQUENCE, ETC.

Frequently	1
Occasionally	2
Rarely	3

BEHAVIOR IS CHARACTERIZED BY SUDDEN UNEXPLAINABLE SHIFTS IN EMOTIONAL STATE BEING CHARACTERIZED BY SUDDEN TEMPER TANTRUMS, EMOTIONAL OUTBURSTS, ETC.

Frequently	1
Occasionally	2
Rarely	3

SOCIAL ADJUSTMENT AND MATURATION MAY BE BEST DESCRIBED AS

Immature for chronological age	1
Average for chronological age	2
Above average for chronological age	3

READING COMPREHENSION IS

Below average for chronological age and/or grade placement	1
Average for chronological age and/or grade placement	2
Above average for chronological age and/or grade placement	3

FIGURE 7. (cont.)

Rating

FAILS TO VOLUNTEER FOR AND ACCEPT RESPONSIBILITIES

Frequently	1
Occasionally	2
Rarely	3

CONFUSES LETTERS WHICH LOOK ALIKE

Frequently	1
Occasionally	2
Rarely	3

ASSUMES UNUSUAL POSTURES WHEN READING OR WRITING, SUCH AS BLINKING OR RUBBING EYES, TILTING HEAD TO ONE SIDE, HOLDING MATERIAL TOO CLOSE, OR ASSUMING UNUSUAL FACIAL EXPRESSIONS

Frequently	1
Occasionally	2
Rarely	3

LOSES HIS PLACE ON THE PAGE

Frequently	1
Occasionally	2
Rarely	3

APPEARS TO BE EXCESSIVELY IRRITABLE AND AGGRESSIVE — SULKING, PICKING FIGHTS, RESISTING AUTHORITY FIGURES

Frequently	1
Occasionally	2
Rarely	3

COMPLAINS OF PHYSICAL PROBLEMS SUCH AS HEADACHES, STOMACHACHES, ETC., ESPECIALLY DURING CLASSROOM ACTIVITIES WHICH HE FINDS MOST CHALLENGING

Frequently	1
Occasionally	2
Rarely	3

TOTAL SCORE _____

THE JANSKY SCREENING INDEX

Jansky (1972) demonstrated in her study that three out of four failing readers can be identified at preschool level. Her approach, which is a follow-up study of her work with de Hirsch (1966), is that of prevention of reading problems rather than remediation after the child has experienced failure. Her index uses scores from a screening index and from the teacher's predictions. It adapts norms, or cutting points, to the academic expectations of a given school.

The screening index includes the following:

1. Bender Motor Gestalt: Cards A, 1, 2, 4, 6, 8
2. Gates Word Matching Subtest from Bates Reading Readiness Battery (selected exercises)
3. Letter naming: six index cards on which letters are printed in capital letters with black ink
4. Picture naming: 22 pictures of line drawings of common items
5. Binet Sentence Memory Test: list of sentences read to the child by the examiner

According to Jansky, the procedure for developing cutting point data in a given school is as follows:

Procedure to follow for prediction

1. In the spring kindergarten teacher ranks students' potential for reading.
2. The teacher divides the list into four categories, one for students who are likely to do well, one for those who will probably do average work, one for those who will probably fall in the "doubtful range," and one for those who are likely to fail.
3. In the late spring the school psychologist, kindergarten teacher *Y*, a first grade teacher, or a paraprofessional administers the screen index to the children of teacher *X*.
4. This tester ranks the children according to their scores on the predictive screening index.
5. The school psychologist or the principal determines the school's expected reading failure rate.
6. This failure rate, inflated by a 10% safety factor is then used to designate the kindergarten children to be considered high risks.
7. The tester and kindergarten teacher *X* then compare lists to settle on a final high-risk group.

A diagnostic test battery should be administered to kindergarten children placed in the high-risk group. These test results provide a profile of a child's weaknesses and strengths in areas related to reading proficiency, and this information is used for remediation planning. Teachers, psychologists, diagnosticians, or paraprofessionals may be trained in a simple, short session to administer the tests. Testing time per child is only about 20 minutes.

SUMMARY

There is a need for teachers to develop diagnostic skills by using screening instruments, checklists, and other assessments. A combination of information obtained through teacher observations and normative data collected by trained diagnosticians sets the optimum situation at the school level for diagnosing learning problems. Physical, social, intellectual, academic, and emotional data is needed to give a total picture of the individual.

To aid the teacher and diagnostician in screening for behavior and learning disabilities, formal and informal screening instruments should be used. The informal ones are checklists devised to simplify observation procedures. Formal screening instruments such as Mills's Learning Test, Giles's Individual Learning Disability Screening Instrument, and the Meeker-Cromwell test are suggested. Some discriminate between three modes of learning, while others cut across several dimensions of behavior and learning disabilities. The LD/Screen-Syllabication test and LD/Screen-Pupil Behavior rating scale provide a convenient means for screening for language and learning disabilities and provide schools a means for establishing their own norms. The Jansky Screening Index for kindergarten children also provides a means of developing local norms and is presented as an aid to the development of preventive techniques at the beginning of first grade. Because of the overlapping of emotional problems with learning disabilities teachers are urged to use their most sensitive observations to check for emotional symptoms. We have included a list that identifies the most commonly observed characteristics of emotional problems in children. All of these methods are to be used by teachers prior to clinical testing for the purpose of making a more accurate diagnosis.

chapter 4

Task Analysis Procedure

After you have studied this chapter, you should be able to

1. Understand task analysis.
2. Differentiate the approaches to task analysis.
3. Discuss the value of using task analysis in diagnosis and remediation.
4. Understand a process of adapting task analysis to a different style of learning.

INTRODUCTION

An educational diagnostician has a responsibility beyond just making a global diagnosis of the learning problem. The diagnosis must lead to remediation procedures. If proper remediation is to be prescribed it is important to know all the steps required in the learning of a task and to pinpoint where in this process a breakdown occurred. Therefore, to the data collected through standardized tests and teacher observation, a new approach to assessment is added — task analysis; i.e., determining the demands of a task to know which approach to use in presenting the material to be learned. (See the continuum shown in Figure 8.)

The structure for task analysis may be based on the arbitrary choices of the planners. They may choose to run a task analysis (1) on any task lesson assignment, (2) on any of the classifications listed in Chapter 1, or (3) on any subtest. Any of these would be effective means of gathering data to help determine the process needed for a child to accomplish a "task."

FIGURE 8A.   Continuum line for learning a task

TASK ANALYSIS ON LESSON ASSIGNMENTS

Let us begin with a reading assignment as an example. Chalfant and Scheffelin (1969) offer as examples two representative approaches to beginning reading. The steps necessary to accomplish the task of reading are analyzed. These are shown in Figures 8B and 9.

Figure 8B shows the task analysis of a whole-word system of reading. The first step, or subtask, requires the reader to attend to the "word";

FIGURE 8B.   A whole-word system of reading:
a task analysis

1. Attends to visual stimuli	CAT
2. Identifies visual stimuli as graphic word unit	CAT
3. Retrieves auditory language signal for graphic word unit	CAT → (/KAET/)
4. Responds by saying /KAET/	/KAET/

Terminal behavior—Given a graphic word unit such as "CAT," the reader says the word name "/KAET/" within five seconds

Legend

CAT   Visual stimulus
CAT   Graphic word unit perceived as a whole visual image
→   Association in the direction indicated
(/KAET/)   Recalled auditory language signal
/KAET/   Spoken word or auditory language signal

---

*Figures 8B and 9 from James C. Chalfant and M. A. Scheffelin, "Central Processing Dysfunctions in Children," *NINDS Monograph No. 9,* H.E.W. (Washington, D.C., 1969).

the next step is to identify it as a graphic word unit. Following this procedure the reader must then be able to retrieve the auditory language signal for the graphic word unit and finally say the word name.

Figure 9 shows an analysis of a sound-symbol system of reading. The first step in this analysis requires the reader to *attend* rather than observe, as in *look at*. (This means to look *at* something rather than to observe and comprehend.) Second, the graphic word unit (visual stimuli) is identified as discrete letters in a sequence. The reader must retrieve (recall and comprehend) a phoneme for each grapheme and place these in a temporal sequence. Finally, the reader must blend the phonemes into a familiar auditory language signal and *say* the "word name." Once the task is analyzed, the appropriate approach to the child's style of learning, whether it deals with a physiological or a psychological problem, may be determined.

FIGURE 9. A sound-symbol system of reading: a task analysis

1.	Attends to visual stimuli	CAT
2.	Recognize stimuli as graphic word unit	CAT
3.	Identified stimuli as sequence of discreet letters	1st = C, 2nd = A, 3rd = T
4.	Retrieves phoneme for each grapheme	C → (/K/) A → (/AE/) T → (/T/)
5.	Recalls phonemes in temporal sequence corresponding to graphic sequence in step 3	$\dfrac{1st}{(/K/)} + \dfrac{2nd}{(/AE/)} + \dfrac{3rd}{(/T/)}$
6.	Blends phonemes into familiar auditory language signal	(/KAET/)
7.	Responds by saying /KAET/	/KAET/

Terminal behavior—Given a graphic word unit such as "CAT," the reader says the word name /KAET/ within five seconds

Legend

CAT   Visual stimulus
C–A–T   Discrete letters in sequence (graphemes)
(/K/)   Recalled auditory sound signal (phoneme)
→   Association or correpondence in the direction indicated
(/KAET/)   Discrete sounds blended into word
/KAET/   Spoken word or auditory language signal

If child *A* is a nonverbal learning child, then the way to start remediation would be to use the whole-word system of reading, which does not demand as much auditory-vocal response. Perhaps child *B* is also a nonverbal learner, but is, in addition, an uncooperative learner. In order to make a proper remediation plan for child *B's* styles of learning, counseling and group or play therapy should be considered in addition to use of the whole-word system. The therapy may include contingency management, as in behavior modification, or it may involve structuring the reading material around what the child likes to read and is able to read.

Johnson (1968) recommends a different task analysis approach, citing spelling as an example. Two cases are discussed. An eight-year-old child with dyslexia and severe visual-memory deficiencies made only three errors on an oral spelling test, but he missed more than half of the words when they were dictated because he could not revisualize letters. The boy was able to associate the spoken letters, *j a m* with the sweet substance he put on bread, but he could not associate the printed word with the object. A high school sophomore girl had a different type of spelling disability. On a multiple choice spelling test she earned a B, but she earned a D on a dictated test. Examine the nature of the task. The first was purely visual and required recognition of the correct spelling. The second called for the conversion of an auditory stimulus to a visual-motor pattern. Because this student was unable to tranduce information from the auditory to the visual modality, she could not write words from dictation. In contrast, some can write but are unable to spell orally because they cannot reauditorize letter names. Throughout the diagnostic study and daily teaching this type of task analysis is invaluable.

A list of functions to be examined in task analysis are provided by Johnson as follows (the definitions are those of the authors):

Intrasensory — discrimination between two sounds with eyes closed
Intersensory — association of picture or letter that goes with a sound, the integration of two modalities
Sensory modality related — visual, auditory, or haptic task
(a)   Verbal — written materials to read and interpret and vocal expression to be interpreted
(b)   Nonverbal — pictorial and concrete instructions with a minimum of verbal directions, whether written or vocal

Johnson, also, suggests that a level of the task should be identified after the functions are analyzed. She designates these levels as follows:

Perception—to be known and identified
Memory—to be recalled

Symbolization or conceptualization—to be generalized and categorized

The use of a procedure that analyzes the suggested functions according to Johnson involves a study of the modality and the *type* of response rather than the developmental aspects required in the process of learning the task.* Both are good procedures and could be used in the planning stages of teacher evaluation.

A last suggestion in terms of analysis is for teachers to decide how they expect the subject to respond — through pointing, gesturing, speaking, or writing. This points out the need for modifying assignments in the classroom. Some children have learning styles different enough to handicap their progress unless consideration is given to the most appropriate means of response (for example, oral spelling instead of written spelling) in individual cases. Not only must alternative presentations be chosen for learning disability children, allowances for different means of expressive communication must also be made.

FIGURE 10. Acquiring auditory receptive language: a task analysis

1. *Attention.* Attend to vocally produced auditory sound units; i.e., noises, speech sounds, words, phrases, sentences

2. *Discrimination.* Discriminate between auditory-vocal sound units

3. *Establishing correspondences.* Establish reciprocal association between the auditory-vocal sound units and objects or events
   (a) Store and identify auditory-vocal sound units as meaningful auditory-language signals—substitute auditory-language signals for actual objects and/or events
   (b) Establish word order sequences and sentence patterns

4. *Automatic auditory-vocal decoding*
   (a) Improve interpretation by analyzing increasingly more complex auditory-language signals
   (b) Increase the speed and accuracy of the reception of auditory-language signals through variation, practice, and repetition to the point of automatic interpretation
   (c) Shift attention from the auditory-language signals to the total meaning that is carried by the signal sequence

5. *Terminal behavior.* Respond appropriately to verbal commands, instructions, explanations, questions, and statements

---

*Chalfant and Scheffelin approach task analysis through developmental aspects.

TASK ANALYSIS OF CLASSIFICATIONS OF
DEVELOPMENTAL TASKS

Figures 10 through 14* show the task analysis procedure, which may be applied to various classifications (Chalfant and Scheffelin, 1969). According to the construct in Figure 10, the learner must initially attend the vocal-sound units and then must discriminate between the sounds made. Step three includes a reciprocal association formed between the sound unit and an experience. This association allows the learner to interpret the vocal sound as a meaningful language signal, which is stored until retrieved when needed. In the fourth step, analysis of more complex signals occurs. This allows for greater refinement of interpretation, and

**FIGURE 11.   Acquiring expressive auditory language:
a task analysis**

1. *Intention*
    (a)   Possess the need to communicate
    (b)   Decide to send message vocally

2. *Formulate message.* Retrieve and sequence the appropriate vocal-language signals

3. *Organize the vocal-motor sequence*
    (a)   Retrieve the vocal-motor sequence for producing the selected vocal-language signals
    (b)   Execute the vocal-motor sequence for producing the vocal-language signal

4. *Automatic vocal encoding*
    (a)   Combine simple vocal-language signals to form more complex vocal-language signal sequences
    (b)   Increase the rate, accuracy, length, total number, and types of vocal-language signal sequences to the point of automatic production
    (c)   Shift attention from the mechanics of producing vocal-language signal sequences to the contents of the message to be sent

5. *Terminal behavior.* To produce appropriate verbal instructions, commands, explanations, descriptions, and questions

---

*Figures 10 through 14 from James C. Chalfant and M. A. Scheffelin, "Central Processing Dysfunctions in Children," *NINDS Monograph No. 9,* H.E.W. (Washington, D.C., 1969).

subsequently, through practice, it encourages automatic interpretation. Following this the emphasis shifts from the mechanics of sequencing the language, or the making of sentences, to the meaning to be conveyed. In the last step appropriate response occurs.

Figure 11 deals with the acquisition of expressive auditory language, which begins with *intention* instead of *attention*. First, the learner must have a need to communicate through vocal-speech. In step two the message is retrieved and the appropriate vocal-language signals are sequenced. Next the vocal-motor sequence is organized. Automatic encoding follows in which the learner combines simple vocal-language signals to form more complex vocal-language signal sequence. The speed, accuracy, length, total number, and types of signal sequences become more automatic through practice. Soon attention is shifted from the mechanics of communication to the meaningfulness of the message. The terminal behavior in step five is to produce appropriate verbal vocalizations.

Three other task analyses are provided by Chalfant and Scheffelin and are shown here in Figures 12, 13, and 14.

**FIGURE 12. Acquiring vocal-motor production:
a task analysis**

1. *Motion.* Random movements of the vocal-motor apparatus produce random vocal-sound units

2. *Attention*
   (a) Attends to kinesthetic stimuli produced by movement of the child's own vocal-motor apparatus
   (b) Attends to vocal-sound units produced by self and others

3. *Repetition.* Begins to repeat vocal-motor movements which result in the repetition of vocal-sound units

4. *Discrimination.* Discriminate between different vocal-sound units and between different motor movements

5. *Establishing correspondences*
   (a) Establish a reciprocal association between a vocal-sound unit and the motor movement which produces that sound unit
   (b) Store and retrieve vocal-sound units and motor movements

6. *Automatic vocal production.* Increase the speed and accuracy of vocal-sound production through variation, practice, and repetition, to the point of automatic reproduction

7. *Terminal behavior.* To deliberately reproduce the appropriate vocal-sound unit

FIGURE 13.   Encoding graphic-language symbols:
a task analysis

1. *Intention*
   (a)   Possess the need to communicate
   (b)   Decide to send the message in graphic form

2. *Formulate the message*
   (a)   Sequence the general content of the message
   (b)   Retrieve the appropriate auditory-language symbols which best express the intent of the communication

3. *Retrieve* the graphic-language symbols which correspond to the selected auditory-language signals

4. *Organize the graphic-motor sequence*
   (a)   Retrieve the appropriate graphic-motor sequence
   (b)   Execute the graphic-motor sequence for producing the graphic-language symbols

FIGURE 14.   Developmental hierarchy of writing tasks

1. *Scribbling*

2. *Tracing*
   (a)   Connected letters or figures
   (b)   Disconnected letters or figures

3. *Copying*
   (a)   From a model
   (b)   From memory
   (c)   Symbolic and nonsymbolic

4. *Completion tasks*
   (a)   Figure
   (b)   Word completion—supply missing letters
        (1)   Multiple choice
        (2)   Recall
   (c)   Sentence completion—supply missing word

5. *Writing from dictation*
   (a)   Writing letters as they are spoken
   (b)   Writing words and sentences
   (c)   Supply missing word
   (d)   Supply missing sentence

6. *Propositional writing*

DEVELOPMENTAL TASKS: SEMANTIC
SYNTACTIC RELATIONS

Specifically important in task analysis at both early and later developmental stages is the function of semantic syntactic relations (sentence development). Among young children who show great difficulty in language, the categories of Bloom, Lightbown, and Hood (1975) can be of great benefit in choosing the proper level and content of sentence structure for planning remediation. Guilford's work with the structure of intellect, which gives particular emphasis to content, is yet to be used extensively. The Bloom, Lightbown, and Hood categories, which also deal with content, may set a new direction, and when used properly in remediation, they may add to the development of intelligence.

The authors introduce their analysis of sentence structure by explaining that studies of children learning language show relationships between the semantics of early sentences and ideas about objects that originate in the development of sensori-motor intelligence in the first two years of life. Children learn that objects exist, do not exist, then recur. They also learn that people do things to objects; that objects can be acted upon and that objects can be located in space. These are the "things" associated with children's first spoken words, according to the research that revealed a group of semantic syntactic relations. Among these are seven categories of verb relations and the category of possession. Verb categories were distinguished (whether or not an actual verb form appeared in the utterances) according to whether or not relevant movement accompanied the utterance and whether or not position was relevant to either action or state (locative v. nonlocative events).

The seven categories of verb relations are listed below, followed by examples of utterances (of children) of each category.

Action
Locative action
Locative state
Notice
State
Intention
Remaining categories

Action. Here *action* refers to two kinds of movement, where the goal of the movement is not a change in the location of the object. For example

	Agent	*Action*	*Affected Object*
(Boy trying to open box)	my	open	that
(Girl opening drawer)	—	open	drawer

Locative Action. This refers to movement where the goal of movement is a change in the location of a person or object.

	Agent	Loc Action	Object	Place
(Child throwing car and truck in box)	—	put	—	in box

Locative State. This relates a person or object and its location.

	Object	Loc State	Place
(Child pointing to overhead light in hallway)	Light	—	hall
(Child looking for toybag)	the bag	go	—

Notice. This refers to attention to a person, object, or event.

	Noticer	Notice	Noticed
(Child talking to an adult)	Mary	watch	Tom

State. Here a reference is made to a transitory state of affairs. Verbs such as *like, want,* and *need* are involved.

	Agent	(Verb)	Object*
(Child standing next to cabinet where object is kept)	I	want	cracker

Intention. This includes such verbs as *want, going to, have to, let's,* in combination with an action, locative action and occasionally a state verb. Example:

	Agent	(Verb)	Object*
(Child picks up necklace)	I	want wear	this

Remaining Categories. This includes verbs of existence, recurrence, attribution, Wh-question[†] nondevelopmental changes, and verbs that are equivocal or anomalous.

	Agent	Action	Object*
(Child having bath)	Baby	swim	bath
(Child returning from store)	—	buy	more grocery store

---

*Headings not reported in original copy
†Why, when, where questions

These categories provide a challenge to those consultants and therapists who must plan language units for children who have difficulty in communication. It is expected that therapists who deal with speech and language problems will have an interest in this particular group, which concerns the semantics of early sentences. Bloom et al. state that children's ability to speak in sentences depends upon the learning of an abstract system of semantic-syntactical structure. This ability is used to linguistically represent events in the world.

TASK ANALYSIS OF SUBTESTS

We have analyzed the auditory association subtest from the ITPA to describe how subtest analyses may be adapted from the Chalfant and Scheffelin guides. Further, to show use of such analyses in a concrete situation, an example using the demonstrator item from the same subtest on the ITPA is provided. These are found in Figures 15 and 16.

FIGURE 15.   Auditory association process: Task analysis of a subtest from the ITPA

1. *Attention.* Attention to vocally produced auditory sound units (i.e., noises, speech sounds, words, phrases, sentences)

2. *Discrimination.* Discriminate between auditory-vocal sound units found in two sets of sentences or phrases

3. *Establishing correspondences.* Establish reciprocal associations between the auditory-vocal sound units and objects or events.
   (a)   Retrieve and identify auditory-vocal sound units as meaningful auditory-language signals. Substitute auditory language signals of the two sets
   (b)   Establish word order sequences and sentence patterns of the two sets

4. *Automatic auditory-vocal decoding.*
   (a)   Shift attention from the auditory-language signals to the total meaning that is carried by the signal sequences
   (b)   Retrieve a common denominator term (aud-vocal symbol) that makes association between the two sets
   (c)   Retrieve the auditory-vocal symbol that stands for the common denominator to fit set two

5. *Terminal behavior.* Respond with appropriate auditory-vocal symbol to complete set two

FIGURE 16.   Application of task analysis to auditory association task

"Grass is green—sugar is _____"

1. *Attention* to vocally produced words and phrases "Grass is green, sugar is _____"

2. *Discriminate* sound units of *grass, is, green, sugar*

3. *Establish correspondence*
    Associate object (*grass*) with color (*green*) and object (*sugar*)
    (a) Retrieve and identify *grass* and *green* and *sugar* as meaningful auditory language signals. Substitute auditory language signals for actual objects and events
    (b) Establish word sequences and sentence patterns of "Grass is green, sugar is _____"

4. *Automatic auditory-vocal decoding*
    (a) Shift attention from auditory language signals to the total meaning that is carried by the sequence "Grass is green, sugar is _____"
    (b) Retrieve a common denominator term (auditory-vocal signal) which makes association between the two sets of signal sequences—*"color"*
    (c) Retrieve the auditory-vocal symbol that stands for the common denominator to fit the second set—*"white"*

5. *Terminal behavior.* Respond with appropriate auditory-vocal symbol to complete second set, "white"

Task analysis may also be used in remediation. Figure 17 is a flow chart for remediation, using the example in Figure 16.

Another means of analyses of subtests is that provided by Hakim, (1974–75), whose purpose is to delineate the critical skills necessary for tasks in the academic areas of reading, writing, and arithmetic. He suggests four dimensions: (1) input; (2) output; (3) cognition; and (4) memory.

Input. Input is the receiving of information and the beginning of the learning process through sensory modalities. Both verbal and nonverbal experiences are included. The sensory modalities to be utilized are auditory and visual.

	Input	
	Verbal	Nonverbal
Auditory		
Visual		

FIGURE 17. Flow chart for remediation

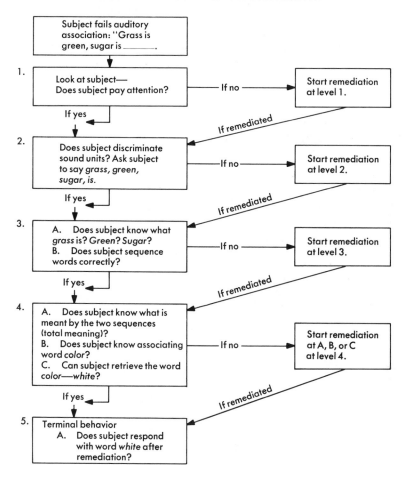

If the task includes the teacher giving verbal information, the input would be auditory-verbal because the child must hear the stimulus and verbal because words are involved.

Output. Output is the expression of information through vocalization or motor expression. The stimulus may be either verbal or nonverbal.

Output		
	Verbal	Nonverbal
Vocal		
Motor		

If the teacher asks a student to write a word, the output is motor-verbal because the child is writing (motor) a word (verbal).

Cognition. The act of knowing involves perceptual, coding, and conceptual levels.

Cognition

Perception	
Coding	
Conceptual	

Hakim identifies the perceptual as the level of differentiation among stimuli, as between "feather" and "father."

The conceptual level involves classifying and categorizing experiences, while the coding level deals with letters that will graphically record the sound of their names.

Memory. The memory dimension incorporates the level of awareness recognition and recall.

Memory

Awareness	
Recognition	
Recall	

At the awareness level a person has a model to copy or reproduce. Clues are present to assist in the solution of the problem at the recognition level, while at the recall level no concrete clues are available to aid the person.

Hakim presents the following model to illustrate his approach to task analysis.

Task. The student is required to write the word that the teacher says on a piece of paper (spelling quiz).

1. *Input* — Auditory-verbal (auditory because the student must hear the word and verbal because a word is used)
2. *Output* — motor verbal (motor because the student must write, and verbal because a word is being written)
3. *Cognition* — Coding (because letter sounds are being transformed into the graphic representation)

4. *Memory* — recall (because no clues are present — we are asking the student to revisualize the word)

The educational diagnostician needs to analyze the tasks involved in the various tests used in the diagnostic process. With this information the diagnostician can pinpoint more precisely the strengths and weaknesses of the student. One example of the use of this task analysis procedure applied to tests has been identified by Hakim.

On subtest 9 of the Detroit Test of Learning Aptitudes, visual attention span for objects, the examiner shows the child a card, removes the card, and asks the child what he/she saw. The analysis can be

1. Input — visual-nonverbal
2. Output — vocal, verbal
3. Cognition — perceptual
4. Memory — recall

It can quickly be determined that this task requires visual input skills with initial nonverbal demands. Then the requirements change. They become vocal-verbal when the student must state through cognition (perceptual) what he/she has recalled (memory).

Such an analysis helps the examiner analyze the data. If the child does not respond to an item, the examiner may, through the process of checks and counterchecks with other analyzed responses, begin to eliminate the dimensions that tend to be true or "hold" when compared with other subtests. Continued analysis can finally highlight which dimensions are being failed most often—visual or auditory input, motor or vocal expression, perception, conceptualization, coding, or the various levels of memory.

The reader may choose, after having read the many possible approaches to task analysis, to modify any of these to meet a particular need. Figures and charts graphically portray the information needed to determine the demands of the task, making it easier to match the cognitive style of learning peculiar to any one student.

SUMMARY

This chapter introduces some relatively new approaches to task analysis. Three areas are covered: (1) task analysis of lesson assignments; (2) task analysis of classification; and (3) task analysis of subtests.

The classification analysis from Chalfant and Scheffelin (1969) deals with developmental demands for learning, as they relate to basic language skills. They are explicit, offering steps to help determine some possible areas where the breakdown in learning may have occurred. The Bloom et al. categories provide analysis of early sentence development.

The Johnson (1967) approach to task analysis offers a framework in which to examine academic tasks like intersensory and intrasensory modal tasks. A flowchart shows the procedure to follow in using task analysis in remediation. The last approach, task analysis of a subtest, is described from Hakim (1974-75).

chapter 5

Criterion-referenced Testing

After you have studied this chapter, you should be able to

1. Understand criterion-referenced testing.
2. Have an introduction to a sample group of criterion-referenced tests.
3. Understand the differences between normed tests and criterion referenced tests.
4. Know the value and the limitations of criterion-referenced testing.

INTRODUCTION

An innovative "shift" in student-evaluation methods is criterion-referenced tests, which are not dependent on norm-references. Rather, they evaluate skills through specific objectives, or criteria; a student's strengths and weaknesses are measured by the number of objectives achieved. The objectives are referenced to content in specific texts or other teaching materials. No assumptions or generalizations are made. Instead the tests measure only what is stated in the objectives. The test results show what students can do relative to the stated criteria and not how they compare to other students. Since criterion-referenced tests evaluate what a student knows or does not know, they provide the basis for instructional procedures appropriate to individual needs. The results can be organized so that appropriate instructional groups can be identified, and if comparisons are desired, the results may be evaluated by comparing records from other schools. This is not the purpose of the testing, but comparison of school achievement levels is possible if desired.

There is a relationship between task analysis and criterion-referenced testing. The goal of task analysis is to examine *where in the task* the individual is failing or succeeding; while the goal of criterion-referenced testing is to determine *what task* the child is failing or passing. Task analysis is an intra-analytic function and criterion-referenced testing is an inter-analytic function.

Criterion-referenced tests use the same basic approach to content validity as do standardized tests. A difference is that the content of the criterion-referenced test is based on a specified set of objectives instead of general curriculum content. The objectives, which are developed by professionals in each academic field, provide a comprehensive approach to content validity.

A major concern of many persons is that the curriculum may be limited to the number of specific objectives outlined in the test. (Of course, a similar concern has been expressed regarding normed tests.) In spite of this limitation, the logic behind a plan that involves assessment of what a person can and cannot do, for use in prescribing remediation seems a worthy attempt in assessment and prescription. If the objectives chosen deal with basic skills and if the whole curriculum is not restricted to a set of limited objectives, it is not expected that the individualized prescription would limit the learning opportunities for the student.

The following tests and their descriptions have been selected to provide an introduction only to this area of testing. Test publishers who do not at present publish criterion-referenced tests will likely place them on the market in the future.

CRITERION-REFERENCED TESTS FOR YOUNG CHILDREN

BASIC SCHOOL SKILLS INVENTORY (BSSI)

An inventory that measures learning and behavior difficulties in young children has been designed by Goodman and Hammill (1975). It is a criterion-referenced test that makes it easy to translate the findings of the evaluation into instructional practice. The BSSI consists of 84 items representing seven areas of school performance.

Basic information
Self-help

Handwriting
Oral communication
Reading readiness
Number readiness
Classroom behavior

Each of the 84 items are stated in question form, and inquire about the child's school-related performance. Each item indicates a desired outcome. An example follows:

> 53. Can the child recognize which of the following pairs of words rhyme: dog—hog, star—pen, blow—slow?
>
> Since rhyming exercises are included in most readiness training programs, you will probably already know the children who do well or poorly on such activities. The example is to be used when you have some doubt about a child's ability in this area. The child must answer all three pairs to pass this item." [Goodman & Hammill, p. 7]

To each item the teacher responds, "Yes the child can do this," or "No the child cannot do this." All items are followed by an explanation that clarifies the expected outcome.

At the beginning of the subscales of the inventory are lists of materials needed to complete the various assessment areas. Pupil record sheets are provided to record individual performances.

The inventory does not encompass a total preschool readiness curriculum. It is recommended that the BSSI be used as a *supplement*. Goodman and Hammill describe their test as follows:

> 1. BSSI was constructed with professional opinions from teachers. . . . It is unfortunate that teachers have had so little input into the development of the construct called "school readiness"; they, more than any other professional group, are most cognizant of the characteristics, skills, and behaviors that contribute to school success. BSSI reflects teachers' judgments of what is educationally important in a child's behavior and performance.
>
> 2. BSSI embodies a behavioral orientation. All the inventory items are presented as behavioral statements of desired learning objectives. The items represent important entrance skills that children who are beginning academic work will need; therefore, they are the terminal behaviors toward which kindergarten and first grade teachers should direct an appreciable amount of their efforts. Presentation of the times as behavioral objectives also increases the specificity, objectivity, and measurability of the instrument. . . . Each item is either directly teachable or

represents a behavior that is subject to modification through training.

3. BSSI is both a norm-reference and a criteria-reference instrument. In the interpretation of the inventory results, you are likely to be concerned with two basic questions: 1.) How does the youngster compare with other children of his age? and 2.) what are the child's specific and educational deficits. The first question, which involves a comparison of the child's performance with the performance of others in his age group requires essentially a norm-referenced interpretation. The second, the child's mastery of the subject content entails a criterion-referenced interpretation. The inventory has been designed to accommodate either type of evalution.

4. BSSI bridges the gap between assessment and training. Having administered the inventory, you can determine some of the performance areas in which the child is having difficulty and can plan a daily program that emphasizes those specific skills which are absent from his repertoire. One of the advantages of this criterion-based approach is that there is no difference between the inventory assessment items and the prescribed training tasks —they are identical. With this kind of consistency, no time is wasted in translating the test results into classroom action.*

EARLY LEARNING SYSTEM†

The Early Learning System (for four-year-olds and five-year-olds), though not specifically classified as a criterion-referenced test, does begin with specific performance objectives, which cover seven areas.

Module A.   Language of Directions: Entry Skills
Module B.   Language of Directions
Module C.   Color Discriminations
Module D.   Shape Discriminations
Module E.   Quantification and Set Concepts
Module G.   Sensory Discriminations

Each module has a beginning diagnostic test for the skills identified therein. Workbooks for each module provide practice in each of the skills. Instruction for the lesson assignments and the posttests is given on cassettes. In addition to teaching basic skills and concepts, the Early

---

*From Libby Goodman and Donald Hammill, *Basic School Skills Inventory* (1975) p. 7.
†See Appendix C.

Learning System is designed to aid children in developing the ability to pursue studies to completion.

INDIVIDUAL CRITERION-REFERENCED TEST (ICRT)*

The ICRT was developed by Educational Progress, a division of the Educational Development Corporation of Tulsa, Oklahoma. The test includes math and reading sections with the objectives referenced to as many as five different instructional programs. Two of the programs are distributed by Educational Progress, but the school district can designate three basal texts or reading series for prescriptive references.

A partial printout, Figure 17a indicates skills the student was able to demonstrate and notes skills to review and learn. The company pro-

FIGURE 17A.   Individualized criterion referenced test report

You Were Able To
Find the difference of a vertical subtraction problem
Find the sum of a horizontal addition problem (to 9)
Find the difference of a horizontal subtraction problem
Match like shapes
Find the figure that represents the fraction ½
Measure an object to the nearest inch
Find the sum of a pictured word problem (to 9)
Identify a subset of a set of 10 members
Identify appropriate symbols to complete a number sentence
Identify the equation for an addition problem
Identify the sum of three addends
Identify the missing addend in an incomplete addition problem
Identify the total value of a set
Identify the number of hundreds, tens, and ones in a number
You Need To Review How To
Find the difference of a pictured word problem (minuend to 9)
Find the product of two three-digit factors
Identify the perimeter of a rectangle
You Need To Learn How To
Find the product of a two-digit factor and a four-digit factor
Solve a multiplication word problem (one-digit and two-digit factors)
Solve a word problem using basic operation on money
Solve a multiplication/subtraction word problem
Find the missing factor of a counting number

*See Appendix C.

vides printouts that prescribe materials to match the diagnosis. ARPL and CLUES are programs distributed by the Parent Company.

PRESCRIPTIVE READING INVENTORY (PRI) AND PRESCRIPTIVE MATH
INVENTORY (PMI) (GRADES 1.5–6)*

The PRI and PMI are criterion-referenced tests distributed by the California Test Bureau of the McGraw-Hill Publishing Company. Since these are referenced to basal texts or series, a school district must specify which series they are using. The printouts will reference the objectives to the pages in the correct series for that school district. (See Appendix R for sample printouts of these tests.)

BEHAVIORAL CHARACTERISTICS PROGRESSION (BCP)*

A criterion-referenced test for the very young and for the retarded is the Behavioral Characteristics Progression (BCP). The instrument is arranged as a matrix of behaviorally stated developmental objectives. Its central element is the behavioral objectives, which allow clients to be assessed on a given trait. There are 59 behavioral areas (strands), each containing up to 50 behavioral steps (characteristic traits). They progress from virtually no abilities in an area to what is considered adult behavior in that area. Examples of two strands identified as "Feeding and Eating" (No. 3) and Math (No. 35) are as follows:

> IDENTIFYING BEHAVIORS: (No. 3, Feeding and Eating) 1–50
> Behaviors
> ☐ Eats only blended or strained foods ☐ Thrusts food out of mouth with tongue ☐ Gags on foods ☐ Sucks food instead of chewing it ☐ Bites down on spoon when inserted into mouth ☐ Chews food only partially before swallowing ☐ Swallows foods w/out chewing them ☐ Chews in other than rotary motion ☐ Takes lg. pieces of food into mouth w/out biting ☐ Eats w/fingers ☐ Crumbles food in hand when finger feeding ☐ Drools while eating ☐ Spits out food ☐ Holds spoon/fork in fist rather than fingers
>
> 1.0   Opens mouth when physically stimulated by spoon held by another.
> 2.0   Opens mouth voluntarily at the sight of food.
> 3.0   Removes semi-liquid food from spoon with mouth when being fed—some rejection.
> 5.0   Allows spoon to be removed from mouth.

---

*See Appendix C.

13.0 Grasps finger foods offered by adult and carries them to mouth.
17.0 Carries finger foods to mouth and bites off smaller pieces.
49.0 Serves self in cafeteria.
50.0 Manages to eat different types of foods: liquids, crisp foods, slippery foods.

Identifying behaviors   (No. 35, Math)   1–50 Behaviors.

☐ Does not add or subtract correctly ☐ Does not multiply or divide correctly ☐ Has difficulty solving word problems ☐ Forgets sequence of steps in long division ☐ Carries and/or borrows from wrong direction in addition, subtraction

1.0   Sorts according to shape, size and length.
2.0   Locates big and little, large and small in groups of two objects.
3.0   Arranges objects in order of size from smallest to largest.
10.0 Counts orally to three.
15.0 Locates front and back, left and right.
20.0 Identifies what number comes before and after a given number or between two numbers (up to 10).
23.0 Reads and writes numerals to 19.
50.0 Multiplies and divides fractions and decimals. Computes simple percentages.*

SUMMARY

Criterion-referenced tests bridge the gap that often exists between diagnosis and remediation. The specific objectives make for definitive diagnosis of skills and identify those behaviors that need remediation or are not yet learned. Since the objectives are referenced to specific texts or other teaching materials the tests provide a basis for individualizing instruction.

Criterion-referenced tests differ from other standardized tests in that they are not normed on a specific population. They are similar to diagnostic tests, however, which may be norm referenced. More criterion-referenced tests will probably be published in the future.

---

*From Santa Cruz County Office of Education, Santa Cruz, California, ESEA Title III.

chapter 6

Clinical Diagnostic Procedure

After you have studied this chapter, you should be able to

1. Describe the information needed (in addition to test data) if a complete diagnosis is to be attempted.

2. Identify the minimum battery of tests to be used at the preschool, elementary, upper elementary, junior high, and high school levels.

3. Describe the tests of intelligence, achievement, and perception (developmental and communication) commonly used to determine learning problems.

4. Understand the individual subtest functions within the *Wechsler Intelligence Scale for Children,* and the *Illinois Test of Psycholinguistic Abilities.*

5. Discuss a clinical procedure to follow in the process of diagnosing learning problems.

NONTEST DATA

By the time the consultant is ready to begin diagnosis, all available information concerning the case study should be gathered. In addition to test data, the consultant should be familiar with the observational data (see Chapter 3), medical information, home environment history, social history, and educational history of a client. The following list itemizes some supplements to test data:

Home environment history

1. Sleep habits
2. Study habits and attitudes
3. Family stability and unity of spirit
4. Parent behavior and attitude toward child
   a) Expectations
   b) Acceptance or rejection
   c) Encouragement or pressure

Medical information

1. Vision
2. Hearing
3. General health
4. History of past illnesses
5. Birth injury

Social history

1. Socioeconomic status needs
2. Social activities
3. Sociogram information
4. Adaptability
5. Peer and sibling relationships
6. Developmental history of personal and social relationships

Educational history

1. Achievement test information
2. Serial observations of consistency of and persistency in behavior patterns
3. Samples of schoolwork (reading and language evaluations)
4. Current school problem as viewed by parent
5. Complete academic history including failures and successes
6. Socioeconomic influences

Intellectual endowment

1. History of motor and language development
2. Intelligence quotients obtained on prior tests
3. Specific and outstanding accomplishments

In most instances much of this information can be obtained from a child's parents without any difficulty. Sometimes this may be impossible, and the consultant must confront the child for the data. Because of a sense of privacy or because of rebelliousness, young people may not wish to reveal significant facts about their lives. Should this be the case, the consultant must go to the school records for background material.

TEST BATTERIES AND DESCRIPTION OF TESTS

To cover in one book every test that could be helpful in diagnosing learning disabilities is impossible. Those described in this chapter are only a sampling. They are in prevalent use in the United States and are highly recommended. For other available tests, please refer to Appendix C. Many of the tests listed, though not related to the studies in this book, have been useful in some unusual cases.

FIGURE 18. Minimum test battery for preschool children

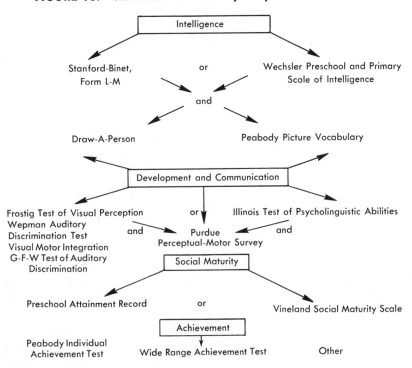

FIGURE 19.   Minimum test battery for elementary children

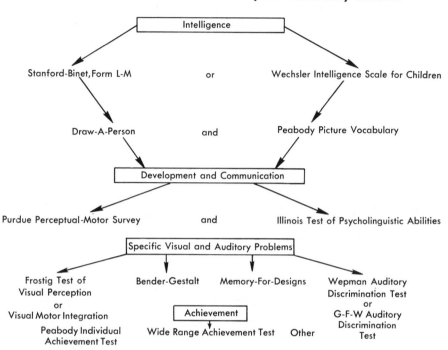

The choice of a test battery should depend on three major factors:
(1) the functions and/or skills needing evaluation in order to plan effective remediation; (2) the stamina of the child; and (3) the time available
for testing. A basic minimum test battery should always be planned;
as the need becomes apparent, other tests can then be added. Generally
the battery should be administered over a period of two days rather than
in one sitting.

For the preschool child, four areas are recommended for testing:
(1) intelligence; (2) achievement; (3) development and communication;
and (4) social maturity. A minimum battery for elementary, junior high,
and high school groups should include: (1) intelligence; (2) achievement; (3) development and/or communication (according to age group);
and (4) specific visual and auditory tests. As measurement becomes
more refined, tests of other communication processes (such as the sense
of touch) will become available. When these new tests are developed,
they should be added to the test battery.

The minimum test battery provides diagnostic information in the two
major areas of learning — perceptual-motor and language. By evaluating
performance from both of these areas, the most direct route to effective

FIGURE 20. **Minimum test battery for upper elementary, junior high, and high school**

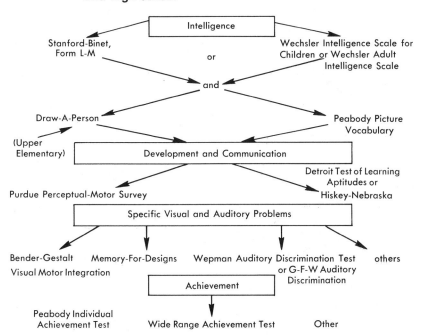

remediation can be determined. Figures 18–20 show possible choices for test selections at different grade levels.

INTELLIGENCE TESTS

WECHSLER INTELLIGENCE SCALE FOR CHILDREN

The *Wechsler Intelligence Scale for Children,* commonly known as the WISC, has now been revised and is identified as the WISC-R. The old and new editions both test the verbal tasks and the performance tasks of a child in order to determine full-scale I.Q. score. The *nature* of the content of the subtests has not been changed; thus the abilities measured remain the same. Some of the significant changes in the WISC-R are listed as follows:

1. Consecutive presentation alternating verbal and performance subtests
2. Identification on the record form of basal and ceiling positions

3. Identification on the record form of questioning procedure
4. Coding and mazes subtests printed on separate supplementary forms
5. Greater variety of aids for discrimination between 0, 1, and 2 credit responses on vocabulary, similarities and comprehension subtests
6. Change in age range—the WISC-R is offered to ages 6-0 through 16-11.

Both the WISC and the WISC-R consist of six verbal and five non-verbal, or performance, subtests covering (1) information; (2) comprehension; (3) arithmetic; (4) digit span (memory for digits forward and backward); (5) similarities; (6) vocabulary; (7) picture completion; (8) picture arrangement; (9) block design; (10) object assembly; and (11) coding. In the WISC the verbal subtests (1-6 above) precede the performance subtests (7-11). The WISC-R alternates the presentation of the verbal and the performance subtests in the administration of the total test.

The *Information Test* measures the limits of a child's general information. The extent of one's general information has long been thought to be closely related to total I.Q.

The *Comprehension Test* can be called a test of common sense, since achievement on it seems to depend upon a certain amount of practical information and a general ability to evaluate past experience. It is frequently valuable in detecting emotional instability, and almost invariably it reveals something about a person's social and cultural backround.

The *Arithmetic Test* tests ability to solve arithmetic problems. Since mathematical aptitude is often indicative of mental alertness, children who do poorly on this test often have difficulty with other subjects. Thus this subtest can be valuable in the evaluation of educational abilities, especially when supplemented by the results of the Information Test. The combined scores of these two tests frequently furnish an accurate estimate of the child's scholastic achievement.

The *Digit Span Test,* as pointed out in the test manual, is perhaps one of the least effective tests of general intelligence. A good rote memory may be practical in many situations, but it certainly is not an integral part of global intelligence.

The *Similarities Test* is a kind of general intelligence test in which the responses reveal the logical character of the thinking processes.

An excellent measure of general intelligence, the *Vocabulary Test,* evaluates learning ability, verbal resources, and general range of ideas through the number of words comprehended. Because brain-damaged patients will often retain words that reflect their past level of performance but not their actual functioning ability, the Vocabulary Test can also estimate the extent of a child's mental deterioration.

The Picture Completion Test requires the subject to discover and identify the missing part of an incompletely drawn picture. The test is particularly good for determining intelligence at the lower levels. Most conspicuously it measures the individual's basic perceptual and conceptual abilities, insofar as these are involved in the visual recognition and identification of familiar objects and forms. In a broader sense, however, the test measures the ability of the individual to differentiate between essential and nonessential details. It has been found to have the highest "general intelligence" loading of any of the performance tests.

The Picture Arrangement Test consists of a series of pictures which, when placed in the right sequence, tell a little story. This test measures ability to comprehend sequence and to reconstruct situations—abilities some theorists have referred to as "social intelligence." Those who do fairly well on this test are rarely mentally deficient, even though they may score poorly on other tests.

The Block Design Test measures ability to perceive and analyze forms and to perceive pattern. An excellent test of general intelligence, the Block Design Test is good for qualitative analysis. How the subject approaches a task in this test can help define if and why he/she has a problem. Patients suffering from mental deterioration, senility, and brain disease have particular difficulty in managing this test, and often, even with repeated efforts, they cannot complete the simplest design.

With the exception of the Digit Span Test, the *Object Assembly Test* correlates with general intelligence less than any of the Wechsler subtests. It does, however, contribute something to the total score. The best features of this test are its qualitative merits. Various examiners have praised it because it tells them something about the thinking and working habits of the subject. When object assembly is analyzed in terms of Guilford's structure of intellect (1959), three factors emerge: spatial orientation, visualization, and figural selection.

The Coding Test shows its most consistent loadings in nonverbal organization and memory. The subject is required to associate certain symbols with certain other symbols, and the speed and accuracy with which the association is completed measures intellectual ability. Reading-disabled children may be handicapped because they read slowly, and unstable people generally may do poorly on this test.

The Wechsler test batteries, among the oldest and most frequently used intelligence tests, are of special importance because of the countless number of studies that have been made with them. Their diagnostic and clinical features contribute greatly to the study of learning disabilities.

THE STANFORD-BINET INTELLIGENCE SCALE, FORM L-M

This test of mental maturity or intellectual ability is so well known that it is unnecessary to deal with it at length. In relation to learning disabilities, its lack of a profile compared to the WISC or WISC-R has reduced its effectiveness in differential diagnosis. However, this does not negate its usefulness. Recent research suggests that it can be quite helpful in the diagnosis of specific problems. Sattler (1965), Meeker (1969), and Valett (1968) have completed studies of the specific factors that are measured by each subtest. Refer to the section for use of the Stanford Binet in diagnosis in Chapter 7.

PEABODY PICTURE VOCABULARY TEST

The *Peabody Picture Vocabulary Test* (PPVT) by Lloyd M. Dunn is an *untimed* individual test that usually takes 15 minutes or less. The test booklet contains 3 practice plates and 150 test plates, each consisting of four numbered pictures. The examiner reads the stimulus word given on the answer sheet, and the subject responds by indicating the number of the picture that best illustrates the stimulus word.

Items are arranged in ascending order of difficulty, and the subject responds only to the items between his "basal" level (eight consecutive correct responses) and his "ceiling" level (six failures out of eight consecutive responses).

Scoring is rapid and objective. The examiner places a marker over the item number of each incorrect response; these marks are counted and subtracted from the ceiling score. The difference can be converted into a mental age, an I.Q., and a percentile rank.

By measuring a subject's vocabulary, the PPVT provides a well-standardized estimate of verbal intelligence. It has been found to correlate with the WISC in the high .70s and low .80s.

PICTORIAL TEST OF INTELLIGENCE

The *Pictorial Test of Intelligence* by Joseph L. French and Donald Greer is another test that may be used with young children, ages three to eight. It is a Binet-type instrument that allows the subject to respond in a multiple choice fashion. The instructions are simple and the subject responds by pointing to one of four pictures on a test card. The examiner records the position of the choice on an answer sheet. The total number of correct items, the raw score, is converted by table to mental age units and to deviation I.Q.'s.

There are six subtests arranged in order of difficulty, and there is no base or ceiling to be obtained. All items are administered (with a few exceptions), regardless of the successes or failures of the subject.

The test is reputed to be of value in measuring motor and speech handicaps and in measuring the learning aptitudes of young children in a molar manner.

GOODENOUGH-HARRIS DRAWING TEST

The *Goodenough-Harris Drawing Test* is a good test of conditioned or learned responses. A child draws a person on a sheet of white 8½- x 11-in. unlined paper. The number of details reproduced in the drawing determines the score, and the comparison of the total number of details with a normal scale determines the child's mental age. From the mental age, one can tabulate the I.Q.

Children with learning disabilities, particularly dyslexia, have considerable difficulty with drawing a person. Whether or not this difficulty is due to problems of self-concept, revisualization, or the inability to organize a complex structure is not known at this time.

McCARTHY SCALES OF CHILDREN'S ABILITIES

A test that is very popular among diagnosticians is the *McCarthy Scales of Children's Abilities*. It is used with young children and provides a scale index for the following areas: verbal (V), perceptual-performance (P), quantitative (Q), memory (Mem), and motor (Mot). From the verbal, perceptual-performance and quantitative scales a general cognitive index (GCI) can be derived. A position for evaluation of laterality is also provided.

The measurements obtained in this test afford the diagnostician a valuable tool for examining individual differences in psychological processes, functions *which must be identified* according to the guidelines of many states before a child may be labeled as learning disabled. The provision of such descriptive indices in the profile make this a very good test for the novice diagnostician. Since this test is for young children, it also helps to meet the assessment need of kindergarten children, which is growing because of the extension of services provided this age child in the public schools.

The *Slosson Intelligence Test for Children and Adults* (SIT), by Richard L. Slosson, is an individual screening instrument made for use by the whole range of school professionals. The items used in this short screening test are similar in nature to the Stanford-Binet tasks, and the estimated time for administering and scoring varies from between ten to thirty minutes. Very complete instructions for determining chronological age, mental age, basal age, and ceiling level are provided. In addition a very handy "I.Q. Finder" is attached to the back of the manual. Scoring is done by checking responses with a plus or minus on the scoring sheet.

DEVELOPMENTAL AND COMMUNICATION TESTS

VISUAL-MOTOR AND PERCEPTUAL-MOTOR

Bender Visual-Motor Gestalt Test

The *Bender Visual-Motor Gestalt Test* is a maturational test in visual-motor gestalt functions. It is useful in exploring retardation, regression, loss of function, and organic brain defects in children and adults. However, this kind of diagnostic exploration should be left to the professional diagnostician. Its use relative to learning disorders should be confined to visual-motor aspects. This point cannot be overemphasized. The role of medicine is to diagnose medical problems, but the role of education is to diagnose academic problems.

The subtest is given a white, unlined sheet of paper, 8½ × 11 in. The subject views a card with a stimulus design and then copies the design. The test has no time limit, and the designs are not removed until the subject reproduces them. Memory is not a factor in this test.

The reproductions are scored based on the amount of distortion of shape, rotation, integration, and perseveration of each design. Total errors are counted and compared with the normal score for the subject's age group. The Koppitz (1964) scoring system is available for use with children up to 11 years of age.

Developmental Test of Visual-Motor Integration

The *Developmental Test of Visual-Motor Integration* (VMI), by Keith Beery is a series of 24 geometric forms to be copied using pencil and paper. The forms are arranged in order of increasing difficulty. The test can be administered to children between 2 and 15 years old, but it was designed primarily for the preschool and the early primary grades. The format is suitable for group and individual administration.

Since visual-motor behavior is a composite of other behaviors including visual perception and motor coordination, techniques for determining specific areas of difficulty are provided. In addition teaching techniques to parallel areas of assessment are suggested. Individual record booklets may be ordered for children ages 2 to 8 years old or for ages 2 to 15 years old. A manual provides instructions for group and individual administration and scoring criteria for the geometric drawings.

Memory-for-designs Test

The *Memory-for-designs Test* (MFD) by Frances Graham and Barbara Kendall involves the reproduction of single geometric designs from memory. In the 1920s the inability to perform such tasks was associated with "organic" impairment, and the MFD was developed to accompany the test battery for the clinical study of possible brain-damaged patients.

The test is composed of 15 cardboard squares with a single black design printed on each. The subject views a card for five seconds and must reproduce the design from memory on a sheet of white 8½ x 11 in. paper. The higher the score received, the poorer the performance. When tabulated from the raw score, the difference score gives an approximate rating of normal, borderline, or critical (possible brain damage).

The Marianne Frostig Test of Visual-Motor Perception

Designed by Marianne Frostig, this test measures five specific areas of visual perception: (1) eye-motor coordination; (2) figure-ground discrimination; (3) form constancy; (4) position in space; and (5) spatial relations. Although it was intended primarily for preschool children, the test can be quite effective in helping to detect specific areas of visual perception weakness in first-grade and second-grade children. Frostig has a well-planned remediation program based on this diagnostic instrument. Her program can also help the consultant to prescribe remediation for visual perception problems.

The Purdue Perceptual-Motor Survey

The Purdue Perceptual-Motor Survey (PMS) by Eugene G. Roach and Newell C. Kephart (1966) is not a test. It is a survey that enables one to observe a broad spectrum of behavior within a structured, but not stereotyped, set of circumstances. The framework originated in Kephart's *The Slow Learner in the Classroom* (1960) and is designed primarily to detect rather than to diagnose perceptual-motor behavior in a series of behavioral performances. The consultant will find it easy to administer and will need little or no equipment.

Consisting of 22 scorable items, the survey is divided into 11 subtests, each measuring some aspect of the child's perceptual-motor development. Basically, these subtests are concerned with laterality, directionality, and the skills of perceptual-motor matching.

From this survey, the consultant may discover subtle areas of weakness that perhaps cannot be detected through tests of linguistic abilities. Thus possibilities for remediation, including physical education programs and tutorial instruction, become even greater. Because the need for physical remediation has become increasingly more evident, many physical education programs are being designed in accordance with structured exercises that help to develop well-rounded gross motor movements.

The Purdue Perceptual-Motor Survey should not be used for children who have specific defects such as blindness, paralysis, or known motor problems. Although designed for children in grades 2 through 4, the survey can also be used with older children who are retarded. The normative scores were determined by using children between the ages of six and ten.

LANGUAGE AND LEARNING APTITUDE TESTS

DETROIT TESTS OF LEARNING APTITUDE

The *Detroit Tests of Learning Aptitude,* by Harry J. Baker and Bernice Leland, is a comprehensive individual psychological examination and a practical diagnostic instrument. It is comprised of nineteen subtests, each a scale by itself, and from these a variety of batteries may be selected for specific cases. These include the blind and visually handicapped, the deaf and the acoustically handicapped, the orthopedically handicapped, the cerebral palsied, the speech handicapped, the neurologically handicapped and brain injured, and the emotionally disturbed and socially maladjusted. The batteries of tests may also measure the special disabilities of both normal and mentally retarded people and the outstanding talents of the mentally gifted. Baker and Leland identify eight mental faculties in their 19 subtests. These are listed here.

Subtests	Mental Faculties	Subtest Numbers
1. Pictorial Absurdities	(a) Reasoning and comprehension	1,2,8,10,15,17
2. Verbal Absurdities	(b) Practical judgement	5,7,10,18
3. Pictorial Opposites	(c) Verbal ability	2,4,11,19
4. Verbal Opposites	(d) Time and space relationships	10,12,17
5. Motor Speed	(e) Number ability	7,14
6. Auditory Attention Span for Unrelated Words	(f) Auditory attentive ability	6,7,13,18
7. Oral Commissions	(g) Visual attentive ability	1,3,9,12,16,17,18
8. Social Adjustment A	(h) Motor Ability	5,7,12,18
9. Visual Attention Span for Objects		
10. Orientation		
11. Free Association		
12. Designs		
13. Auditory Attention Span for Related Syllables		
14. Number Ability		
15. Social Adjustment B		
16. Visual Attention Span for Letters		
17. Disarranged Pictures		
18. Oral Directions		
19. Likenesses and Differences		

ILLINOIS TEST OF PSYCHOLINGUISTIC ABILITIES

Many investigators have studied acquisition and use of language. Until recently remedial work on linguistic deficiencies has been limited to speech correction and testing for educational and remedial programs has been done on a trial basis only. To facilitate educational evaluations for remedial purposes, the *Illinois Test of Psycholinguistic Abilities* (ITPA) can be used as a diagnostic tool. Its design originated from Hull's formulations and Osgood's psycholinguistic model (Kirk, 1969). In the following explanation, subtest titles from the 1961 and the 1968 editions of the test are listed, with the 1961 titles in parentheses.

Three major factors determine any given psycholinguistic ability: level of organization, psycholinguistic processes, and channels of communication.

Levels of Organization refers to the functional complexity of an organism. Some psycholinguistic activities exhibited by humans appear to demand much higher levels of organization than others. Two levels are important for language acquisition—representational and automatic-sequential. The representational level includes activities that require the meaning or significance of linguistic symbols. Tests that measure this are Auditory Reception (Auditory Decoding) and Visual Reception (Visual Decoding), Associational-Auditory Association (Auditory-Vocal Association) and Visual Association (Visual-Motor Association), Expression-Verbal Expression (Vocal Encoding) and Manual Expression (Motor Encoding). The automatic-sequential level includes activities that require the retention of linguistic symbol sequences and the execution of the automatic action that follows different linguistic structures. The redundancies within a language make certain responses automatic. Tests that measure this are Automatic-Grammatic Closure (Auditory-Vocal Automatic) and Visual Closure (1968 revision only), Sequential—Auditory Memory (Auditory-Vocal Sequencing) and Visual Memory (Visual-Motor Sequencing).

Psycholinguistic processes refer to the acquisition and use of all the habits required for normal language usage. There are three main sets of habits: reception (decoding), association, and expression (encoding). The process of reception consists of the sum of those habits necessary for the attainment of meaning through either visual or auditory linguistic symbols or stimuli. The process of association consists of the sum of those habits necessary for manipulating linguistic symbols internally. Tests that demonstrate the presence of associative ability include word association tests, analogies tests, and similarities and differences tests.

The process of expression consists of the sum of those habits necessary for expression in words or gestures.

Channels of communication indicates the sensory-motor path by which linguistic symbols are transmitted, received, and responded to. The ITPA is divided into two parts — reception and response. Pure receptive ability requires only a mode of reception — hearing or sight. How the subject responds has no relevancy to a test of receptive ability. Similarly, expressive ability requires only a mode of response — speech or gesture. Associative ability or any combination of abilities, however, requires the interaction of all the channels of communication.

There are nine psycholinguistic abilities tests in the 1968 edition. Following is a definition of each test.

The representational level. These tests assess the subject's ability to receive and interpret meaningful symbols (reception or decoding), relate symbols on a meaningful basis (association), or express meaningful ideas in symbols (expression or encoding).

Reception

1. Auditory Reception (Auditory Decoding) examines the ability to comprehend the spoken word.
2. Visual Reception (Visual Decoding) examines the ability to comprehend pictures and written words.

Association

1. Auditory Association (Auditory-Vocal Association) examines the ability to relate auditory symbols in a meaningful way.
2. Visual Association (Visual-Motor Association) examines the ability to relate visual symbols in a meaningful way.

Expression

1. Verbal Expression (Vocal Encoding) examines the ability to express ideas through spoken words.
2. Manual Expression (Motor Encoding) examines the ability to express ideas through gestures.

The Automatic-sequential level. These tests assess nonmeaningful uses of symbols; i.e., long-term retention and short-term memory of symbol sequences. Automatic tests make frequent use of language's numerous redundancies, which lead to highly overlearned or automatic habits for directing syntax and inflection without conscious effort.

Automatic tests

1. Grammatic Closure (Auditory-Vocal Automatic) helps in predicting future language abilities from past achievements. It is specifically related to the correct use of grammar.
2. Visual Closure (1968 edition only) measures the perception interpretation of any visual object when only a part of it is shown.

Sequential tests

1. Auditory Memory (Auditory-Vocal Sequencing) examines the ability to correctly repeat a sequence of auditory symbols. A modified digit repetition test measures this linguistic skill.
2. Visual Memory (Visual-Motor Sequencing) examines the ability to correctly reproduce a sequence of visual symbols. The subject duplicates the order of a sequence of pictures or geometrical designs, which are shown and then removed.

Supplementary tests (1968 edition only) for purposes of remediation

1. Auditory Closure measures the perceptual interpretation of any sound when only some of it is heard.
2. Sound Blending measures the communication of sound blends by determining how well the person is able to blend together the sounds he/she hears.

HISKEY-NEBRASKA TEST OF LEARNING APTITUDE

The *Hiskey-Nebraska Test of Learning Aptitude* was designed to evaluate the learning ability of deaf children. The present edition is a revision of another test (1941), and both were developed by Dr. Marshall S. Hiskey at the University of Nebraska (1966). The revision has been expanded to cover age norms for those who can hear. It was standardized according to results for children ranging in age from two years six months to seventeen years five months.

The Hiskey-Nebraska Test is included in this battery of tests for learning disabilities because it has subtests that measure psycholinguistic abilities. Since it may be given to children older than ten, which is the maximum range of the *Illinois Test of Psycholinguistic Abilities,* this test supplements the test battery. The following subtests are administered to children between ages three and ten:

Bead Pattern
Memory of Color

Picture Identification
Picture Association
Paper Folding

When used in conjunction with such tests as the WISC and the Stanford-Binet, the following subtests are practical for discovering learning disabilities. These can be administered to children of all ages.

Visual Attention Span
Block Patterns
Completion of Drawings
Memory for Digits
Puzzle Blocks
Picture Analogies
Spatial Reasoning

The test can be administered as a whole in place of or in addition to the other tests in the battery. In many cases four subtests from the latter group are used more often than the remaining three to avoid duplication of the WISC and Stanford Binet. These are the subtests that measure visual attention span, completion of drawings, picture analogies, and spatial reasoning.

Although the test manual does not elaborate on what these subtests purport to measure, experience with similar tests points to the following possibilities:

Visual attention span measures the ability to sequence picture objects. Memory is a major factor (similar to visual memory on the ITPA).

Completion of drawings measures a kind of visual closure. More specifically, it measures an ability to discriminate essential from nonessential detail, thus making the term visual discrimination applicable to the subtest.

Picture analogies, similar to the visual association subtest of the ITPA, is a psycholinguistic subtest that measures the ability to see relationships between different visual stimuli.

Spatial reasoning measures just that. It is similar to the spatial relationship measure found on Frostig's visual perception test.

Listed below are the other Hiskey-Nebraska subtests with their corresponding descriptions of measurement.

1. Bead pattern — visual memory and visual memory for designs
2. Memory of color — visual memory and memory for visual patterns
3. Picture identification — perception and visual discriminations

4. Picture association — conceptual ability to see similarities between different visual stimuli
5. Paper folding — a visual-motor ability that involves sequencing
6. Block patterns — perceptual organization, depth perception, and spatial relationships
7. Puzzle blocks — perceptual organization and spatial relationships.
8. Memory for digits — memory for sequencing visual digits

A word of caution — if a single test score is very high in comparison to the other scores in the battery it should be reported as above average rather than as gifted ability. Because of the wide gap in age range between one-unit steps in raw scores, a child's score may be elevated beyond expectancy causing an artificial profile to occur. When handled judiciously this test provides valuable information in the diagnosis of psycholinguistic abilities in children over ten years of age.

THE PICTURE STORY LANGUAGE TEST

The *Picture Story Language Test* measures skill with the written word. The intent is to furnish a developmental scale for children, and it is also useful in the study of adults. The test consists of a *picture about which a story is to be written.* According to Myklebust (1965) clinical and educational situations in which the test can be applied are as follows:

1. As a diagnostic instrument for the study of children with language disorders and other types of learning disabilities
2. As a research tool to investigate the relationships between written language and aspects of behavior such as intelligence
3. To determine the achievement level of a given class or of a larger group in order to note the progress made from one year to another
4. To compare the advantages of various educational methods
5. To study the range and nature of written language abilities geographically
6. To ascertain levels of written language ability for purposes of grouping and teaching
7. To define errors of written language which characterize the performances of the deaf, asphasic, mentally retarded, speech defective, emotionally disturbed, dyslexic and dysgraphic
8. To obtain data for comparatively analyzing facility with the spoken, read and written word
9. As a tool for studying grammar and the syntactical development of sentence structure
10. As a measure of the geriatric deterioration of verbal behavior

11. As a means for comparing the languages used in various countries psycholinguistically
12. As an indication of literacy*

The test is comprised of three scales. One measures length (productivity scale), another measures correctness (syntax scale), and the third measures content or meaning (abstract-concrete scale).

The productivity scale measures total number of words, total number of sentences, and the number of words per sentence. The syntax scale measures accuracy of word usage, use of word endings, and punctuation. The abstract-concrete scale is concerned with the nature of the thoughts expressed. It is divided into five levels, each representing an increment in the extent to which the content of the story manifests use of abstract ideas.

A person of any age can be compared with the norms, which indicate the extent to which an average child between 7 and 17 years of age is successful in communicating ideas. Average testing time is 20 minutes, however, there are no time limits and rarely does a child require more than 30 minutes.

THE VISUAL-AURAL DIGIT SPAN TEST (VADS)

The VADS Test, developed by Elizabeth M. Koppitz in 1970, is designed to measure visual memory, auditory memory, and written and oral reproduction of remembered information. It consists of four subtests:

1. Aural (Oral) — auditory presentation and oral recall of digits
2. Visual (Oral) — visual presentation and oral recall of digits
3. Aural (Written) — auditory presentation and written reproduction
4. Visual (Written) — visual presentation and written reproduction

On each subtest three to seven digits are presented on successive trials. When a child reproduces a given series of digits correctly, the next higher series of digits is presented. When a child misses a trial with a given number of digits a second trial is given with different digits. A subtest is discontinued when a child fails both trials of a given number of series. This test is valuable in determining input and output styles of learning.

---

*By permission from H. R. Myklebust, *The Development of Disorders of Written Language, Vol. 1* (New York: Grune & Stratton, 1965) p. 70-71.

AUDITORY DISCRIMINATION TESTS

AUDITORY DISCRIMINATION TEST

The *Auditory Discrimination Test,* by Joseph M. Wepman, helps to identify children at the early elementary level who are slow to develop auditory discrimination. The test also makes a differential diagnosis of reading and speech difficulties in older children. The child listens to the examiner read pairs of words and indicates whether the words are the same (a single word repeated) or different (two different words). The child exercises no visual ability; just nods his head or verbally responds to indicate an affirmative or negative answer. The Wepman test requires little time to administer, and it adds significant data to a test battery.

GOLDMAN-FRISTOE-WOODCOCK TEST OF
AUDITORY DISCRIMINATION (G-F-W)

Among the more recent tests designed to measure deficiencies is the *Goldman-Fristoe-Woodcock Test of Auditory Discrimination* (G-F-W). This test is designed to provide measures of speech-sound discrimination ability, relatively unconfounded by other factors. While the test is designed for use with children as young as four years of age, it also can be used with adults. It provides a measure of auditory discrimination under ideal listening conditions plus a comparative measure of auditory discrimination in the presence of controlled background noise.

The test is comprised of three parts. The first is the Training Procedure, which familiarizes the subject with the word-picture associations to be used during the two subtests and permits the examiner to establish the presence of these associations. The second part is the Quiet Subtest, which provides a measure of auditory discrimination in the absence of background noise. Third is the Noise Subtest, which provides a measure of distracting background noise. Separate norms are provided for each subtest from age 3 years 8 months to age 70 and over.

ACHIEVEMENT TESTS

WIDE RANGE ACHIEVEMENT TEST

The *Wide Range Achievement Test* (WRAT), by J.F. Jastak and S.R. Jastak, tests the basic school subjects. Designed to supplement tests of intelligence and of behavioral adjustment, the WRAT aids in the accurate diagnosis of reading (word recognition), spelling, and arithmetic (computation) disabilities for people of all ages and in the determination of instructional levels for school children.

Consisting of two levels (I and II), both of which are printed on the same blank, the test may be used to examine a person twice, once before and once after the age of eleven. Three kinds of scores are available: grade ratings, percentiles, and standard scores (comparable to the I.Q. of standard tests). The test requires only about 30 minutes.

Clinical analysis of learning disabilities as a result of the WRAT cannot be overrated.

DURRELL-SULLIVAN READING ACHIEVEMENT TEST

The *Durrell-Sullivan Reading Achievement Test,* a group reading test for grades 3 through 6, evaluates the child's performance in word meaning, paragraph meaning, spelling (optional), and written recall (optional). It is approximately a 45-minute test, and provides norms in both grade equivalent and age equivalent. These norms run continuously and are comparable from one grade level to another.

This test is most valuable because its subjective analysis can suggest the nature of a child's reading difficulty.

KEYMATH DIAGNOSTIC ARITHMETIC TEST

An individualized test of arithmetic skills is the *KeyMath Diagnostic Arithmetic Test,* by A. J. Connolly, W. Nathman, and E. M. Pritchett. It is designed for children from the preschool level through the sixth grade. No upper limits are offered for use in individual remediation. The test is untimed, and it usually takes 30 minutes. The responses are recorded on a form that graphically profiles arithmetic skills. The following areas are covered:

Content	*Operations*	*Applications*
A. Numeration	D. Addition	J. Word problems
B. Fractions	E. Subtraction	K. Missing elements
C. Geometry	F. Multiplication	L. Money
and Symbols	G. Division	M. Measurement
	H. Mental computation	N. Time
	I. Numerical reasoning	

The four subtests on fundamental computations contain some problems of a "pencil and paper" variety. Other subtests in KeyMath require the child to respond orally to open-ended items that are presented by the examiner. The examiner is provided (1) a grade equivalent score based on the total test performance; (2) a diagnostic profile depicting the child's relative performance in the 14 skill areas; and (3) a description of each item's content and an indication of whether the child has mastered it.

Because of the diagnostic structure of KeyMath, it is particularly useful for children with learning problems. It is similar to a criterion-referenced test, since it readily identifies the successes and failures of the subject, however it is grade normed.

CALIFORNIA ACHIEVEMENT TESTS

The *California Achievement Tests* (CAT), by Clark and Tiegs, is one of many group tests. They are presented in this test battery because of the diagnostic analysis of learning difficulties provided on the back of the profile sheet. Frequently school files contain good diagnostic tools, but they are often overlooked or not used to the fullest extent. If it is available, the consultant should study the CAT profile in relation to other test data. The reading areas test ability to follow directions, reference skills, and interpretation of materials. Also tested are mathematics fundamentals, mathematics reasoning, and mechanics of English.

In particular, the reading tests explore specific areas of learning difficulties. An incorrect response to a test question in mathematical vocabulary, scientific vocabulary, reference skills, or interpretation of material may signify a definite weakness. A child who has difficulty in sequencing the events in the interpretation of materials section, will probably have comparable difficulty in sequencing the pictures on the WISC picture arrangement test or the ITPA visual motor sequencing test. In other words, the strength of a diagnosis depends upon the completeness of the test battery and its resulting checks and counterchecks on the test data.

PEABODY INDIVIDUAL ACHIEVEMENT TEST (PIAT)

The PIAT, by Lloyd M. Dunn and Frederick C. Markwardt (1970), is designed for children of kindergarten age through age 12 years. It provides six scores; mathematics, reading recognition, reading comprehension, spelling, general information, and total score. The testing time required is between 30 to 40 minutes. This test evaluates the general level of achievement of a pupil and may be followed by a more comprehensive evaluation if necessary.

SUMMARY

In order to make an accurate diagnosis, the consultant must have more than one or two test scores on which to rely. For children under ten years of age, the *Illinois Test of Psycholinguistic Abilities* can help in identifying specific linguistic weaknesses. The Picture Language Test can be used for both children and adults. For children over the age of ten, either the Hiskey-Nebraska or the *Detroit Tests of Learning Aptitude* may be used. From the Hiskey-Nebraska tests, the subtests, picture analogies, spatial reasoning, visual attention span, and the completion of drawings are specifically recommended to confirm the seriousness of visual-motor and/or visual-spatial dysfunctions pointed out by either a low WISC coding score or any other WISC performance subtest score. From the *Detroit Test of Learning Aptitude,* subtests that measure visual attention span for letters, visual attention span for objects, and sequencing of disarranged pictures provide help in determining visual-spatial and/or visual-memory problems. Other subtests that measure auditory attention span for unrelated words, auditory attention span for related syllables, and ability to follow oral directions aid in the assessment of auditory problems, while motor speed and orientation subtests help diagnose eye-hand coordination and directionality problems.

The Purdue Perceptual-Motor Survey tests the elementary school child for gross motor problems, which are partially responsible for fine motor disorders that may be inferred from the WISC or another test.

Tests for other learning problems include the Memory-For-Designs, the *Bender Visual-Motor Gestalt Test,* and the *Developmental Test of Visual-Motor Integration.* These measure visual-motor problems. For measurement of auditory discrimination problems, the *Wepman Auditory Discrimination Test* and the G-F-W Test of Auditory Discrimination are suggested. The *Peabody Picture Vocabulary Test* and the WISC/WISC-R vocabulary subtest may be used for comparing differences between picture and spoken vocabulary; the DAP (for children under the age of 12) may also be used for measurement of visual-motor coordination.*

---

*Seven years of observation by Bush at the Kilgore Children's Psychiatric Hospital in Amarillo, Texas showed that clinical cases tend to score lower on the DAP than on other I.Q. tests because the children's self-concepts may be immature or because they have been poorly oriented to detail.

In addition to intelligence tests, achievement tests of reading, spelling, and arithmetic estimate a child's performance in relation to his achievement capacity (psychometric data). The WRAT, in order to detect underachievement, equates its standard scores with I.Q. scores. The reading test on the WRAT is a test of word recognition that requires no reading comprehension. Therefore, if the consultant wishes to test a child in reading comprehension, the PIAT test may be used. The PIAT and KeyMath add several scales to aid in math achievement evaluations.

Refer to Appendix C for a list of learning disabilities tests that are not included in this chapter.

chapter 7

Interpreting Test Data

After you have studied this chapter, you should be able to

1. Discuss the categories that have been classified from test pattern profiles.

2. Compare the functions of the WISC, as reported by Wechsler and by Glasser and Zimmerman, as they relate to the Structure of Intellect by Guilford.

3. Discuss the difference between specific dyslexia and complex dyslexia according to the findings of McGlannan.

4. Determine spatial, conceptual, sequencing, perceptual organization, verbal comprehension and freedom from distractability strengths or weaknesses from the WISC.

5. Identify strengths and weaknesses and their relationship to learning components from the use of the Stanford Binet.

6. Graph and highlight strengths and weaknesses found when the Stanford Binet is used in diagnosis.

7. Understand the possibilities in using the Meeker SOI codes to aid in the differential diagnosis of learning skills.

8. Identify the specific learning components classified under perceptual-motor functions and language functions.

INTRODUCTION

After a test battery has been selected and administered, the data collected must be interpreted. This interpretation entails considerably more responsibility than merely determining intelligence quotients or mental ages.

In beginning a study of psychometric data, students inadvertently seek some global pattern from the WISC, WISC-R, WAIS, or Stanford-Binet, hoping it will *pinpoint* a learning problem. But these test patterns, like an I.Q. score, only suggest a particular global feature. They are not accurate in diagnosing minimal brain injury, emotional disturbance, or learning disorder, although trained clinicians can often combine them with other data from the test battery to reach valid conclusions concerning these disabilities. However, consultants who have had little or no experience in testing will not be able to make such a judgement until they have studied the science of diagnosis.

FIGURE 21.   Comparison of nonreader and adolescent sociopath test patterns

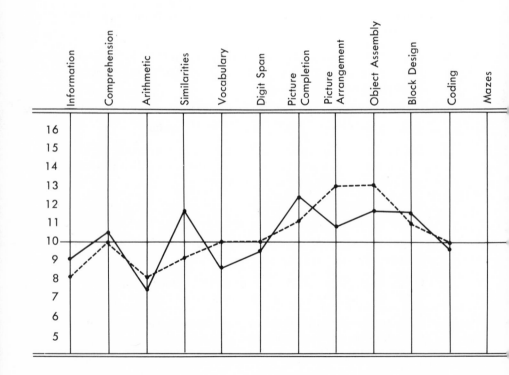

PROBLEMS OF TEST PATTERNS

The following sections include test patterns that are similar in design but different in their category designations. The difficulty in using test patterns for diagnosis is shown in the studies made by Graham, Wechsler, McGlannan, and Clements. Graham (1952, p. 270) found that some nonreaders have performance I.Q.'s higher than their verbal I.Q.'s and that other nonreaders have verbal I.Q.'s higher than their performance I.Q.'s. He also found a similarity between the higher performance I.Q. group and the Wechsler pattern of the adolescent sociopath (Graham, 1958, p. 172). Figure 21 shows a graph of Graham's nonreader pattern superimposed on Wechsler's pattern.

TABLE 9. Mean scale scores of sociopaths and nonreaders

	Wechsler Adolescent Sociopath Mean-Scaled Scores	Graham's Nonreader (High Performance) Mean-Scaled Scores
Information	9.0	9.0
Comprehension	9.5	10.5
Arithmetic	9.0	7.0
Similarities	10.0	12.0
Vocabulary	10.0	8.5
Digit span	9.0	9.0
Picture completion	11.0	12.2
Picture arrangement	13.0	11.0
Block design	11.0	11.6
Object assembly	13.0	11.5
Coding	9.0	9.5

Clements found three patterns typical of MBI children (Clements, 1966, pp. 47–48). In Graham's and Wechsler's studies, the patterns of the nonreader and the sociopath (representing different categories) are similar (Figure 21 and Table 9). To further complicate the situation, McGlannan (1968) designates two patterns for dyslexic children, which she calls specific dyslexia and complex dyslexia, and both show scores that fall into patterns much like the others. Figure 22 shows the relative positions of these five patterns.

In 1974 Jeanne McCarthy and Elkins completed studies made in five different states to determine homogeneous clusters among language-disabled and learning-disabled children. Twenty-two subscores from the WISC and the ITPA were used. The authors sought to determine

FIGURE 22.   Similarity of test patterns identifying six behaviors

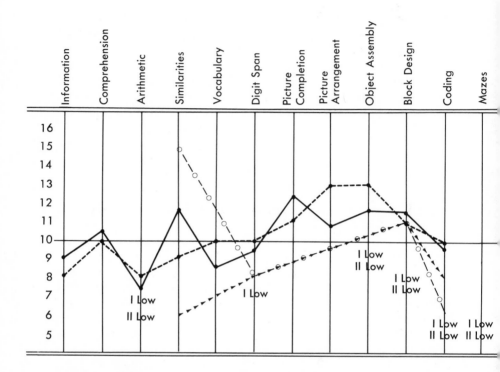

whether there were clusters of subtest scores that could accurately identify specific learning disabilities.

The results of their study suggested "that psychiatrists, psychologists, or psychoeducational diagnosticians need to be very cautious about the entire profile literature in which profiles of specific strengths and weaknesses on the WISC and ITPA are said to be indicative of problems in academic achievement." They found no pattern on the WISC typical of learning-disabled children. Evidence showed that patterns on the WISC may vary among locales. Significantly, children who fail in a linguistic reading program may have different patterns from those who fail in phonetic reading. The patterns McCarthy and Elkins found on the WISC among the learning-disabled children were similar to those found

---

*According to Clements, MBI pattern III does not differentiate the interest scatter; therefore, it is not included in his figure.

by Clements among minimally brain-injured children. Children who are learning disabled or have a minimal brain injury may exhibit a number of different patterns on the WISC.

The following variety of patterns was found on the WISC by McCarthy and Elkins:

1. A profile showing few discrepancies between scaled scores or between verbal and performance scores with above-average scores
2. A profile of low-verbal, high-performance scores
3. A profile of high-verbal, low-performance scores
4. A profile showing extreme discrepancies on both scales, but little difference between verbal and performance scores
5. Low scores on all subtests

THE USE OF TEST PATTERNS

Learning-disorder categories, although important for administrative planning, do not help in planning curricula for the variety of problems found in any homogeneous group. For example, any one language-learning-disabled child is different from all others. Thus teachers work with children whose learning problems are different but whose classifications are the same. They must plan more individualized curricula. Even though a category like language disability or perceptual-motor impairment designates the area of weakness, it does not identify the kind of language or perceptual-motor problem. (It is significant that the McCarthy-Elkins study did show that subgroups do exist on psychometric variables of importance, and future studies may delineate these variables.)

At this point the consultant can be of help to the teacher. If the consultant accepts the premise that the classification that directed school placement describes the *general* behavior of the child, then he/she can study the subtest scores, in order to make a discrete differential diagnosis.

An examination of a hypothetical case, using the following scaled scores, offers some idea of how the subtest scores on the WISC or WAIS might be used.

In this list of scores there is no significant difference between verbal and performance abilities; however, performance abilities hold a slight edge over verbal abilities. One could say that this person tested

Information	9	Picture completion	12
Comprehension	10	Picture arrangement	11
Arithmetic	7	Block design	11
Similarities	12	Object assembly	10
Vocabulary	8	Coding	9
Digit symbol	9		

adapted better in the use of perceptual-motor abilities than in the use of language abilities. The lowered arithmetic and digit span scores suggest easy distractibility;* the lowered scores on the coding or digital symbol tests suggest slow psychomotor speed and slow pencil manipulation ability; and the lowered information and vocabulary scores suggest a lack of reading experience and an indifference to word meaning. The subject has learned to effect greater control over perceptual-motor functions, although the coding test scores hint at some perceptual-motor problem.

According to the test scores, the subject needs remedial aid in arithmetic and in memory for digits. The slow psychomotor speed indicates more time is needed to complete work assignments. When the subject fully understands the principles or procedures involved in the assignment, the quantity of the work required could be reduced to compensate for slow psychomotor speed. The need for remedial reading is apparent, although the kind of remediation should be determined by additional test data, which would reveal whether the verbal problem is visual or auditory.

To have a better understanding of what the subtest scores measure, the consultant should be familiar with Guilford's factors on the WISC (1959)—(Table 10) and with the factors analyzed by Wechsler (1958). Glasser and Zimmerman (1967) provide additional information useful in the interpretation of the WISC.† The reader is also referred to the diagnostic information on the WISC and WAIS reported by Lutey (1967). Subtest descriptions and reports of research on the subtests are given extensive coverage.

Table 10 is a list of factors associated with the WISC subtests.

---

*Clements questions anxiety as a cause for distraction. He suggests that anxiety cannot be this selective and therefore these lowered subtest scores are probably the result of a faulty system.

†Glasser and Zimmerman's analysis was taken from a study by Marcella R. Bonsall and Mary M. Meeker, *Structure of Intellect Components in the WISC* (Los Angeles County Superintendent of Schools, Division of Research and Guidance Programs for the Gifted, 1964), in which they placed each WISC subtest under one of Guilford's structure of intellect components. Glasser and Zimmerman then interlaced these with the actual factor analysis of Jacob Cohen. [See "Factorial Structure of the WISC at Ages 7–6, 10–6, and 13–6," *Journal of Consulting Psychology* 23 (August, 1959) 285–99.]

TABLE 10

WISC *Subtest Scores*	*Wechsler's Factors*	*Guilford's Factors*
Information	Range of information picked up through the years, memory (cultural milieu inferred), verbal comprehension	Memory for ideas, verbal comprehension, associational memory, semantic relation selection
Comprehension	Verbal comprehension, judgment, understanding	Judgment, verbal comprehension, sensitivity to problems
Arithmetic	Arithmetical reasoning, concentration, memory, numerical fluency	General reasoning, symbol facility
Similarities	Concept formation, abstract thinking vs. functional and concrete, verbal comprehension	Associational fluency, semantic relations, expressional fluency
Vocabulary	Vocabulary, word meaning (cultural milieu inferred), verbal comprehension	Verbal comprehension (all items)
Digit span	Memory — attention (automatic factor)	Memory span (forward), memory for symbol patterns (backward)
Picture completion	Discrimination between essential and nonessential detail, memory	Visual or auditory cognition, perceptual foresight, figural relation selection (lack of evidence as yet)
Picture arrangement	Social alertness, common sense, planning and anticipating, sequencing, ability to synthesize	Convergent production, evaluation
Block design	Perception, analysis, synthesis, reproduction of abstract designs (logic and reasoning applied to space relationships)	Figural relations, figural redefining, figural selection
Object assembly	Perception, visual-motor coordination, visual imagery, synthesis of concrete forms, flexibility of working toward a goal, spatial relationships	Spatial orientation, visualization, figural selection

TABLE 10 (cont.)

Coding	Psychomotor speed, eye-hand coordination, pencil manipulation	Symbolic possibilities, symbolic facility
Mazes	Ability to plan in a new situation (problem solving), ability to delay action, visual-motor coordination	Perceptual foresight

At the Child Guidance Center, University of Arkansas Medical Center, Sam Clements found three test patterns typical of the minimal brain-injured child (Clements, 1964, pp. 189-90).

WISC Pattern A

1. Scatter in either or both verbal and performance scales.
2. Low scores (relative to the others) most frequently in arithmetic, block design, object assembly, digit span, coding, and mazes.
3. Final verbal and performance I.Q. scores often nearly equal. (Note internal inconsistency.)
    (a) Not uncommon to find comprehension 5 to 10 points higher than arithmetic.
    (b) Not uncommon to find picture completion 5 to 10 points higher than block design.

WISC Pattern B

1. Verbal I.Q. 15 to 40 points higher than performance I.Q. (In this instance the achievement on the other verbal tasks is sufficiently high to obscure or to compensate for a drop in arithmetic. If the arithmetic score is excluded, the difference is more pronounced, this test being another type of symbol process.)
2. Trouble with most of the performance scale items, particularly with the pure visual-motor tasks, which include block design, object assembly, coding, and mazes — less difficulty with picture arrangement and picture-completion. (Often the performance I.Q. falls within the mentally deficient range, while the verbal I.Q. falls within or above the normal range).

WISC Pattern C

1. Least frequent pattern.
2. Performance I.Q. 10 to 30 points higher than verbal I.Q. (This child, generally considered to have dyslexia, has difficulty with

verbal expression and must actively search for the words necessary to express a usually concrete solution to a "thought" problem. On the other hand, this child is quite proficient at the
subtests that constitute the performance scale.)

McGlannan cites two patterns that identify dyslexia (1968, pp. 186-
87), (Figures 23 and 24).

Jastak and Jastak report the following possibilities for diagnosing
dyslexia (1965, pp. 27-29). These were made in connection with studies
involving both the WISC and WRAT. (Study the WRAT manual for
a better understanding.)

   1. Intelligence as a criterion.
      (a) A standard reading score ten points lower than spelling on
           WRAT AND WISC. (The larger the discrepancy, the
           greater the probability of dyslexia.)

FIGURE 23. Specific dyslexia

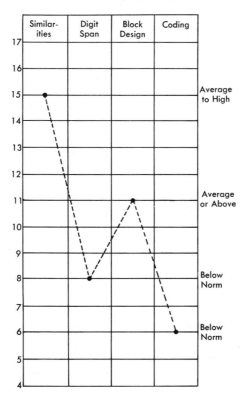

FIGURE 24.   Complex dyslexia

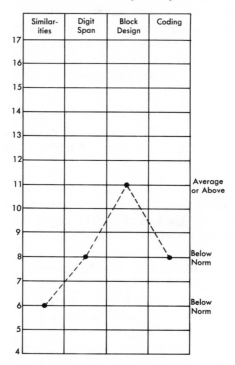

(b) Performance quotients higher than full scale Wechsler I.Q.
     or Stanford-Binet I.Q.
2. Cognition as a criterion
    (a) Comprehension and Similarities tests of WISC and WAIS
         nearly always significantly higher than WRAT reading and
         spelling quotients.
3. Arithmetic computation as a criterion
    (a) WRAT arithmetic quotient significantly higher than WRAT
         reading quotient.

USE OF INTERTEST COMBINATIONS TO AID DIAGNOSIS

Consultants thoroughly familiar with the factors measured on the
WISC will not need assistance in determining where the problem lies.
Beginners, however, may need additional aids. The following may give the
advantage of discovering specific individual weaknesses recorded in the
test data. Bannatyne (1968, p. 243) suggests the following:

1. Spatial abilities can be determined from the results of the picture completion, block design, and object assembly subtests. Add the three scaled scores and divide by 3.

Picture completion	6
Block design	8
Object assembly	6
	20

$$20 \div 3 = 6.7$$

2. Conceptual abilities can be determined from the results of the comprehension, similarities, and vocabulary subtests. Add the three scaled scores and divide by 3.

Comprehension	11
Similarities	12
Vocabulary	9
	32

$$32 \div 3 = 10.6$$

3. Sequencing abilities can be determined from the results of the digit span, coding (digit symbol), and picture arrangement subtests. Add the three scaled scores and divide by 3.

Digit span	7
Coding	5
Picture arrangement	9
	21

$$21 \div 3 = 7$$

If any quotient falls below the person's mean score, a weakness in the area which the subtests represent is obvious. The lowest quotient designates the greatest weaknesses. Begin by calculating the child's mean score for groups 1, 2, and 3 and determine whether any of the quotients fall below the child's mean. If the child is an underachiever, this will help to show the weak areas that may be influencing the level of underachievement.

Money (1962, p. 292) suggests, as follows, that according to the Cohen factor analysis:

1. Preceptual organization problems can be determined by adding the scaled scores from the block design and object assembly tests and dividing by 2.

Block design	10
Object assembly	9
	19

    $$19 \div 2 = 9.5$$

2. Verbal comprehension can be determined by adding the scaled scores from the information, comprehension, similarities, and vocabulary tests and dividing by 4.

Information	4
Comprehension	8
Similarities	6
Vocabulary	5
	23

    $$23 \div 4 = 5.7$$

3. Freedom from distractibility can be determined by adding the scaled scores from the arithmetic and digit span tests and dividing by 2.

Arithmetic	6
Digit span	4
	10

    $$10 \div 2 = 5$$

Money's combinations expose weaknesses in verbal comprehension, concentration, and attention relative to numbers and problem solving; those of Bannatyne expose weaknesses in spatial, conceptual, and sequencing abilities. When used together they systematically review strengths and weaknesses of the child. However, there is probably a small percentage of error in each subtest score. Because of this and because of variation in day-to-day performance, use of the term *tendency toward* is more suitable than a specific conclusive statement concerning a child's abilities. Refer to Table 11 annd Figure 25 with patterns from the *case of D* as an example.

TABLE II. Scaled score combinations for the case of D

		SCALED SCORES		
Spatial	Picture Completion	13		
	Block Design	10	Mean	10.0
	Object Assembly	7		
Conceptual	Comprehension	13		
	Similarities	17	Mean	13.66
	Vocabulary	11		
Sequencing	Coding	15		
	Digit Span	10	Mean	14.0
	Picture Arrangement	17		
Perceptual Organization	Block Design	10	Mean	8.5
	Object Assembly	7		
Verbal Comprehension	Information	15		
	Comprehension	13	Mean	14.0
	Similarities	17		
	Vocabulary	11		
Freedom from Distractibility	Arithmetic	13	Mean	11.5
	Digit Span	10		
		MEAN SCALED SCORE		13.5

The mean scaled score from all subtest scores is 13.5. According to Bannatyne's combination, D's weakness is in spatial ability, and according to Cohen, D's greatest weakness is lack of perceptual organization with freedom from distractibility, showing a *tendency for D* to become distracted from the major task at hand. The consultant may want to copy this form in order to facilitate use of these combination patterns.

Bush and Mattson (1973) report their findings on WISC underachiever patterns at two different levels of intelligence, the normal level and the bright and gifted level. Figure 26 shows the scaled score differences between achievers and underachievers with normal intelligence. Figure 27 shows the scaled score differences between achievers and underachievers with bright and gifted intelligence. As was hypothesized, some significant differences were found in both cases. In the normal intellect group, underachievers tended to show significantly less aptitude on the following subtests: information, arithmetic, vocabulary, digit span, and

FIGURE 25. Case of D, an underchiever with WISC full scale I.Q. of 123

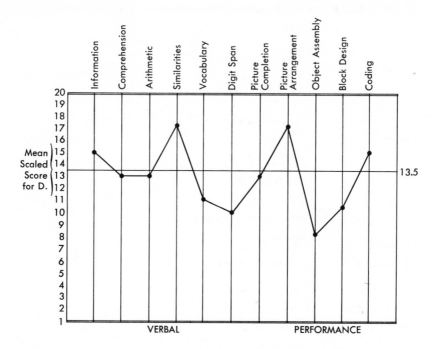

FIGURE 26. A comparison of WISC scaled scores of achievers and underachievers with normal intelligence

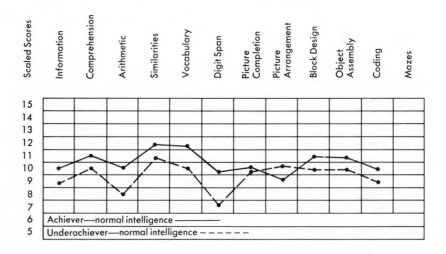

FIGURE 27.   A comparison of WISC scaled scores of bright/gifted underachievers and bright/gifted achievers

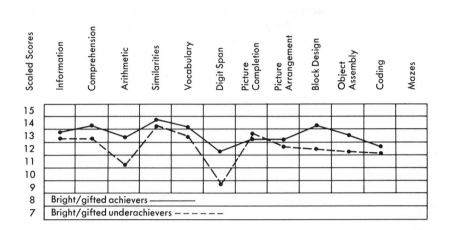

picture arrangement. In the bright and gifted group underachievers showed significantly less aptitude on arithmetic, digit span, and block design subtests.

A Wilcoxson Rank-Sum Test was made between the deviations of the subtests in the underachievers at the different levels of intelligence. The one significant difference was found to be on the deviations of the information subtests. Where normal-level underachievers showed negative deviations from the mean of their group, the bright and gifted underachievers showed positive deviations from the mean of their group.

Most other subtests tended to deviate from their means in the same directions. When there was a difference among the others, it was not significant. A plausible inference was made for the deviation of the information subtest. Among underachievers who do not read extensively and do not store as much information from that source as their achieving peers, it would appear logical that the bright and gifted underachiever with higher intelligence would have more "going for him" and, therefore, would retain more than would the underachiever with normal intelligence.

It can be helpful in a diagnosis to examine research that has been completed on profiles of various groups. The diagnostician can make comparisons and determine whether the profiles of individual cases compare with those of others in the same categories. Such comparisons can often generate questions that may cause the examiner to pursue a different path for further analysis and can also aid in planning remediation.

USE OF THE STANFORD BINET IN DIAGNOSIS

Sattler's model, to be used with the Stanford Binet, affords a profile for purposes of analysis (Sattler, 1965, pp. 174–75). By analyzing the subtests and classifying them under factors or kinds of abilities, one can easily identify a subject's strengths and weaknesses. The model is as follows:

(L)		Language
(M)		Memory
	(mM)	Meaningful memory
	(nmM)	Nonmeaningful memory
	(vM)	Visual memory
(CT)		Conceptual thinking
(R)		Reasoning
	(vR)	Verbal reasoning
	(nvR)	Nonverbal reasoning
(NR)		Numerical reasoning
(VM)		Visual motor
(SI)		Social intelligence

The general abilities measured and identified by Sattler can be examined in terms common to the study of learning disability. Adjacent to and more descriptive of each general factor, in accordance with this framework, is a specific learning disability "clue" (learning component). These clues are commonly used in other tests and aid in identifying the problem. This is necessary for purposes of remediation. For example, the measurement of language in Test 1, Year II–6, can be identified as auditory comprehension or auditory reception. Or in Test 5, Year II, the measurement of language can be identified as both visual reception and expressive language. This profile analysis of the test data is a good diagnostic tool, since the learning mode, such as hearing or sight, is also noted. The factors and their locations in the test are indicated at each age level by the subtest number.

Graphs following Table 12 may provide additional assistance for a profile analysis of the Stanford Binet. Figure 28, p. 142 is a sample worksheet for the tester's initial arrangement of scores. Each vertical column represents a test year, and each horizontal column represents a test factor. Successes and failures are indicated at each age level with plus (+) and minus (−) signs in the lines of the corresponding test factors.

When scores from a case study are recorded on this graph (Figure 29, p. 143), each vertical column should have a total of six plus or minus signs, except for the average adult level, which should have eight.

TABLE 12. Year levels of the Stanford Binet with learning components for each subtest*

Test	Factor	Learning Components
		Year II
1	VM	Visual discrimination
2	nmM	Visual imagery
3	L	Visual discrimination
4	VM	Depth perception
5	L	Visual reception and expressive language
6	L	Word fluency
A	L	Expressive language
		Year II-6
1	L	Auditory reception
2	L	Visual discrimination
3	L	Visual perception
4	L	Visual reception and expressive language
5	nmM	Auditory sequencing
6	SI	Auditory reception
A	VM	Visual discrimination
		Year III
1	VM	Eye-hand coordination and perceptual motor
2	L	Visual reception and expressive language
3	VM	Depth perception
4	vM	Perceptual memory
5	VM	Eye-hand coordination and perceptual motor
6	VM	Eye-hand coordination and perceptual motor
A	nmM	Auditory sequencing
		Year III-6
1	nvR	Perceptual discrimination
2	nvR	Spatial relationship
3	nvR	Visual discrimination
4	SI	Verbal expression and visual reception
5	nvR	Color discrimination
6	SI	Auditory reception
A	nvR	Visual discrimination

*The abbreviations for the adult levels that follow Year XIV are AA for average adult and SA for superior adult.

*An alternate graph showing the number of the tests at each level may be found in Appendix A, page 269.

TABLE 12. (cont.)

Test	Factor	Learning Components
		Year IV
1	L	Visual reception and expressive language
2	mM	Visual memory
3	CT	Auditory association
4	L	Auditory discrimination and visual reception
5	nvR	Visual discrimination
6	SI	Auditory reception
A	mM	Auditory memory
		Year IV-6
1	SI	Visual reception and visual discrimination
2	CT	Auditory association
3	nvR	Visual association and visual discrimination
4	SI	Auditory reception
5	mM	Auditory memory and sequence
6	SI	Auditory reception
A	L	Auditory discrimination and visual perception
		Year V
1	VM	Perceptual motor
2	VM	Spatial and perceptual motor
3	L	Auditory reception
4	VM	Perceptual motor
5	nvR	Visual association and visual discrimination
6	nvR	Spatial relationship and perceptual motor
A	VM	Perceptual motor
		Year VI
1	L	Auditory reception and expressive language
2	CT	Meaningful auditory discrimination
3	nvR	Spatial discrimination
4	NR	Problem solving
5	CT	Auditory association
6	VM	Perceptual motor
A	SI	Expressive language and visual reception
		Year VII
1	SI	Visual reception
2	CT	Auditory association

TABLE 12.   (cont.)

TEST	FACTOR	LEARNING COMPONENTS
3	VM	Perceptual motor
4	SI	Auditory reception
5	CT	Auditory association
6	nmM	Auditory memory and sequencing
A	nmM	Auditory memory for patterns and sequencing

Year VIII

1	L	Auditory reception and expressive language
2	mM	Auditory memory and sequencing
3	vR	Auditory reception and expressive language
4	CT	Auditory association
5	SI	Auditory reception
6	SI	Auditory sequencing
A	SI	Auditory reception

Year IX

1	VM	Perceptual motor and spatial reasoning
2	vR	Auditory reception
3	vM	Perceptual motor
4	L	Auditory and memory association
5	NR	Problem solving
6	nmM	Auditory sequencing and pattern memory
A	L	Auditory association

Year X

1	L	Auditory reception and expressive language
2	NR	Spatial reasoning
3	L	Auditory reception and expressive language
4	SI	Auditory reception and verbal expression
5	L	Word fluency and memory
6	nmM	Auditory sequencing
A	vR	Auditory reception

Year XI

1	vM	Memory and perceptual motor
2	vR	Auditory reception and expressive language
3	L	Auditory reception and expressive language
4	mM	Auditory memory
5	SI	Verbal expression

TABLE 12. (cont.)

Test	Factor	Learning Components
6	CT	Auditory association
A	SI	Auditory reception and expressive language

Year XII

Test	Factor	Learning Components
1	L	Auditory reception and expressive language
2	vR	Auditory reception
3	SI	Visual reception
4	nmM	Sequencing
5	L	Auditory reception and expressive language
6	L	Memory and visual association
A	vM	Memory and perceptual motor

Year XIII

Test	Factor	Learning Components
1	nvR	Spatial reasoning
2	L	Auditory reception and expressive language
3	mM	Auditory memory
4	vR	Auditory reception and expressive language
5	L	Visual reception and visual relation
6	vM	Visual memory for patterns and perceptual motor
A	VM	Spatial reasoning

Year XIV

Test	Factor	Learning Components
1	L	Auditory reception and expressive language
2	NR	Spatial reasoning
3	vR	Auditory reception
4	NR	Auditory reception
5	nvR	Position in space and spatial reasoning
6	CT	Auditory association
A	NR	Auditory reception

Year AA

Test	Factor	Learning Components
1	L	Auditory reception and verbal comprehension
2	NR	Problem solving
3	L	Auditory association
4	NR	Problem solving
5	CT	Verbal comprehension
6	nvR	Position in space
7	CT	Auditory association
8	L	Expressive language and auditory reception
A	VM	Spatial reasoning

TABLE 12. (cont.)

Test	Factor	Learning Components
		Year SAI
1	L	Expressive language and auditory reception
2	NR	Problem solving
3	L	Memory and visual association
4	nmM	Memory for patterns
5	L	Verbal expression and auditory reception
6	CT	Auditory association
A	CT	Auditory association
		Year SAII
1	L	Expressive language
2	vR	Expressive language and auditory reception
3	CT	Auditory association
4	NR	Auditory reception
5	CT	Auditory association
6	mM	Auditory memory
A	vR	Auditory reception
		Year SAIII
1	L	Expressive language and verbal comprehension
2	CT	Auditory association
3	CT	Auditory association
4	nvR	Position in space
5	vR	Problem solving
6	mM	Auditory memory
A	CT	Auditory association

If Figure 29 is too cluttered for the teacher, Figure 31, p. 145, is a clean bar graph, and it reads more easily. Dittoed copies of the original form (Figure 30, p. 144) do not include the test years or the bar graph, since these are individually determined. Figure 31 is a sample bar graph that analyzes the results of the case scores recorded in Figure 29. It shows that the subject has a basal age (BA) of eight years; any task prescribed for a child of eight years should be within this subject's ability. The subject's chronological age (CA) is nine years and five months, but he/she does not consistently perform at this age level in language, nonmeaningful memory, verbal reasoning, and social intelligence.

Note in Figure 31 that some of the factors have a dashed line extending to a higher level. The highest year to which the dashed line reaches is the highest year at which the child performed on the test. Failures, however, do occur at or below this level. In representing an erratic reaction

FIGURE 28. Stanford Binet worksheet

Year of Test										
Factors	Language									
M E M O R Y	Meaningful									
	Non-meaningful									
	Visual									
	Conceptual Thinking									
R E A S O N I N G	Verbal									
	Nonverbal									
	Numerical									
	Visual-Motor									
	Social Intelligence									

the dashed line may perhaps indicate overachievement. No dotted line has been drawn for visual-motor factors because there are no visual-motor tests (except for the average-adult alternate) above the ten-year level. The dashed histogram ordinate suggests that the child's ceiling level relative to ability cannot be accurately measured.

A mental age (MA) of ten years and ten months is indicated from the child's ability in meaningful memory, visual memory, conceptual thinking, and nonverbal reasoning. Together with some possible overachievement, these strengths influence this advanced mental age. Even though the Stanford-Binet scores indicate that the child has an I.Q. of 112, the graphical representation indicates several weak areas. Some other tests, such as the ITPA, can further explore and substantiate the diagnosis of a child's mental abilities.

THE USE OF THE STRUCTURE OF INTELLECT (SOI) IN DIAGNOSIS

In 1959 Guilford reported his factored construct of the intellect (SI) showing the 120 functions within the three "faces" of *operations, content,*

FIGURE 29.   Stanford Binet worksheet

Factors		Year of Test	8	9	10	11	12	13	14
		Language	+	+	− − +	−	− −	−	−
	M E M O R Y	Meaningful	+			+		+	
		Non-meaningful		−		+		−	
		Visual		+		+		−	
		Conceptual Thinking	+			+			+
	R E A S O N I N G	Verbal	+	+		−	+	+	−
		Nonverbal						+	−
		Numerical			+	+			− −
		Visual-Motor	+						
		Social Intelligence	+ +			−	+	−	

and *products*. These three-dimensional functions are the product of factor-analytic research conducted by J. P. Guilford and his associates at the University of Southern California. Meeker's research (1963) showed SI factors were also found in school age children. In her book, *The Structure of Intellect: Its Uses and Interpretation* she demonstrated that analyses of the WISC, WPPSI, and the Stanford-Binet measured factors identified in the Guilford model. The nature of the Stanford-Binet norms readily identifies 56 different intellectual functions measured, while the WAIS, WISC-R show only 28 factors. Instead of mental ages, Meeker shows expectancy norms for the various functions measured on these tests. Code sheets to be used with the *Illinois Test of Psycholinguistic Abilities,* the *Slosson Intelligence Test* and the *Detroit Test of Learning Aptitudes* (See Appendix B) identify factors at learning-age levels. Talley sheets and arrangements of the SOI factors identified by Meeker are found in Appendices H and K.*

---

*We suggest using the Meeker SOI analysis and/or the Tucker analysis to gain a profile of an examiner's individual learning pattern for purposes of curriculum development.

FIGURE 30.   Stanford Binet worksheet converted to bar graph form

Year of Test		
Factors Language		
MEMORY	Meaningful	
	Non-meaningful	
	Visual	
Conceptual Thinking		
REASONING	Verbal	
	Nonverbal	
	Numerical	
Visual-Motor		
Social Intelligence		

Tucker (1972), basing his procedure on Meeker's work, provides an analysis of the SOI for the Stanford Binet Test. He uses a punch-hole technique that shows all items missed on the Stanford Binet. The booklet form is designed so that each punched item identifies factors from which one may determine age equivalents on the SOI.

SUMMARY

In Chapter 1 the learning-disorder classifications are identified. The study of test patterns in this chapter reveal, according to an examination of the psychometric data, that the WISC patterns indicate a great deal of similarity between categories such as nonreader, emotional disturbance, minimal brain injury, and learning disability. Research findings from Clements, Wechsler, McGlannan, and Graham are included for the reader to make comparisons. Consultants are advised to be cautious about making category diagnoses from a single test pattern. Test interpretation can be approached through the study of intertest scatter to determine strengths and weaknesses. WISC test pattern combinations are presented

FIGURE 31. Stanford Binet bar graph

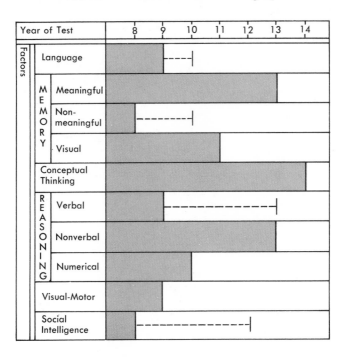

as a means for better understanding the test data. Use of the Stanford Binet in differential diagnosis is also explained.

A new trend offers an exciting frontier in diagnosis and evaluation. Ideas such as Guilford's structure of the intellect (1959) have lead to new interpretations of the WISC, the Stanford Binet, the *Detroit Test of Learning Aptitude,* the Slosson and the *Illinois Test of Psycholinguistic Abilities.* Guilford says of his cubicle construct that it is only a beginning and that educators may look forward to more and varied factors for describing individual behavior. The work of Meeker has made the SOI applicable to the education process.

For effective diagnosis the diagnostician/consultant is responsible for: (1) understanding learning disability terms (defined fully in the Glossary); (2) relating these to the various subtests of a test battery; and (3) following through with suggestions for the teacher.*

---

*A tutor also needs the advice of a consultant. Some cases, because of the severity and the need for individual attention, cannot be handled by the teacher who must share her time with all the children in the classroom. The private tutoring that some children require often exceeds the responsibilities of the teacher.

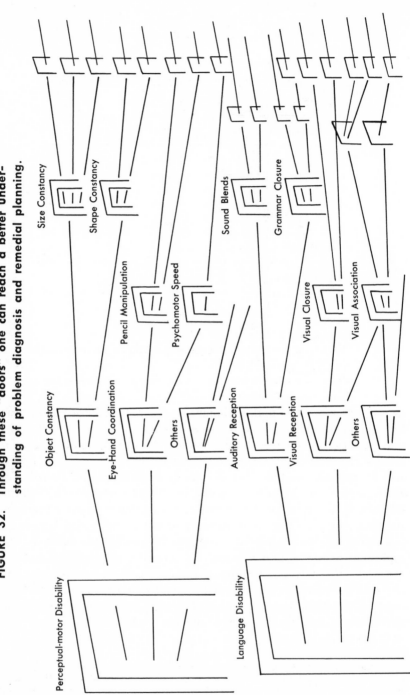

FIGURE 32. Through these "doors" one can reach a better understanding of problem diagnosis and remedial planning.

146

chapter 8

Reporting Test Data

After you have studied this chapter you should be able to
1. Determine the correct length of the report and the terminology appropriate for the reader.
2. Understand reasons why simple terms should be used in writing.
3. Correctly use qualifying words in report writing.
4. Understand the ethical aspects of reporting scores to parents.
5. Understand the legal aspects of reporting to parents and teachers.
6. Develop a format to be used in reporting.
7. Report levels of function by use of checklists.

INTRODUCTION

A major part of any evaluation process is the report of the findings, whether oral or written. Most diagnosticians and consultants agree on some basic procedures for reporting information. The case study should begin with identification of the subject and end with a summary of the test or observation findings. But the symbols and technical jargon used often varies. Format is not a critical issue; most formats are devised to meet the needs of particular situations.

The authors believe that there are three major factors to be considered when a report is to be written: (1) terminology, length, and design for target populations; (2) ethical aspects of reporting symbols; and (3) legal aspects of decisive commitments.

TERMINOLOGY, LENGTH, AND DESIGN FOR TARGET POPULATIONS

A report should be written to be understood by everyone involved— from lawyers, doctors, and teachers to parents of all professions and levels of education. The teacher should be able to understand the terms used and relate them to teaching materials and to the learning of the child. Parents should also be able to understand the terms and relate them to practical experiences in the home. Zimmerman and Woo-Sam (1973) suggest that technical jargon should be minimized and that the writer should be able to communicate even the most difficult concept in simple language. Huber (1961) states that the most difficult skill to acquire in report writing is the knack of writing in a straightforward way. Identifying simple terms that will be interpreted in the same manner by people from different disciplines is not as easy as it would appear. For example, the simple term *rote memory* can be defined several different ways. To a teacher it can mean memory for numbers, as in counting, or memory for letters, as in repeating the alphabet, while to a psychologist rote memory could be interpreted as memory for a list of nonsense syllables. In order to facilitate communication the writer should provide specific definitions so that any target population will understand the terms used. An example would be

> John's rote memory for numbers, *as in counting to 15,* was found to be inconsistent and thus unreliable.

The length of the report will of course vary among cases. However, a safe guideline is that it should not cover more than two typewritten pages single spaced and with double spacing between paragraphs. The length of any report may influence whether the busy reader will read all of it or only portions of it. If the design does not have topics clearly separated, the reader may do no more than scan the report for scores or read the last few lines. Headings should separate observation of overt behavior from the discussion of test results.

Qualifiers tend to weaken a report, particularly if used in any excess. Huber (1961) states that terms like *appears to be, might be,* and *seems to be* make the results indecisive.

Contrary to this viewpoint, people opposed to use of standard tests in schools unwittingly present a reason for the use of qualifiers when they argue that tests are unfair to different socioeconomic and cultural groups. Their premise is that data is inaccurate if it comes from standardized tests. To avoid the pitfall of inaccurate reporting the use of *appears to be, seems to be,* and *might be* becomes appropriate in many instances. The use of these terms in clinical reporting in the past has been an arbitrary choice, and this use often has added to the fluency of the report. In the final analysis, in order to evaluate for accuracy, all qualifiers might be omitted in the initial writing, and then those that would make the statements more accurate in terms of what is actually known could be added to the report. The trend toward accountability and increased awareness of the law demands a careful look at what can and cannot be proved.

Use of the names of tests or subtests in reports is also important. To diagnose is to examine all the test data and "rule out" all evidence which would contradict such findings (Weed, 1969). In medicine a doctor may observe fever and sore throat in a child but will rule out measles in favor of mumps if the jaws are swollen. Using this as a guideline, it should be logical to weigh one possibility against the other when one is trying to determine weaknesses or strengths in the different modalities of learning. In educational diagnosis the different modalities of learning are measured by the variety of tests used. Thus it is logical and reasonable that one may report by crosschecking and by calling tests by name. When reporting to parents, the reporter may need to consider whether this much information will be of interest and understood. Some parents would appreciate the opportunity to learn about normative data on their children.

ETHICAL ASPECTS OF REPORTING SYMBOLS

Reporting of actual test scores to parents and teachers has not been accepted by many authorities. This has been particularly true of I.Q. scores. Wilson (Bonder & Wilson) lists the following reasons for not telling parents their childrens' I.Q.'s: (1) limited test results may not be reliable; (2) interpretation of test results is too complex; and (3) parents may put pressure on children or give up hope if they know the scores. Lagerman (1961) in his argument against I.Q. tests points out that knowledge of such scores may discriminate against some youth in terms of choice of studies.

Bonder (Bonder & Wilson) counters this by saying that if parents know the scores they can be shown how to work with their children who have high I.Q.'s and can avoid the habit of making odious comparisons between siblings who differ significantly in intellectual functioning. Cannon (1973) reports that many psychologists are now providing parents with copies of their reports on students and are receiving favorable

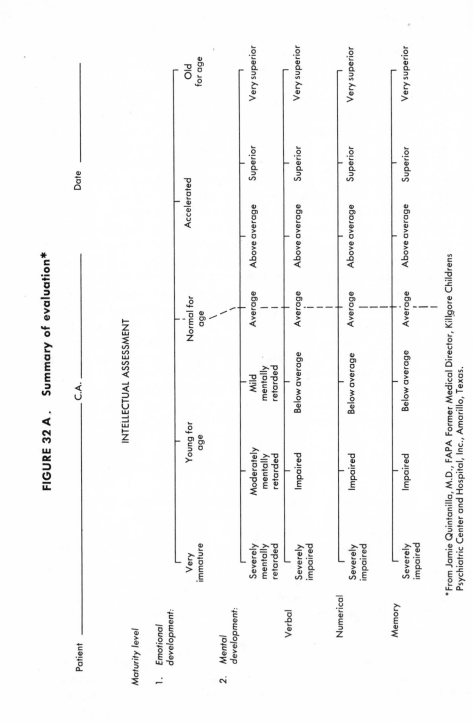

FIGURE 32 A. Summary of evaluation*

Patient _____ C.A. _____ Date _____

INTELLECTUAL ASSESSMENT

Maturity level

1. *Emotional development:*

| Very immature | Young for age | Normal for age | Accelerated | Old for age |

2. *Mental development:*

| Severely mentally retarded | Moderately mentally retarded | Mild mentally retarded | Average | Above average | Superior | Very superior |

Verbal

| Severely impaired | Impaired | Below average | Average | Above average | Superior | Very superior |

Numerical

| Severely impaired | Impaired | Below average | Average | Above average | Superior | Very superior |

Memory

| Severely impaired | Impaired | Below average | Average | Above average | Superior | Very superior |

*From Jamie Quintanilla, M.D., FAPA Former Medical Director, Killgore Childrens Psychiatric Center and Hospital, Inc., Amarillo, Texas.

150

FIGURE 32. (cont.)

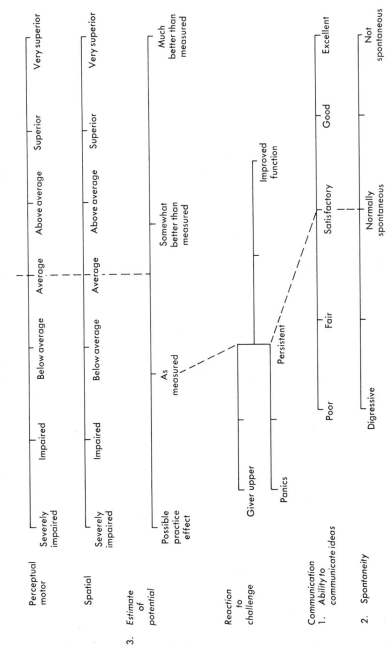

feedback from them. Since passage of Section 438 of the General Education Provisions Act dealing with privacy rights of parents and students, commonly known as the Buckley Amendment, this philosophical argument may have been rendered irrelevant.

Teachers should know their students' I.Q.'s. Since they have access to many standardized group tests, which may or may not provide valid I.Q.'s, scores provided by trained diagnosticians or psychologists dispel invalid information obtained from less reliable sources. Knowledge of I.Q. scores also aids in prescriptive planning. It helps teachers choose materials that will challenge but not inundate the slow learner and motivate the gifted child. Of course, I.Q. scores should be reported with an explanation of their standard errors.

Whether scores should be reported in specific symbols (numerical) or as levels (above average, average) should be a matter of school policy and should reflect community demands. Once this has been established the consultant should follow the accepted standards.

The summary graphs, Figures 32 and 33, show a convenient way to report data in levels and can be checked according to the levels of function. They will not give the teacher discrete normative data regarding achievement, but they do provide adequate information concerning the severity of the functions evaluated. If these are used as the final reporting instruments, the writer should add a final summary in essay form. This essay should be free of jargon and easily understood by both parents and teachers (Erwin & Cannon, 1974). The case studies in Chapter 9 *do report* both scores and levels. They were made available to parents upon request and to schools and doctors after the release had been permitted by the parents.

The following "psychological examination" is one other example of final reporting. It omits all numerical data explanation of the rationale behind its conclusions and recommendations. Only minor mention is made of the problem. Instead the emphasis is placed on what should be done.

PSYCHOLOGICAL EVALUATION

BEHAVIOR AND APPEARANCE

WD was a nice-looking five and a half year old child who appeared normal in all physiological aspects of growth and development. He was dressed in good clothes and was clean and neat.

There was no separation problem from his mother and he appeared willing to remain in the testing room. It was, however, a demanding chore

FIGURE 32. (cont.)

Patient _____ C.A. _____ Date _____

SENSORY-MOTOR
AND PERCEPTUAL-MOTOR SUMMARY

Language

Understanding of words	Poor	Fair	Average	Good	Superior
Use of words	Poor	Fair	Average	Good	Superior
Speech	Poor	Fair	Average	Good	Superior

Defects		
Stuttering		Poor articulation
Baby talk		
Hesitations		
Mannerisms		
Substitutions		
Omissions		

| Hearing | Apparently normal | Questionable |
| Vision | Apparently normal | Questionable |

Motor skills

Fine motor	Impaired	Below average	Average	Above average	Superior
Gross motor	Impaired	Below average	Average	Above average	Superior
Laterality and directionality	Impaired	Below average	Average	Above average	Superior

153

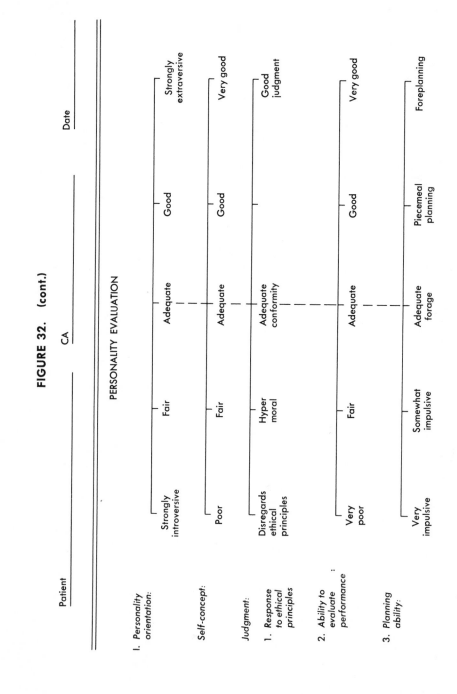

FIGURE 32. (cont.)

154

FIGURE 32. (cont.)

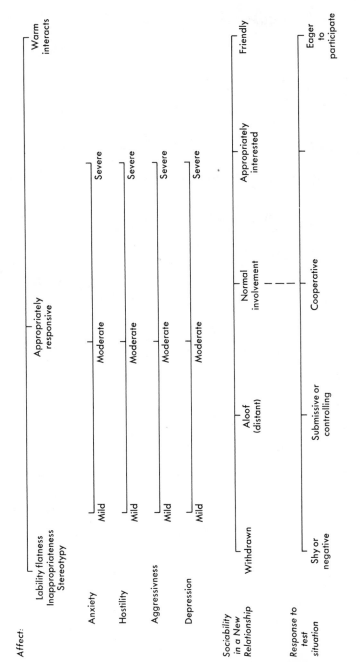

155

FIGURE 33. Behavior summary

ACTIVITY

Hyperactive	*Fidgeting*	*Average*	*Quiet*	*Relaxed*
Constantly moving— movement varies with task			Unless requested to move	

EFFORT

Refuses to make effort	Effort varies with task	Average	Applies self effectively	Works to best of ability

COOPERATION

Refuses	Reluctant	Average	Cooperates compliantly	Works with eagerness

ATTENTION

Very impulsive— acts without instruction	Does not attend	Average	Attends	Very alert

CONCENTRATION

Quits task after few minutes	Easily distracted from task	Average perseverance of task	Distracted only by extreme circumstances	Concentrates on one task for long time

MOTOR SKILLS

Defective coordination	Clumsy	Average motor coordination	Above average control	Unusual motor coordination control

CONVERSATIONAL SKILL

Refuses to speak	No spontaneity— not relevant	Average skills appropriate	Talkative— relevant	Talkative— highly skilled

SELF IMAGE

Extremely critical of work	Satisfied with inadequate work or apologetic	Average recognition of poor work	Accepts mistakes with regret	Good self-esteem

COMPREHENSION

Rarely understands instructions	Needs much elaboration	Average— may require elaboration	Above average— does not need elaboration	Quickly grasps problem— anticipates

to keep him occupied with the tasks. Though he was quiet and obedient, he was distracted by the external stimuli of the room, such as the articles on the desk, the typewriter, and books stacked on the shelves. When his task was not a writing task, he often marked on any paper nearby.

By presenting a new test to him immediately after having finished one, it was possible to keep him working for one and one-half hours. After this period of time, he began to tire. The testing was completed on the second day.

In both sessions WD spoke much too softly to be heard distinctly. There seemed to be no articulation problem, but it was necessary to have him repeat his words and sentences often.

Summary and Recommendations

WD was examined and found to be functioning between the retarded range and the low-normal range of intellectual ability. His quotient score placed him in the retarded range, but his range of functions showed that he could not be classified as a true retardate, since he showed some capacity to function at the (low) normal level.

He was shown to have a perceptual problem, which has no doubt influenced his communication and motor skills to the degree that he is immature in fine motor skills, as in pencil manipulation.

It is recommended that he be given the following remedial help. The asterisks at different numbers designate the activities that should be performed on a daily basis five days a week.

*1. WD should trace geometric designs like circles, squares, crosses, and diamonds on template if available. If not, the remediation teacher (RT) should take WD's hand and trace over the designs until WD can consistently follow the patterns with his forefinger, independent of help. (It is a good practice to have the third finger lap over the forefinger in training.)

2. WD should have a triangle pencil guard to aid his grasp. Following the tracing, the RT should hold his hand, helping him to draw these designs until he has mastered the tasks. (Diamonds are not generally mastered independently until a mental age of seven years is reached.)

3. The entire perceptual program in the Nunn- Jones book, *The Learning Pyramid: Potential Through Perception,* should be gradually built into his daily training. The program is easy to follow and the equipment shown can be modified to make the training tasks available.

4. Every request made of WD should be made in short, simple statements. It should be determined that WD has understood the request by showing or repeating.

*5. WD should be provided opportunities to see and discriminate two colors at a time. Select different colors for discrimination and practice until he can call them correctly ten days consecutively. Use a variety of colored objects as well as colored shapes and designs.

6. WD's routine should be structured in a way that he can learn *what to count on next.*

*7. Train for auditory skills by presenting opportunity to discriminate sounds of horns, whistles, barking, and other such common noises.

8. Do not begin any formal reading program until WD has mastered well the visual discrimination of large geometric designs and auditory discrimination of gross sounds (as in #7 above). His formal training should be put off for a year; then introduce some late kindergarten and first-grade tasks such as recognition of letters, numbers, and letter sounds.

9. If WD behaves in inappropriate ways, he should not be made to feel guilty but *should understand that he cannot engage in such behavior.*

Consistency and *firmness* are essential. Be certain before making rules that the one in authority can see that the rules are carried out. Otherwise WD can learn that he can "get away" with his inappropriate behavior.

Consultant

LEGAL ASPECTS OF REPORTING

In many states the legal rights of parents and their children have long been clearly defined. The courts have ruled that parents have the right to any data which dictate grade placement, special services, or categories for their children. In addition, parents have been given the right to the control of and release of the data. Mordock (1971) questions any practice that withholds written reports from parents on professional or ethical grounds. He says that the purpose of any evaluation is to facilitate the learning process, which requires the joint effort of parents, teacher, and diagnosticians. Machowsky (1973), Robbins and Carrigan (1971), and Hyman (1972) stress the liability involved should diagnosticians withhold information from parents or release it to others without proper consent. Martin (1972) has excellent coverage of the specifics of privileged information.

Whereas many states have had rulings regarding open school records, the mandate from the national level dispels any question as to whether closed records may continue to exist. The Buckley Amendment to the Educational Provisions Act of 1974 gave parents access to their child's records. A person 18 and older not only has access to his/her own records, but also with certain exceptions is the *only* one who can authorize their release.

It is now common for school systems to seek the advice of the legal profession to eliminate misuse of student records and to set standards for future use of information in these records (Johnson, 1974). While no hard and fast rules can be set, there are a few guidelines that will help eliminate possible harm to students.

Observations should be carefully and factually reported, and interpretations of the incident being recorded should be avoided. Consultants and teachers should avoid drawing conclusions about a child's behavior that they are not academically qualified to make. Labeling, which may inadvertently cause a receiving teacher to react inappropriately to students without giving them a chance, should be avoided.

It is also recommended that when parents view their child's records, a professional person should be present to explain the information. Isolated bits of numerical data, such as achievement scores and I.Q.'s, are of little value to the parent unless they are correctly interpreted. Those who have written articles on special education and the law are E.Y. Zedler, (1952); Ross, DeYoung, and Cohen (1971); and A. Abeson (1972).

THE FINAL FORM OF THE REPORT

The form of the final report will probably vary and is influenced by one's training and the needs of a particular situation. The following is provided to aid the reader in choosing the relevant areas to be covered in designing formats for specific locales:

1. *Identification*
   Name
   Sex
   Birthdate
   Chronological age
   Examiner's name
   Date of examination

2. *Reason for referral*
   Purpose
   Source
   Circumstances

3. *History of case*

   School behavior
   (Home influences and behavior are usually obtained by a social worker and more often found in psychological rather than educational evaluations.)

4. *Psychometric information*
   Tests used
   Scores (when appropriate) or levels of function

5. *Behavior and appearance of subject*
   Attitudes
   Dress
   Method of approach to tasks

6. *Summarization of test results*
   Level of intellectual functioning and impressions of reliability or validity

7. *Recommendations*

8. Evaluator's signature and identifying role as psychologist, consultant, or educational diagnostician

SUMMARY

Examination of the issues involved in reporting test data brings into focus the problem of educational jargon. A report must be understood by parents, teachers, and people in other professions. Also the content of reports should be examined in terms of the legality of withholding or releasing test findings. Many states are explicit in their rulings regarding confidentiality and individual rights. It is clearly apparent that diagnosticians must first acquaint themselves with the laws and regulations of their state and then make their reporting plans accordingly.

Summary forms for report writing are provided to aid the reporter in designating levels of function and/or activity after making a careful analysis of the test results. In addition a design for a report format is provided.

chapter 9

Case Studies

After you have studied the case studies in this chapter, you should be able to

1. Understand a general approach to reporting information obtained from a test battery.
2. Understand the means of reporting psychometric data with an evaluation.
3. Discuss similarities and differences in case studies to highlight or emphasize the major points in diagnosis.

INTRODUCTION

The following case studies are grouped according to grade levels. Since scores seem to cluster in relation to performance versus verbal areas of function, some of the evaluations are also grouped to show these differences so that the reader has an opportunity to view the wide scatter of abilities within each cluster. Identifying terms indicate the outstanding features of each case so that consultants may easily locate any sample that they may need. For example, at the elementary level among the high performance group, a case may emphasize a difficulty in visual-motor or auditory performance, whereas, another may emphasize the subject's tendency to overproduce or to underproduce.

According to Chapter 7, two cases may have the same problem emphasis but a different test pattern, or vice versa. Case A, showing a severe perceptual-motor deficiency in one task yet a high performance score in an area that includes perceptual-motor functions, differs from case B, which is made distinctive by the same perceptual-motor weakness. The latter case, however, may show a low performance score, revealing weaknesses in other functions of that area.

Case A—Perceptual-motor deficiency
High performance I.Q.

Case B—Perceptual-motor deficiency
Low performance I.Q.

Similarly, note how a child with a very high vocabulary ability who is categorized as a nonreader differs from a nonreader with a very low vocabulary ability. The complexities of like behavioral results stemming from unlike sources and unlike behavioral results stemming from like sources demonstrate that classification according to test patterns is not necessarily indicative of the appropriate category.

When medical information, such as an EEG, is provided, some classifications may be assigned on the basis of cause. However, Chapter 9 is concerned rather with the practice of differential test analysis in relation to future planning for academic improvement. Each case is individual and requires the kind of diagnosis that will lead to individual remediation. For this reason, the term "brain damage" rarely occurs in the case studies. Unless medically diagnosed, indications of dysfunction in various psychological tests (for example, the Bender-Gestalt test) are referred to as visual-motor problems. According to Bender (1938), in the final analysis a visual-motor disorder is the only valid deduction that can be made from the reproduction of geometric designs. The consultant who is qualified to make only an educational diagnosis should stay within the framework of educational terminology. The school's responsibility is academic, and the academic problem is the one to be identified. The case studies that mention brain damage do so only in the context of reporting from other sources.

The cases are divided into kindergarten, elementary, junior high, and senior high school levels. The time available, the requests of the referring source, and the individual circumstances of the case determine the test selection.

KINDERGARTEN

The three cases for study at this level differ in their reasons for referral. Recommendations were made on the basis of initial requests.

1. Case of CC. *Slow language and motor development.*

The parents referred CC because they were concerned about slow development and possible difficulties when she begins school.

NAME CC   EXAMINER Jane Doe

DATE OF BIRTH   DATE OF
EXAMINATION   C.A. 4–1

EVALUATION FOR LEARNING DISABILITIES

BEHAVIOR AND APPEARANCE

CC was a blond, blue-eyed child of normal height and weight for the age of four years and one month. She was very neat, clean, and well dressed. Although normally quick in her movements, CC demonstrated a mild instability in her walk and a mild tremor in her hand movements when writing or handling any of the materials. She cooperated well at the beginning, but after an hour she started to tire. In fact, she would try to end the tasks by saying "I'm frough!" Enough information was obtained, however, to establish a valid range for her.

TEST RESULTS

See Psychometric Summary.

SUMMARY

CC was examined and found to be functioning in the dull range of intellectual ability with a Stanford-Binet I.Q of 80, a PPVT I.Q. of 82, and a DAP I.Q. of 86. On the Stanford-Binet her basal fell at the three-year level where she passed all the tests with ease, and her ceiling fell at the five-year level where she failed all the tests. Therefore, her functioning level was established at three to five years. The PPVT and the DAP substantiated this general level of functioning.

An examination of the functions tested shows CC to be operating at the three-year level in vocabulary, reasoning, visual memory, and number concepts, while her meaningful memory and social intelligence functions fall at about the four-year level. This indicates her strengths and implies that her slowness is not global.

The final analysis suggests borderline retardation in some functions and normal capacity in others. Since her attention span is short and will probably cause her to be slow in picking up nonmeaningful symbols, CC should be subjected to numerous experiences with kinesthetic aids to learning. In order to facilitate her vocabulary and visual-motor learning, the Peabody Language Development Program is recommended. In addition, the Kephart exercises may not only promote better motor functions but also aid her in understanding directions. Because her achievement lies at the nursery school level, all beginning activities should be uncomplicated. She should have formal kindergarten training structured according to the specific needs indicated in this evaluation.

Consultant

PSYCHOMETRIC SUMMARY

Intelligence Tests:

Wechsler Intelligence Scales

_____WPPSI   _____WISC   _____WAIS

WPPSI Scaled Scores

Verbal	Performance
Information_____	Animal House_____
Comprehension_____	Picture Completion_____
Arithmetic_____	Mazes_____
Similarities_____	Geometric Design_____
Vocabulary_____	Block Design_____
(Sentences)_____	Animal House (Retest)_____

WISC and WAIS Scaled Scores

Verbal	Performance
Information_____	Picture Completion_____
Comprehension_____	Picture Arrangement_____
Arithmetic_____	Block Design_____
Similarities_____	Object Assembly_____
Vocabulary_____	Coding or Digit Symbol_____
Digit Span_____	Mazes_____

Verbal Scale I.Q._____
Performance Scale I.Q._____
Full Scale I.Q._____

Stanford-Binet (Form L-M)	Draw-A-Person Test	Peabody Picture Vocabulary
C.A. _4-1_	C.A. _4-1_	C.A. _4-1_
M.A. _3-4_	M.A. _3-6_	M.A. _3-1_
I.Q. _80_	I.Q. _86_	I.Q. _82_

Wide Range Achievement Test *No norms for age 4-1.*

Reading Grade Level _Nursery Level_ Standard Score_____Percentile_____
Spelling Grade Level _Nursery Level_ Standard Score_____Percentile_____
Arithmetic Grade Level _Nursery Level_ Standard Score_____Percentile_____

Purdue Perceptual-Motor
  Survey_____

Wepman Auditory Discrimination
  Test_____

Children's Apperception
  Test_____

Memory-For-Designs Test
  _____

Bender Visual-Motor
  Gestalt Test_____

Illinois Test of Psycholinguistic
  Abilities (See ITPA Profile)
    Total Language_____
    Scaled Score_____

Hiskey-Nebraska Test

Bead Pattern_____	Visual Attention Span_____
Memory for Colors_____	Block Patterns_____
Picture Identification_____	Completion of Drawings_____
Picture Association_____	Memory for Digits_____
Paper Folding_____	Puzzle Analogies_____
	Spatial Reasoning_____

Other Tests:

2. Case of MJB. *Above average intelligence—difficulty with proper balance.*

This case was referred by a medical doctor in order to determine intelligence and motor control.

NAME MJB   EXAMINER Jane Doe

                                          DATE OF
DATE OF BIRTH   EXAMINATION   C.A. 5–5

EVALUATION FOR LEARNING DISABILITIES

BEHAVIOR AND APPEARANCE

MJB had light brown hair, deep blue eyes, and long eyelashes. His height and weight seemed normal, but a slightly enlarged forehead suggested a hydrocephalic condition. He was a very polite child, and separating him from his mother created no problem. He asked her where she would be and seemed satisfied with the answer that she would be shopping. He was quite apathetic, never smiling or seeming actively interested in the tasks. Although compliant throughout the period, he showed no spontaneous enthusiasm for any of the activities.

TEST RESULTS

See Psychometric Summary.

SUMMARY

MJB was examined and found to be functioning in the superior range of intellectual ability with a Wechsler Preschool and Primary Scale of Intelligence (WPPSI) I.Q. of 129. DAP I.Q. of 106 and the PPVT. I.Q. of 109 do not correlate with his major I.Q. test. They do, however, correlate with some of the subtests on the WPPSI. A score of 12 on the vocabulary subtest relates closely to a PPVT I.Q. of 109. Since the PPVT is a vocabulary test and since all his other verbal task scores were higher, this correlation suggests a weakness for him in vocabulary. (The vocabulary tests often reflect cultural milieu.)

An immature self-concept could possibly produce a lowered DAP I.Q. score; among such clinical cases, this is not unusual. The only other indication of function at the normal level is a score of 11 on the picture completion subtest of the WPPSI, a pictorial test which measures an aptitude for differentiating essential from nonessential visual detail. All other subtest scores place this child at a functioning level of above average to superior. MJB showed a unique development in arithmetical reasoning. When he didn't know what the " + " sign meant, he asked, "Does that mean what are all of these together?" He then calculated the answers on his fingers. (Note in the Psychometric Summary that he achieved in arithmetic as though he had an I.Q. of 147.) The high-scaled score of 18 on the WPPSI Arithmetic subtest is commensurate with this level of function. His comprehension, range of information, and concept formation all showed superior performances.

In the performance area, there was a mild but not significant drop in ability. This suggests that his eye-hand coordination is slightly slower than most of his verbal responses. However, he has two strong areas; his work with mazes and with geometric designs was above average. Thus his fine motor ability, as it relates to the reproduction of visual stimuli, is apparently superior, even though he cannot recall visual stimuli or differentiate between details in the same way that he is able to function in the other visual-motor tasks.

The WRAT reveals an arithmetic level of grade 2.4 and a reading and spelling level of grade 1.3. The former has been explained by the child's ability for arithmetical reasoning. But with a verbal I.Q. of 130, he did not perform as well in reading and spelling as he should have. Since he has not been in a formal, structured training program, however, his reading and spelling achievements may increase to a commensurate I.Q. level after kindergarten experiences.

The ITPA (1961 edition) reveals scores that suggest superiority in receptive abilities, such as comprehension of what he sees and hears. His ability to remember both auditory and visual symbols and to make associations of meaningful visual and auditory language stimuli is normal. The significant drop in linguistic functions was found in the encoding process (expressive operations). In both vocal and motor areas, he is functioning below the other measured areas.

In order to examine other functions, the Purdue Perceptual-Motor Survey and parts of various aphasia and dominance measures were used. According to the latter measures, he has mixed hand and mixed feet dominance but left eye dominance. There is no evidence of finger agnosia or nonverbal apraxia since he has no trouble recognizing his fingers by touch when his eyes are closed or expressing ideas with his hands. On the motor encoding test of the ITPA he had to view pictures and re-create them. On the aphasia test his performance was directed by auditory cues. In accordance with the Purdue scale, he can (1) identify body parts readily; (2) imitate movements; (3) establish body balance in the Kraus-Weber exercise; (4) move his arms and legs at command (angels-in-the-snow, performed on the back while lying on the floor); and (5) draw geometric designs well for his age. From this, it seems apparent that his eye-hand coordination as well as body manipulation are normal.

The problem became evident when MJB was asked to walk the balance beam (a 2- by 4-inch beam on 2-inch concrete blocks). He could not take even one step without stumbling or falling off. Neither could he walk sideways or backwards. Thus, it appears that his motor problem is related to his vertical balance. In all other tasks he performed adequately though not perfectly, but perfect performance should not be expected from a five-year-old. At his age, however, he should have the ability to walk the length of the balance beam satisfactorily. But he cannot. There is also a mild irregularity in his ocular pursuit, although when tested this did not seem to slow down his visual-motor coordination. Some exercises are recommended, however, in order to make his eye movements more regular.

Thus MJB appears to be a very intelligent boy. Except for the severe weakness in vertical body balance he shows strengths that range into the superior level and weaknesses (as measured by the WPPSI) that do not fall below normal. As previously discussed, his eye-hand coordination appears normal. (The Bender record was also normal; the Koppitz score was ten.) Expressive operations are among his noted weaknesses, even though they do not fall below the normal level. Thus, the medical diagnosis of ataxia is substantiated and calls for remedial exercises in balance and ocular pursuit, as described in *The Slow Learner in the Classroom* by Kephart (1960.) MJB should be encouraged to express himself using both verbal and motor skills. This can be discussed with his mother at a later conference.

Consultant

PSYCHOMETRIC SUMMARY

Intelligence Tests:

Wechsler Intelligence Scales

__✓__WPPSI   _____WISC   _____WAIS

WPPSI Scaled Scores

Verbal		Performance	
Information	_15_	Animal House	_13_
Comprehension	_15_	Picture Completion	_11_
Arithmetic	_18_	Mazes	_14_
Similarities	_14_	Geometric Design	_16_
Vocabulary	_12_	Block Design	_13_
(Sentences)		Animal House (Retest)	

WISC and WAIS Scaled Scores

Verbal	Performance
Information	Picture Completion
Comprehension	Picture Arrangement
Arithmetic	Block Design
Similarities	Object Assembly
Vocabulary	Coding or Digit Symbol
Digit Span	Mazes

Verbal Scale I.Q.____ _130_
Performance Scale I.Q.__ _123_
Full Scale I.Q.___ _129_

Stanford-Binet (Form L-M)	Draw-A-Person Test	Peabody Picture Vocabulary
C.A.____	C.A. _5-5_	C.A. _5-5_
M.A.____	M.A. _5-9_	M.A. _5-11_
I.Q.____	I.Q. _106_	I.Q. _109_

Wide Range Achievement Test

Reading Grade Level___ _1.3_ ___Standard Score _117_ Percentile____
Spelling Grade Level___ _1.3_ ___Standard Score _117_ Percentile____
Arithmetic Grade Level _2.4_ ___Standard Score _147_ Percentile____

Purdue Perceptual-Motor Survey_____

Wepman Auditory Discrimination Test_____

Children's Apperception Test_____

Memory-For-Designs Test
_____

Bender Visual-Motor Gestalt Test _Normal_____

Illinois Test of Psycholinguistic Abilities (See ITPA Profile)
Total Language_____
Scaled Score_____

Hiskey-Nebraska Test

Bead Pattern_____	Visual Attention Span_____
Memory for Colors_____	Block Patterns_____
Picture Identification_____	Completion of Drawings_____
Picture Association_____	Memory for Digits_____
Paper Folding_____	Puzzle Analogies_____
	Spatial Reasoning_____

Other Tests:

Name __CASE OF MJB__   Age __5-5__   Birthdate _____

ILLINOIS TEST OF PSYCHOLINGUISTIC ABILITIES

(Experimental Edition, 1961)

Language Age	REPRESENTATIONAL LEVEL						AUTOMATIC-SEQUENTIAL LEVEL			Language Age
	DECODING		ASSOCIATIONAL		ENCODING		AUTOMATIC	SEQUENTIAL		
	Auditory	Visual	Auditory Vocal	Visual-Motor	Vocal	Motor	Auditory Vocal	Auditory Vocal	Visual-Motor	
	1	2	3	4	5	6	7	8	9	
9-0										9-0
8-6										8-6
8-0										8-0
7-6										7-6
7-0										7-0
6-6										6-6
6-0										6-0
5-6										5-6
5-0										5-0
4-6										4-6
4-0										4-0
3-6										3-6
3-0										3-0
2-6										2-6
	7-1	7-10	6-1	6-1	5-4	5-10	7-3	6-3	6-0	
	Comprehension of spoken word.	Comprehension of picture and written word.	Ability to relate spoken words in a meaningful way (auditory symbols)	Ability to relate visual symbols in a meaningful way	Ability to express ideas in spoken words	Ability to express ideas in gestures	Ability to predict future linguistic events from past experiences	Memory of auditory symbols	Memory of visual symbols	

CA:

3. Case of W.L. *Auditory communication problem.*

This case was referred by a speech therapist.

NAME WL   EXAMINER Jane Doe

DATE OF BIRTH _____ DATE OF EXAMINATION _____ C.A. 3–2

EVALUATION FOR LEARNING DISABILITIES

BEHAVIOR AND APPEARANCE

With blue eyes and curly blond hair, WL was quite small for a three-year-old. She was very clean, neat, and attractively dressed. She readily adjusted to the new situation, for she was not shy with strangers and there was no hint of a separation problem when her mother left. She worked well on all the tasks for about an hour. But then she began to experience some fatigue, and several times she refused to work. At times, her speech became inarticulate, but when she knew the answers, she spoke clearly enough to be understood. Through jesting and other forms of diversion, it was possible to collect the data necessary to complete the evaluation.

TEST RESULTS

See Psychometric Summary.

SUMMARY

Examination found WL to be functioning in the normal range of intellectual ability with a Stanford-Binet I.Q. of 102 and a PPVT I.Q. of 94. Since her picture vocabulary was an obvious strength on the Stanford-Binet, expectation was for the PPVT I.Q. to be higher. However, on this test she exhibited signs of fatigue. Perhaps the added effort of making correct picture choices confused her more than the mere naming of items in single pictures.

She passed all tasks on the three-year level, establishing her basal at this point. Her ceiling was established at the five-year level since she failed all tests at this level. Her greatest strengths lie in the area of meaningful memory, for these tasks she passed at the four- and four-and-one-half-year levels. One task pertained to visual memory and the other to auditory memory. In the latter, the directions related to her knowledge of words to the degree that she could respond by acting out the activities. Otherwise, her auditory reception was found to be below normal.

All intellectual functions, motor and language, are normal, and her meaningful memory is above average. The ITPA (1961 edition) found visual perception (visual decoding) to be her only communication strength. Her communication problem as determined by the ITPA revealed that she cannot articulate correctly. The test data did not show whether the cause is minimal brain injury or developmental lag. Be it either disorder, her ability to discriminate between sounds is poor, even though she has no apparent hearing problem. Fatigue may have influenced her visual association (Test 4 on the ITPA), but the Stanford-Binet supports her low auditory functioning on the ITPA, since she needed to have the test directions repeated over and over. Consequently, without remediation of her deficiency in sound discrimination, WL will probably find learning difficult by the first grade. The parents should consult the four areas of auditory training at the first-grade level in the book *Aids to Psycholinguistic Teaching* (1969). Speech therapy should be beneficial, especially for future academic and social adjustment.

—————————————————————

Consultant

PSYCHOMETRIC SUMMARY

Intelligence Tests:

Wechsler Intelligence Scales

_____WPPSI   _____WISC   _____WAIS

WPPSI Scaled Scores

Verbal	Performance
Information_____	Animal House_____
Comprehension_____	Picture Completion_____
Arithmetic_____	Mazes_____
Similarities_____	Geometric Design_____
Vocabulary_____	Block Design_____
(Sentences)_____	Animal House
	(Retest)_____

WISC and WAIS Scaled Scores

Verbal	Performance
Information_____	Picture Completion_____
Comprehension_____	Picture Arrangement_____
Arithmetic_____	Block Design_____
Similarities_____	Object Assembly_____
Vocabulary_____	Coding or Digit Symbol_____
Digit Span_____	Mazes_____

Verbal Scale I.Q._____
Performance Scale I.Q._____
Full Scale I.Q._____

Stanford-Binet (Form L-M)	Draw-A-Person Test		Peabody Picture Vocabulary
C.A. _3-2_	C.A._____	_would_	C.A. _3-2_
M.A. _3-4_	M.A._____	_not_	M.A. _2-10_
I.Q. _102_	I.Q._____	_respond_	I.Q. _94_

Wide Range Achievement Test

Reading Grade Level_____ Standard Score_____ Percentile_____
Spelling Grade Level_____ Standard Score_____ Percentile_____
Arithmetic Grade Level_____ Standard Score_____ Percentile_____

Purdue Perceptual-Motor	Wepman Auditory Discrimination
Survey_____	Test_____

Children's Apperception	Memory-For-Designs Test
Test_____	_____

Bender Visual-Motor	Illinois Test of Psycholinguistic
Gestalt Test_____	Abilities (See ITPA Profile)
	Total Language_____
	Scaled Score_____

Hiskey-Nebraska Test

Bead Pattern_____	Visual Attention Span_____
Memory for Colors_____	Block Patterns_____
Picture Identification_____	Completion of Drawings_____
Picture Association_____	Memory for Digits_____
Paper Folding_____	Puzzle Analogies_____
	Spatial Reasoning_____

Other Tests: _Preschool Attainment Record (PAR)_
_CA: 3-2   AA: 3-7   AQ: 111_

175

Name ___CASE of WL___ Age ___3-2___ Birthdate ___

ILLINOIS TEST OF PSYCHOLINGUISTIC ABILITIES

(Experimental Edition, 1961)

CA:

	REPRESENTATIONAL LEVEL						AUTOMATIC-SEQUENTIAL LEVEL			
	DECODING		ASSOCIATIONAL		ENCODING		AUTOMATIC	SEQUENTIAL		
Language Age	Auditory	Visual	Auditory Vocal	Visual-Motor	Vocal	Motor	Auditory Vocal	Auditory Vocal	Visual-Motor	Language Age
	1	2	3	4	5	6	7	8	9	
9-0										9-0
8-6										8-6
8-0										8-0
7-6										7-6
7-0										7-0
6-6										6-6
6-0										6-0
5-6										5-6
5-0										5-0
4-6										4-6
4-0										4-0
3-6										3-6
3-0										3-0
2-6										2-6
	0	4-1	2-3	2-5	3-0	2-3	2-6	2-7	2-7	

Subtest descriptions:
- Comprehension of spoken word.
- Comprehension of picture and written word.
- Ability to relate spoken words in a meaningful way (auditory symbols)
- Ability to relate visual symbols in a meaningful way
- Ability to express ideas in spoken words
- Ability to express ideas in gestures
- Ability to predict future linguistic events from past experiences
- Memory of auditory symbols
- Memory of visual symbols

ELEMENTARY

High Verbal — Low Performance Group

4. Case of DHT. *Combination of visual-motor and auditory problems.*

Referral source was a medical doctor who wanted information to complete his own case study.

NAME DHT   EXAMINER Jane Doe

DATE OF
DATE OF BIRTH   EXAMINATION   C.A. 7–4

EVALUATION FOR LEARNING DISABILITIES

BEHAVIOR AND APPEARANCE

DHT, a nice-looking boy with ash-blond hair, was normal in height and weight for his age. His casual clothing was very clean and neat. Being very outgoing, even impulsively so, he immediately began asking questions about my family. As we started the testing, he demonstrated a normal amount of interest, and it was not difficult to keep him working at his tasks. If the activities stopped for only a few minutes, he began asking questions and making remarks, easily adjusting to any new stimulus. Although he showed some signs of slight disinterest by asking when we would be finished, he cooperated for the full two-hour period.

TEST RESULTS

See Psychometric Summary.

SUMMARY

Examination of DHT found him to be functioning erratically between dull and high normal intelligence. The wide gap between his DAP I.Q. of 85 and his Peabody Picture Vocabulary I.Q. of 127 would be difficult to understand without the intertest scatter of the WISC. The WISC Full Scale I.Q. of 95 suggests a low normal global intelligence. However, the great difference between the performance I.Q. of 80 and the verbal I.Q. of 109 indicates verbal strengths and performance weaknesses. A scaled score of 13 on the WISC Vocabulary and the PPVT I.Q. of 127 suggest an above average vocabulary ability. Other verbal measures suggest above average concept formation and normal arithmetical reasoning, memory for digits, comprehension, and range of information. In the performance area only two subtests, coding and picture arrangement, revealed normal scores. All other visual-motor functions were rated dull or below. The very low picture completion scaled score indicates that DHT misses many of the essential details of visual stimuli. Thus a rather serious visual-motor problem seems obvious. This is further substantiated by the rotation of design 8 on the Bender-Gestalt and by a difference score of 5 on the MFD. This latter score place DHT on the borderline of severe visual-motor dysfunction.

The WRAT placed his level of achievement at the first grade with accomplishments in arithmetic several months above those in reading and spelling (all, however, at the first-grade level). The standard arithmetic score of 96 suggests that he is achieving at a level commensurate with his arithmetic ability, but his reading and spelling fell slightly below expectancy. Several problem areas such as reversals and memory for symbols were detected by his response to the spelling test. He changed the *d* in the word *and* to *b* after a glance and stated, "I can't remember which one is right." Then he spelled *boy* as *booewe.* He first wrote down *boo,* then asked me how to spell *we.* I simply sounded the word *boy* for him, and he completed the above spelling. It was evident that he had tried to spell the word phonetically.

Since there was obvious evidence of a rather critical visual-motor problem and since the Auditory Discrimination Test revealed that he also misunderstands some sounds, the ITPA was not given. Instead, to determine any emotional overlay, the Children's Apperception Test was administered. In all ten stories he portrayed normal feelings. No family triangle, hostility, or fear was detected. Therefore, if DHT had experienced emotional trauma, it did not effect reaction at this time.

A critical visual-motor problem together with evidence of a learning difficulty due to poor sound discrimination suggests that he is not receiving, understanding, or associating written words with objects or experiences.

The data reveals a normal intellectual potential with strengths in vocabulary and concept formation, but with little ability to recall symbols previously seen or heard. DHT requires remediation such as recommended in the ITPA aids book (see Appendix B); specifically, he requires remediation with the auditory and the visual sequencing tasks, the visual-motor association tasks, and the visual decoding tasks. Also, his slowness in developing a dominant laterality and his poor coordination require a highly structured perceptual-motor program of physical education exercises. Most elementary school systems offer these structured exercises upon recommendation.

Consultant

Intelligence Tests:

Wechsler Intelligence Scales

_____WPPSI   __✓__WISC   _____WAIS

WPPSI Scaled Scores

Verbal	Performance
Information_____	Animal House_____
Comprehension_____	Picture Completion_____
Arithmetic_____	Mazes_____
Similarities_____	Geometric Design_____
Vocabulary_____	Block Design_____
(Sentences)_____	Animal House
	(Retest)_____

WISC and WAIS Scaled Scores

Verbal	Performance
Information_____9_____	Picture Completion_____3___
Comprehension____11____	Picture Arrangement___9___
Arithmetic_____10_____	Block Design_____7___
Similarities_____14_____	Object Assembly____7___
Vocabulary_____13_____	Coding or Digit Symbol__10__
Digit Span_____9_____	Mazes_____

Verbal Scale I.Q.____109____

Performance Scale I.Q.__80___

Full Scale I.Q._____95____

Stanford-Binet (Form L-M)	Draw-A-Person Test	Peabody Picture Vocabulary
C.A._____	C.A._7-4__	C.A._7-4__
M.A._____	M.A._6-3__	M.A._10-0_
I.Q._____	I.Q._85__	I.Q._127_

Wide Range Achievement Test

Reading Grade Level___1.4____Standard Score__88__Percentile_____

Spelling Grade Level___1.2____Standard Score__85__Percentile_____

Arithmetic Grade Level__1.9____Standard Score__96__Percentile_____

Purdue Perceptual-Motor
Survey_____

Wepman Auditory Discrimination
Test____X = $^{17}/_{30}$ Y = $^0/_{10}$

Children's Apperception
Test____See Summary_____

Memory-For-Designs Test
__Borderline visual-motor problem

Bender Visual-Motor
Gestalt Test__Borderline visual-motor problem

Illinois Test of Psycholinguistic
Abilities (See ITPA Profile)
Total Language_____
Scaled Score_____

Hiskey-Nebraska Test

Bead Pattern_____	Visual Attention Span_____
Memory for Colors_____	Block Patterns_____
Picture Identification_____	Completion of Drawings_____
Picture Association_____	Memory for Digits_____
Paper Folding_____	Puzzle Analogies_____
	Spatial Reasoning_____

Other Tests:

5. Case of HK. *Visual-motor and memory problems.*

The school referred HK because an evaluation was needed to plan remediation within the school situation.

NAME HK   EXAMINER Jane Doe

DATE OF BIRTH   DATE OF EXAMINATION   C.A. 8–9

EVALUATION FOR LEARNING DISABILITIES

BEHAVIOR AND APPEARANCE

HK, a nice-looking boy with brown eyes and brown hair, seemed physiologically normal. His school clothes were neat and clean. Since he was willing to be tested, rapport was easily established. His speech was normal, and his communication good; therefore, the testing moved along naturally and smoothly.

TEST RESULTS

See Psychometric Summary.

SUMMARY

HK's examination found him to be functioning within the average to bright range of intellectual ability with a PPVT I.Q. of 104 and a Full Scale WISC I.Q. of 109. The DAP I.Q. of 80 is not representative of his overall intelligence but substantiates a visual-motor problem which other test data revealed.

The boy's greatest strengths lie in his verbal ability, for his verbal I.Q. of 116 on the WISC was significantly higher than his performance I.Q. of 99. Scoring above average in comprehension, reasoning, and concept formation and significantly below average in vocabulary suggests that HK does not understand the meaning of words as well as he reasons, comprehends, or associates ideas.

HK's performance area contained a great deal of scatter, suggesting that he functions inconsistently when engaged in visual-motor tasks. He was slow in discriminating between essential and nonessential detail and in planning and anticipating social procedure, but with practice he was able to work with designs. He scored normally on the block design test, but his approach to the tasks was unusual. He often copied a design using the wrong color. When asked to study a design, he would note the mistake and attempt to correct it. He corrected several mistakes within the time limit but had to be prompted before recognizing them. The prompting was done by asking him to study his design carefully.

While showing a language ability score within the average to above average range, the ITPA language age scores (1961 edition) of 6–2 and 6–4 on the auditory decoding test and the visual-motor sequencing test also showed two weaknesses. The latter score substantiates his visual-motor problem and indicates difficulty in recalling the sequencing of written symbols, while the former score suggests that he also has a problem in understanding what he hears. These scores are commensurate with his lowered vocabulary score on the WISC.

The Bender-Gestalt and the MFD tests substantiate the visual-motor problem, though both scores fell within the normal range. Despite the results of the Bender (Koppitz), he rotated designs 3 and 4 by 90° and made five small circles instead of dots on design 7. Because of developmental visual-motor maturation, normal irregularities were expected; however, HK's rotations and alterations of designs are not normal.

Nevertheless, this difficulty has not caused HK any unsurmountable academic problems, for he has been achieving at a level commensurate with his ability and his age. For example, his reading, spelling, and arithmetic scores fell at the third-grade level. HK is apparently intelligent enough to work around his problems, but some remediation techniques structured around his weaknesses could assist his present efforts.

Consultant

ADDENDUM

The physical education instructor administered the *Purdue Perceptual-Motor Survey* and made the following evaluation:

1. Balance and posture slightly unsteady
2. Differentiation problem and slow response to identification of body parts
3. Poor perceptual-motor match
4. Ocular pursuit unsteady and jerky

The instructor recommended that HK report to perceptual-motor class for remediation of these problem areas.

Intelligence Tests:

Wechsler Intelligence Scales

_____WPPSI   ✓ WISC   _____WAIS

WPPSI Scaled Scores

Verbal	Performance
Information_____	Animal House_____
Comprehension_____	Picture Completion_____
Arithmetic_____	Mazes_____
Similarities_____	Geometric Design_____
Vocabulary_____	Block Design_____
(Sentences)_____	Animal House (Retest)_____

WISC and WAIS Scaled Scores

Verbal		Performance	
Information	12	Picture Completion	7
Comprehension	14	Picture Arrangement	9
Arithmetic	14	Block Design	13
Similarities	14	Object Assembly	10
Vocabulary	9	Coding or Digit Symbol	10
Digit Span	10	Mazes	

Verbal Scale I.Q. ___116___
Performance Scale I.Q. ___99___
Full Scale I.Q. ___109___

Stanford-Binet (Form L-M)	Draw-A-Person Test	Peabody Picture Vocabulary
C.A._____	C.A. 8-7	C.A. 8-8
M.A._____	M.A. 7-6	M.A. 9-6
I.Q._____	I.Q. 80	I.Q. 104

Wide Range Achievement Test

Reading Grade Level	3.8	Standard Score 103	Percentile_____
Spelling Grade Level	3.7	Standard Score 102	Percentile_____
Arithmetic Grade Level	3.9	Standard Score 104	Percentile_____

Purdue Perceptual-Motor
Survey___See Profile___

Wepman Auditory Discrimination
Test_____

Children's Apperception
Test_____

Memory-For-Designs Test
___Normal Record___

Bender Visual-Motor
Gestalt Test___Borderline visual-
motor problem___

Illinois Test of Psycholinguistic
Abilities (See ITPA Profile)
Total Language___9-1___
Scaled Score_____

Hiskey-Nebraska Test

Bead Pattern_____	Visual Attention Span_____
Memory for Colors_____	Block Patterns_____
Picture Identification_____	Completion of Drawings_____
Picture Association_____	Memory for Digits_____
Paper Folding_____	Puzzle Analogies_____
	Spatial Reasoning_____

Other Tests:

Name CASE OF HK   Age 8-8   Birthdate

ILLINOIS TEST OF PSYCHOLINGUISTIC ABILITIES
(Experimental Edition, 1961)

ca.:

	REPRESENTATIONAL LEVEL						AUTOMATIC-SEQUENTIAL LEVEL		
	DECODING		ASSOCIATIONAL		ENCODING		AUTOMATIC	SEQUENTIAL	
Language Age	Auditory	Visual	Auditory-Vocal	Visual-Motor	Vocal	Motor	Auditory-Vocal	Auditory-Vocal	Visual-Motor
	1	2	3	4	5	6	7	8	9
9-0									
8-6									
8-0									
7-6									
7-0									
6-6									
6-0									
5-6									
5-0									
4-6									
4-0									
3-6									
3-0									
2-6									
	6-2	8-9	9-0	8-11	AN	AN	9-6	AN	6-4
	Comprehension of spoken word.	Comprehension of picture and written word.	Ability to relate spoken words in a meaningful way (auditory symbols)	Ability to relate visual symbols in a meaningful way	Ability to express ideas in spoken words	Ability to express ideas in gestures	Ability to predict future linguistic events from past experiences	Memory of auditory symbols	Memory of visual symbols

Name _Case of HK_   Date of birth _____

Address _____   Sex _M_   Grade _3_

_____   School _____

Examiner _Jane Doe_   Date of examination _____

Score	4	3	2	1	
Walking Board:					Balance
Forward		✓			
Backward					and
Sideways					
Jumping		✓			Posture
Identification of Body Parts			✓		
Imitation of Movement			✓		Body Image
Obstacle Course					and
Kraus-Weber	✓				Differentiation
Angels-in-the-Snow			✓		
Chalkboard					
Circle	✓				
Double circle		✓			Perceptual-
Lateral line					
Vertical line					Motor
Rhythmic Writing					Match
Rhythm		✓			
Reproduction		✓			
Orientation		✓			
Ocular Pursuits					
Both eyes		✓			Ocular
Right eye		✓			Control
Left eye		✓			
Convergence	✓				
Visual Achievement Forms					Form
Form	✓				
Organization		✓			Perception

6.   Case of SB.   *Perceptual-Motor problem.*

The parents were the referral source. A conference was held after-
wards to answer their questions.

NAME SB_____   EXAMINER Jane Doe_____

                                  DATE OF
DATE OF BIRTH_____   EXAMINATION_____   C.A. 9–0

EVALUATION FOR LEARNING DISABILITIES

BEHAVIOR AND APPEARANCE

SB, a nice-looking boy with ash-brown hair and brown eyes, was
neatly dressed in school clothing. His physiological growth and development seemed normal. During the testing he was well mannered and spoke
in a low voice. However, he was easily distracted by other objects close
to the table. Several times he turned from the tasks and placing his hands
on the typewriter, remarked that he and a friend could type. He also
stood up and handled the back of the chair as he answered questions. His
attempts to try to leave the tasks and move on to something else suggested his desired to control and manipulate the session. In order to
hold his attention and to counteract his controlling tendencies, it was
necessary to proceed quickly.

TEST RESULTS

See Psychometric Summary.

SUMMARY

Examination of SB found him functioning in the superior range of
intelligence with a Full Scale WISC I.Q. of 120 and a PPVT I.Q. of 129.
Conversely, SB completed the Goodenough-Harris Test similar to a
child of six years and six months. Irregularities on this test suggest
difficulty in making proper alignment and in recalling obvious detail
such as hands.

The verbal area revealed a very stable high level of function; that is,
his range of information, comprehension, arithmetical reasoning, concept
formation, and vocabulary almost all bordered on the superior range and
higher. The digit span test score felt significantly below the other verbal
abilities though still in the normal range.

The performance area scores were significantly lower than the verbal area scores. The 20-point difference strongly suggests that the boy's perceptual-motor development is slower than his verbal development. The block design and coding scores show his greatest weaknesses to be slow psychomotor speed, pencil manipulation, depth perception, and/or visual-motor coordination.

The WRAT revealed underachievement, with reading and spelling scores at the fourth-grade level and arithmetic scores at the second-grade level. Analysis of the arithmetic test revealed such careless errors as adding instead of subtracting. Since the WISC showed superior arithmetic ability, it seems feasible to assume that poor visual discrimination as a part of the lowered perceptual-motor function is causing his mistakes.

The revised edition (1968) of the ITPA was administered to find that SB's psycholinguistic age is normal at 9–3. This level, however, was still below the capacity achieved on the WISC and the PPVT. It can therefore be assumed that he is not communicating adequately. The profile locates his greatest language weaknesses in the visual aspects of learning, since his visual reception and visual sequential memory were both very low, while his visual association fell below most of the other ITPA scores (although not below normal for his age). The low verbal expression score suggests difficulty in expressing ideas under some conditions.

This data strongly suggests a perceptual-motor problem, since the low visual scores on the ITPA, the lowered performance I.Q. on the WISC, the critical area score on the Bender, and the borderline MFD difference score all show related functional weaknesses. A review of the Frostig Visual Perception Program and of the visual-motor exercises for the third-grade level in *Aids in Psycholinguistic Teaching* (Bush & Giles, 1969) is recommended. In addition, structured perceptual-motor exercises according to *The Slow Learner in the Classroom* (Kephart, 1960) are recommended as a part of SB's daily routine.

_____

Consultant

PSYCHOMETRIC SUMMARY

Intelligence Tests:

Wechsler Intelligence Scales

_____WPPSI   ___√___WISC   _____WAIS

WPPSI Scaled Scores

Verbal		Performance	
Information_____		Animal House_____	
Comprehension_____		Picture Completion_____	
Arithmetic_____		Mazes_____	
Similarities_____		Geometric Design_____	
Vocabulary_____		Block Design_____	
(Sentences)_____		Animal House	
		(Retest)_____	

WISC and WAIS Scaled Scores

Verbal		Performance	
Information___ _15_		Picture Completion___ _12_	
Comprehension___ _15_		Picture Arrangement___ _12_	
Arithmetic___ _13_		Block Design___ _11_	
Similarities___ _15_		Object Assembly___ _13_	
Vocabulary___ _14_		Coding or Digit Symbol__ _8_	
Digit Span___ _10_		Mazes_____	

Verbal Scale I.Q._____ _128_
Performance Scale I.Q. _108_
Full Scale I.Q._____ _120_

Stanford-Binet (Form L-M)	Draw-A-Person Test	Peabody Picture Vocabulary
C.A._____	C.A. _9-0_	C.A. _9-0_
M.A._____	M.A. _6-6_	M.A. _12-9_
I.Q._____	I.Q. ___—___	I.Q. _129_

Wide Range Achievement Test

Reading Grade Level___ _4.8_ ___Standard Score _107_ Percentile_____
Spelling Grade Level___ _4.7_ ___Standard Score _106_ Percentile_____
Arithmetic Grade Level__ _2.8_ ___Standard Score _88_ Percentile_____

Purdue Perceptual-Motor
Survey_____

Wepman Auditory Discrimination
Test_____

Children's Apperception
Test_____

Memory-For-Designs Test
Borderline visual- motor problem

Bender Visual-Motor
Gestalt Test _Critical Range for_
visual- motor problem

Illinois Test of Psycholinguistic
Abilities (See ITPA Profile)
Total Language___ _9-3_
Scaled Score_____

Hiskey-Nebraska Test

Bead Pattern_____	Visual Attention Span_____
Memory for Colors_____	Block Patterns_____
Picture Identification_____	Completion of Drawings_____
Picture Association_____	Memory for Digits_____
Paper Folding_____	Puzzle Analogies_____
	Spatial Reasoning_____

Other Tests:

Date of Examination _____ Name __CASE of SB__ Age __9-0__

PROFILE OF ABILITIES Mean Scaled Score = 36 Standard Deviation = 6

ITPA SCORES

	Representational Level									Automatic Level				
	Reception		Association		Expression			Closure		Sequential Memory		Supplemental Tests		
	Auditory	Visual	Auditory	Visual	Verbal	Manual	Grammatic	Visual	Auditory	Visual	Auditory Closure	Sound Blending	
Scaled Scores	Comprehension of spoken word.	Comprehension of picture and written word.	Ability to relate spoken words in a meaningful way.	Ability to relate visual symbols in a meaningful way.	Ability to express ideas in spoken words.	Ability to express ideas in gestures.	Ability to use correct grammar.	Ability to perceive objects in incomplete form.	Memory of auditory symbols in sequence.	Memory for visual symbols in sequence.	Automatic function to understand difficult and incomplete speech.	Automatic function in synthesizing parts of words.

Scaled Scores: 64 60 56 52 48 44 40 36 32 28 24 20 16 12 8 4

| AN | 6-10 | 10-6 | 9-4 | 7-10 | 10-4 | 9-8 | 10-6 | AN | 5-10 | 10-0 | AN |

189

7. Case of James.   *Visual-motor problem.*

The parents referred this case because they wished information to help in determining reasons for the child's academic slowness.

NAME James   EXAMINER Jane Doe

                                         DATE OF
DATE OF BIRTH   EXAMINATION   C.A. 7–11

EVALUATION FOR LEARNING DISABILITIES

BEHAVIOR AND APPEARANCE

James had black hair and blue eyes, and physiologically he appeared normal. One upper front tooth had a silver cap which he exhibited naturally when he smiled. He was relaxed, compliant, and easy to work with, and he maintained an outgoing, good-natured attitude throughout the period. Thus the testing moved along very swiftly.

TEST RESULTS

See Psychometric Summary.

SUMMARY

Examination of James found him to be functioning in the bright range of intellectual ability with a Full Scale WISC I.Q. of 119. The PPVT I.Q. of 125 (a verbal test) was higher than the Full Scale WISC I.Q. and at the same level (superior) as his WISC verbal I.Q. of 126. The scatter in both the verbal and the performance areas shows that his greatest strengths lie in vocabulary and range of information. However, there are no actual weaknesses in the verbal area; in fact, his comprehension, reasoning, and concept formation are above average. His arithmetic score was the lowest of the verbal area, suggesting that his reasoning is slightly weaker than the other abilities.

The significant drop of 19 points in the performance I.Q. suggests James' problem area. Because of the apparent fluctuation in visual-motor abilities, they are considered unpredictable. Two scores in this area, picture arrangement and coding, were above average, while the other three scores were normal to low normal. The picture arrangement score suggests that he knows how to plan and how to anticipate results, the coding score implies an alert psychomotor speed, and the object assembly and the picture completion scores show a tendency for slow visual-motor organization and poor perception of environmental detail. In effect, he cannot readily discriminate essential from nonessential detail.

The ITPA (1961 edition) reveals an overall above average linguistic ability, although his memory for symbols score fell at a significantly low level and his visual and auditory reception scores fell at the normal level, giving evidence that James has difficulty decoding what he sees and hears. Mild anxiety could be influencing his achievement, but some remediation would probably initiate a fairly quick change.

The Wide Range Achievement Test showed that with reading and arithmetic at the third-grade level and spelling at the high second-grade level, James is well within the level of achievement commensurate with his age group. However, with a verbal I.Q. of 126 he should be working at the high fourth-grade level. This underachievement is probably due to the visual-motor problem that several different tests have revealed.

The Harris Tests of Lateral Dominance reveal another perhaps related problem area. Although James showed primarily left-hand dominance — in two of the activities he used his right hand — he has mixed eye and mixed foot dominance. The result is cross dominance. The *Purdue Perceptual-Motor Survey* further differentiates this problem area by revealing problems of laterality and directionality. Emphasis should be placed on the exercises concerning ocular pursuit as found in *The Slow Learner in the Classroom* (Kephart, 1960), but part of each remediation period must be devoted to a variety of balance exercises and differentiation of body part exercises. In addition, chalkboard activities involving a variety of motifs should be part of his daily routine.

Consultant

PSYCHOMETRIC SUMMARY

Intelligence Tests:

Wechsler Intelligence Scales

_____WPPSI   __✓__WISC   _____WAIS

WPPSI Scaled Scores

Verbal	Performance
Information_____	Animal House_____
Comprehension_____	Picture Completion_____
Arithmetic_____	Mazes_____
Similarities_____	Geometric Design_____
Vocabulary_____	Block Design_____
(Sentences)_____	Animal House
	(Retest)_____

WISC and WAIS Scaled Scores

Verbal		Performance	
Information	_15_	Picture Completion	_9_
Comprehension	_13_	Picture Arrangement	_13_
Arithmetic	_12_	Block Design	_11_
Similarities	_14_	Object Assembly	_9_
Vocabulary	_17_	Coding or Digit Symbol	_13_
Digit Span	_10_	Mazes	

Verbal Scale I.Q._____ _126_
Performance Scale I.Q. _107_
Full Scale I.Q._____ _119_

Stanford-Binet (Form L-M)	Draw-A-Person Test	Peabody Picture Vocabulary
C.A._____	C.A._7-11_	C.A._7-11_
M.A._____	M.A._—_	M.A._10-8_
I.Q._____	I.Q._—_	I.Q._125_

Wide Range Achievement Test

Reading Grade Level_____3.8_____Standard Score___114_ Percentile_____
Spelling Grade Level_____2.9_____Standard Score___102_Percentile_____
Arithmetic Grade Level____3.5_____Standard Score___110_Percentile_____

Purdue Perceptual-Motor
  Survey___*Atypical Record*___
	Wepman Auditory Discrimination
	  Test_____

Children's Apperception
  Test_____
	Memory-For-Designs Test
	  ___*Normal Record*_____

Bender Visual-Motor
  Gestalt Test___*Normal Record*___
	Illinois Test of Psycholinguistic
	  Abilities (See ITPA Profile)
	    Total Language___*AN*_____
	    Scaled Score_____

Hiskey-Nebraska Test

Bead Pattern_____	Visual Attention Span_____
Memory for Colors_____	Block Patterns_____
Picture Identification_____	Completion of Drawings_____
Picture Association_____	Memory for Digits_____
Paper Folding_____	Puzzle Analogies_____
	Spatial Reasoning_____

Other Tests:

Name ___ CASE of JAMES ___ Age __ 7-11 __ Birthdate _____

ILLINOIS TEST OF PSYCHOLINGUISTIC ABILITIES

(Experimental Edition, 1961)

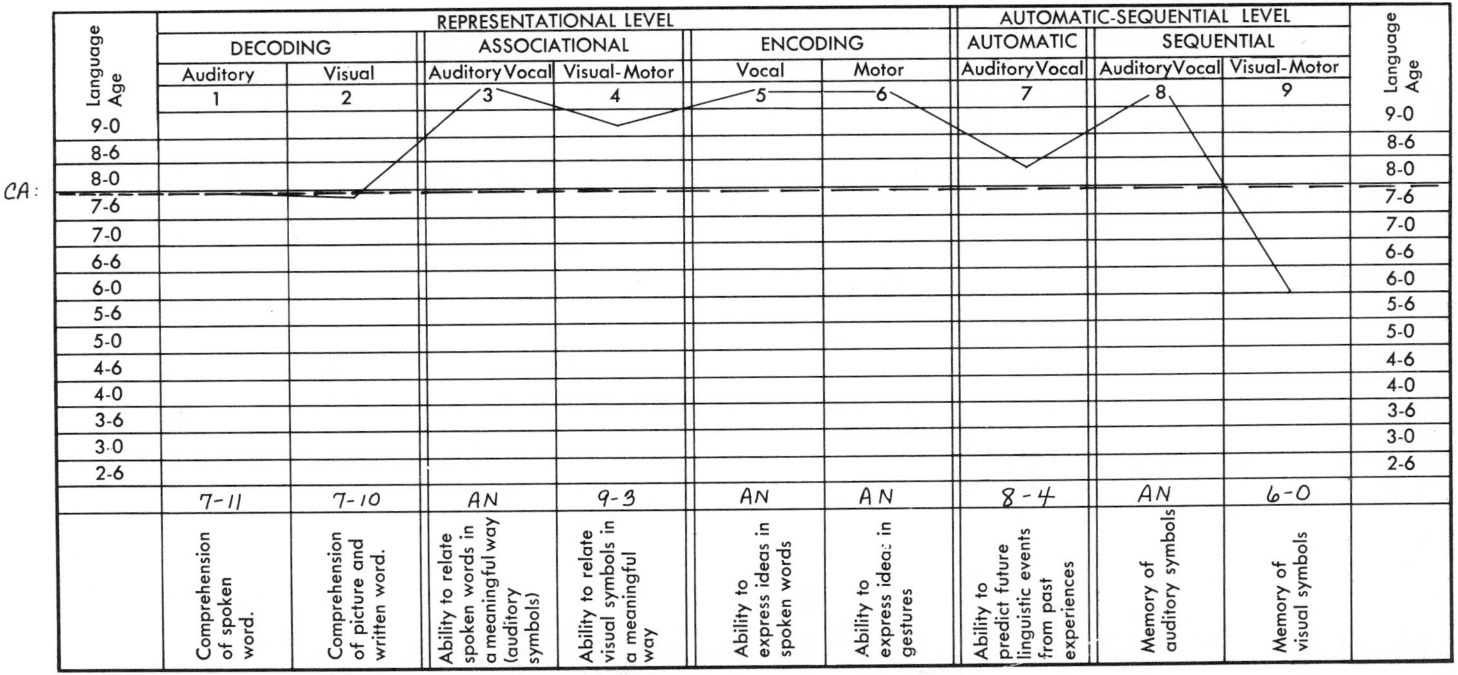

	REPRESENTATIONAL LEVEL							AUTOMATIC-SEQUENTIAL LEVEL			
	DECODING		ASSOCIATIONAL			ENCODING			AUTOMATIC	SEQUENTIAL	
	Auditory	Visual	AuditoryVocal	Visual-Motor		Vocal	Motor		AuditoryVocal	AuditoryVocal	Visual-Motor
	1	2	3	4		5	6		7	8	9

Age / Language Age column values (top): 9-0, 8-6, 8-0, 7-6, 7-0, 6-6, 6-0, 5-6, 5-0, 4-6, 4-0, 3-6, 3-0, 2-6

Bottom labels and scores:

- Comprehension of spoken word. — 7-11
- Comprehension of picture and written word. — 7-10
- Ability to relate spoken words in a meaningful way (auditory symbols) — AN
- Ability to relate visual symbols in a meaningful way — 9-3
- Ability to express ideas in spoken words — AN
- Ability to relate ideas in gestures — AN
- Ability to predict future linguistic events from past experiences — 8-4
- Memory of auditory symbols — AN
- Memory of visual symbols — 6-0

CA:

Name _Case of James_ Date of birth _____
Address _—_ Sex _M_ Grade _—_
_____ School _—_
Examiner _Jane Doe_ Date of examination _____

Score	4	3	2	1	
Walking Board:					
Forward	✓				Balance
Backward		✓			and
Sideways			✓		Posture
Jumping					
Identification of Body Parts	✓				
Imitation of Movement			✓		Body Image
Obstacle Course	✓				and
Kraus-Weber	✓				Differentiation
Angels-in-the-Snow			✓		
Chalkboard					
Circle	✓				
Double circle					
Lateral line	✓				Perceptual-
Vertical line	✓				Motor
Rhythmic Writing					Match
Rhythm			✓		
Reproduction			✓		
Orientation			✓		
Ocular Pursuits					
Both eyes		✓			Ocular
Right eye		✓			Control
Left eye			✓		
Convergence			✓		
Visual Achievement Forms					Form
Form		✓			
Organization	✓				Perception

8. Case of Tom. *A minimal brain injury case with normal achievement.*

Referral was made by the mother to check on the relationship between Tom's ability and his achievement.

NAME Tom   EXAMINER Jane Doe

DATE OF BIRTH   DATE OF EXAMINATION   C.A. 8–8

EVALUATION FOR LEARNING DISABILITIES

BEHAVIOR AND APPEARANCE

Tom was a nice-looking boy with red hair, blue eyes, and light freckles sprinkling his face. His physiological development seemed quite normal. Dressed in school clothes and cowboy boots, he was very clean and neat. At first, Tom displayed some apprehension by wanting his mother to remain during the testing; but this was very quickly overcome as he became actively interested in the tasks. The testing moved along normally with only minor distractions. Periodically he picked up a pencil and played with it as he answered questions. But discreet removal of all external stimuli from his reach allowed the testing to progress more smoothly.

TEST RESULTS

See Psychometric Summary.

SUMMARY

Examination found Tom to be fuctioning in the normal to above normal intellectual range with a WISC Full Scale I.Q. of 112 and a PPVT I.Q. of 116. His verbal intelligence was significantly higher than his performance ability with his vocabulary ability, in particular his expressive vocabulary, rating superior. Although still above average, his picture vocabulary ability rated lower than his expressive vocabulary ability. He apparently misses some visual cues and thus does not respond as astutely as when reciting orally. His range of information, comprehension, concept formation, and memory for digits fell at the high average level, while his arithmetical reasoning fell at the mean normal position.

His performance ability reveals a general normal-level pattern. One test revealed above average functioning in the ability to discriminate essential from nonessential detail. Because the objects involved were familiar to him, they were probably less distracting than unfamiliar geometric designs. Other tests revealed normal functioning, the overall score however falling below the verbal test scores. The Bender-Gestalt did not discriminate the minimal brain injury reported by the mother because Tom achieved a normal quantitative score. Some mild deviations were noted, but generally he has learned to compensate very adequately. The MFD Test did however make this discrimination, for he achieved a difference score of six, placing him on the border line of brain damage. He performs inadequately in response to some memory patterns. But when pencil manipulation is not required, he performs much better, as he did on the memory for visual tasks of ITPA. Tom fluctuates in regard to tasks involving visual memory, so for this reason, achievement to overlearning is recommended for him.

The ITPA (1968 edition) revealed another score suggesting fluctuation in auditory processes. His response to the half-second digit patterns fell below his language age level. Yet his response to the one-second digits on the WISC was above average. There are two possible explanations for this difference. Either he fluctuates erratically in his response to auditory patterns, or with an extra half second to process his data, he is capable of better performance. Since the ITPA reveals weakness in discrimination of sound blends and auditory closure, the latter explanation should receive serious consideration in regard to Tom's need for slow and deliberate directions and explanations.

The WRAT reveals that Tom is achieving in reading, spelling, and arithmetic at expectancy for his age. Therefore, specific tutoring seems unnecessary at this time. The PMS was not administered in this session, since the request was for discovering the relationship between academic achievement and intellectual functioning. Tom's mother gave information relative to neurological examination on the EEG and reported the problem Tom has had in ocular pursuit and balance. It is recommended that he be subjected to the exercises related to these two areas as found in *The Slow Learner in the Classroom* (Kephart, 1960), and *Motoric Aids to Perceptual Training* (Chaney & Kephart, 1968). In addition, the exercises in *Remedial Reading Drills* (Hegge, Kirk & Kirk, 1940), may be beneficial for the improvement of sound discrimination.

Consultant

PSYCHOMETRIC SUMMARY

Intelligence Tests:

Wechsler Intelligence Scales

_____WPPSI   ___✓___WISC   _____WAIS

WPPSI Scaled Scores

Verbal	Performance
Information_____	Animal House_____
Comprehension_____	Picture Completion_____
Arithmetic_____	Mazes_____
Similarities_____	Geometric Design_____
Vocabulary_____	Block Design_____
(Sentences)_____	Animal House
	(Retest)_____

WISC and WAIS Scaled Scores

Verbal		Performance	
Information	12	Picture Completion	13
Comprehension	12	Picture Arrangement	9
Arithmetic	10	Block Design	10
Similarities	12	Object Assembly	9
Vocabulary	19	Coding or Digit Symbol	11
Digit Span	13	Mazes	

Verbal Scale I.Q.____119____
Performance Scale I.Q.__103____
Full Scale I.Q.____112____

Stanford-Binet (Form L-M)	Draw-A-Person Test	Peabody Picture Vocabulary
C.A._____	C.A._____	C.A. _8-8_
M.A._____	M.A._____	M.A. _10-10_
I.Q._____	I.Q._____	I.Q. _116_

Wide Range Achievement Test

Reading Grade Level____4.2_____ Standard Score_110__Percentile_____
Spelling Grade Level____3.7_____ Standard Score_105__Percentile_____
Arithmetic Grade Level____3.9_____ Standard Score_107__Percentile_____

Purdue Perceptual-Motor
Survey_____

Wepman Auditory Discrimination
Test_____

Children's Apperception
Test_____

Memory-For-Designs Test
Borderline visual-motor problem

Bender Visual-Motor
Gestalt Test_Minor visual - motor deviations

Illinois Test of Psycholinguistic
Abilities (See ITPA Profile)
Total Language___AN_____
Scaled Score_____

Hiskey-Nebraska Test

Bead Pattern_____	Visual Attention Span_____
Memory for Colors_____	Block Patterns_____
Picture Identification_____	Completion of Drawings_____
Picture Association_____	Memory for Digits_____
Paper Folding_____	Puzzle Analogies_____
	Spatial Reasoning_____

Other Tests:

Date of Examination _____ Name CASE of Tom _____ Age 8-8

PROFILE OF ABILITIES   Mean Scaled Score = 36   Standard Deviation = 6

ITPA SCORES

	Representational Level						Automatic Level				
Reception		Association		Expression		Closure		Sequential Memory		Supplemental Tests	
Auditory	Visual	Auditory	Visual	Verbal	Manual	Grammatic	Visual	Auditory	Visual	Auditory Closure	Sound Blending
Comprehension of spoken word.	Comprehension of picture and written word.	Ability to relate spoken words in a meaningful way.	Ability to relate visual symbols in a meaningful way.	Ability to express ideas in spoken words.	Ability to express ideas in gestures.	Ability to use correct grammar.	Ability to perceive objects in incomplete form.	Memory of auditory symbols in sequence.	Memory for visual symbols in sequence.	Automatic function to understand difficult and incomplete speech.	Automatic function in synthesizing parts of words.
AN	9-3	10-1	8-11	8-10	AN	AN	8-3	6-6	AN	6-5	7-7

Scaled Scores: 64, 60, 56, 52, 48, 44, 40, 36, 32, 28, 24, 20, 16, 12, 8, 4

9. Case of Mary. *Visual perception problem.*

Referred by a teacher in order to determine aids which may help her eye-hand coordination.

NAME Mary   EXAMINER Jane Doe

DATE OF BIRTH _____   DATE OF EXAMINATION _____   C.A. 6–5

EVALUATION FOR LEARNING DISABILITIES

BEHAVIOR AND APPEARANCE

Mary was very attractive with brown hair and brown eyes. She was neatly dressed in a Brownie uniform and appeared physiologically normal. A little shy, Mary spoke softly and often grinned over her mistakes. She gripped her pencil tightly while at work and frequently turned her paper as she copied the designs. However, she cooperated, and the testing progressed smoothly.

TEST RESULTS

See Psychometric Summary.

SUMMARY

Mary's examination found her to be functioning in the normal range of intellectual ability with a Stanford Binet I.Q. of 101 and a PPVT I.Q. of 110. Her DAP I.Q. of 90 does not represent her global intelligence but instead reflects her major weakness, visual-motor ability.

The test results locate her basal at the four-and-one-half-year level and her ceiling at the nine-year level. Although there was much scatter, her strengths are in the language area. She passed the vocabulary and the comprehension tests at the eight-year level. These were commensurate with her PPVT I.Q. of 110. Along with the other verbal tasks, she passed the conceptual thinking test for her age level, establishing a normal to above normal language ability.

Her weaknesses lie in the performance area with a failure at the five-year level on one visual-motor task for which she did not fold the triangle properly. At the seven-year level, she was not able to draw the diamond, and she put "dog-ears" at the angles on each attempt. Her drawings on the Bender were very irregular. She rotated figures 2 and 3 and distorted design A and figures 4 and 7. On the MFD her difference score of 10 placed her visual-motor coordination in the critical area. The evidence suggests that there is a specific problem of design dyspraxia. Mary was able to print her name but had great difficulty when asked to reproduce various designs.

In reading, spelling, and arithmetic Mary's scores, which fell at the kindergarten level, mark her as an underachiever for her age.

The *Frostig Test of Visual Perception* was administered and specifically established Mary's visual-motor problems as poor spatial relations ability, poor figure-ground discrimination, and poor eye-motor coordination. Mary should be placed on the Frostig Developmental Visual Perception program, and PMS should be administered within a week.

_____

Consultant

ADDENUM

The PMS, administered by the physical education teacher, found that Mary is having difficulty in ocular pursuit and body differentiation. Training to remediate these weaknesses is recommended. (Please refer to *Motoric Aids to Learning* (Chaney & Kephart, 1968).) Kinesthetic techniques along with the Frostig program are specifially recommended.

PSYCHOMETRIC SUMMARY

Intelligence Tests:

Wechsler Intelligence Scales

_____WPPSI   _____WISC   _____WAIS

WPPSI Scaled Scores

Verbal		Performance	
Information	_____	Animal House	_____
Comprehension	_____	Picture Completion	_____
Arithmetic	_____	Mazes	_____
Similarities	_____	Geometric Design	_____
Vocabulary	_____	Block Design	_____
(Sentences)	_____	Animal House (Retest)	_____

WISC and WAIS Scaled Scores

Verbal		Performance	
Information	_____	Picture Completion	_____
Comprehension	_____	Picture Arrangement	_____
Arithmetic	_____	Block Design	_____
Similarities	_____	Object Assembly	_____
Vocabulary	_____	Coding or Digit Symbol	_____
Digit Span	_____	Mazes	_____

Verbal Scale I.Q. _____
Performance Scale I.Q. _____
Full Scale I.Q. _____

Stanford-Binet (Form L-M)	Draw-A-Person Test	Peabody Picture Vocabulary,
C.A. _6-5_	C.A. _6-5_	C.A. _6-5_ Form B
M.A. _6-6_	M.A. _—_	M.A. _6-10_
I.Q. _101_	I.Q. _90_	I.Q. _110_

Wide Range Achievement Test

	Grade Level	Standard Score	Percentile
Reading Grade Level	Kg .7	89	_____
Spelling Grade Level	Kg .8	92	_____
Arithmetic Grade Level	Kg .1	76	_____

Purdue Perceptual-Motor
Survey _See Summary_

Wepman Auditory Discrimination
Test _____

Children's Apperception
Test _____

Memory-For-Designs Test
_____

Bender Visual-Motor
Gestalt Test _____

Illinois Test of Psycholinguistic
Abilities (See ITPA Profile)
Total Language _____
Scaled Score _____

Hiskey-Nebraska Test

Bead Pattern	_____	Visual Attention Span	_____
Memory for Colors	_____	Block Patterns	_____
Picture Identification	_____	Completion of Drawings	_____
Picture Association	_____	Memory for Digits	_____
Paper Folding	_____	Puzzle Analogies	_____
		Spatial Reasoning	_____

Other Tests: _Frostig Test of Visual Perception (See Summary)_

Case of Mary. Stanford Binet test scores

Year of Tests	4-6	5	6	7	8	9
Factors — Language						
MEMORY — Meaningful						
MEMORY — Nonmeaningful						
MEMORY — Visual	(NO TESTS IN THIS AGE RANGE)					
Conceptual Thinking						
REASONING — Verbal						
REASONING — Nonverbal						
REASONING — Numerical						
Visual-Motor						
Social Intelligence						

High Performance — Low Verbal Group

10. Case of Ginger. *Minimal brain injury with language deficit.*

The parents requested a battery of tests to determine intellectual and communication weaknesses. The medical report revealed brain damage in the left temporal and in both the right and left parietal lobes. There was also dissymmetry of rhythm in the left occipital lobe.

NAME Ginger _____ EXAMINER Jane Doe _____

DATE OF BIRTH _____
DATE OF EXAMINATION _____ C.A. <u>6–9</u>

EVALUATION FOR LEARNING DISABILITIES

BEHAVIOR AND APPEARANCE

Ginger had dark hair and for her six years and nine months was normal in height and weight. Although slightly thin, she had good coloring in her cheeks and in general appeared quite healthy. She displayed temporary, mild apprehension, even though she was normally outgoing, friendly, and warm. She held her pencil correctly, but wrote with more hand movement than necessary. The testing progressed smoothly as a result of Ginger's full cooperation.

TEST RESULTS

See Psychometric Summary.

SUMMARY

Examination found Ginger to be functioning within the normal range of intellectual ability with a WISC Full Scale I.Q. of 93 and a PPVT I.Q. of 106. Her immature self-concept probably contributed to a lowered DAP I.Q.

Ginger's overall verbal ability is slightly lower than her performance ability. However, she has some verbal strengths and some performance weaknesses. In the verbal area her numerical ability, vocabulary, comprehension, and memory for digits are normal, while her range of information and concept formation are within the dull range. In the performance area all visual-motor tasks are within the normal range with the exception of the block design subtest. Although Ginger is very slow in abstracting the designs, she is learning to compensate for this existing visual-motor problem.

The pattern of test scores suggests that Ginger's problem lies more specifically in the ability to differentiate among nonmeaningful visual stimuli; she is unable to assemble designs quickly if they are not of meaningful content. Thus, her problem involves the interpretation of the meaning of spatial relationships. Ginger was able to copy designs normally on the coding test, to discriminate essential detail on the picture completion test, and to work the puzzles and picture arrangements adequately, all suggesting a normally controlled eye-hand coordination except as related to block designs. The Bender and MFD records substantiate this borderline problem area. Thus Ginger has less control over her visual-motor problem when she has to see relationships between symbols.

The ITPA (1961 edition) reveals all psycholinguistic abilities to be slightly below normal with the greatest drops in the comprehension of visual and auditory stimuli. The equally low vocal encoding score suggests that she is slow in expressing ideas. It is recommended that first-grade level auditory reception, visual reception, visual-motor association, and verbal expression tasks from *Aids to Psycholinguistic Teaching* (Bush & Giles, 1969) be given special emphasis in her structured tutoring sessions.

The WRAT reveals that Ginger is achieving in arithmetic and spelling at a level commensurate to her I.Q. However, her reading level fell below expectancy. Specific kinesthetic techniques are recommended in order to help facilitate her capacity to work with symbols.

———————————

Consultant

PSYCHOMETRIC SUMMARY

Intelligence Tests:

Wechsler Intelligence Scales

_____WPPSI   __✓__WISC   _____WAIS

WPPSI Scaled Scores

Verbal		Performance	
Information_____		Animal House_____	
Comprehension_____		Picture Completion_____	
Arithmetic_____		Mazes_____	
Similarities_____		Geometric Design_____	
Vocabulary_____		Block Design_____	
(Sentences)_____		Animal House	
		(Retest)_____	

WISC and WAIS Scaled Scores

Verbal		Performance	
Information____7____		Picture Completion____11____	
Comprehension____8____		Picture Arrangement____10____	
Arithmetic____10____		Block Design____7____	
Similarities____7____		Object Assembly____11____	
Vocabulary____9____		Coding or Digit Symbol____11____	
Digit Span____8____		Mazes____	

Verbal Scale I.Q.____89____

Performance Scale I.Q.____100____

Full Scale I.Q.____93____

Stanford-Binet (Form L-M)	Draw-A-Person Test	Peabody Picture Vocabulary
C.A._____	C.A.__6-9__	C.A.__6-9__
M.A._____	M.A.__5-3__	M.A.__7-8__
I.Q._____	I.Q.__78__	I.Q.__106__

Wide Range Achievement Test

Reading Grade Level__PK__.9__	Standard Score_____	Percentile_____	
Spelling Grade Level__1.2__	Standard Score_____	Percentile_____	
Arithmetic Grade Level__1.2__	Standard Score_____	Percentile_____	

Purdue Perceptual-Motor
Survey_____

Wepman Auditory Discrimination
Test_____

Children's Apperception
Test_____

Memory-For-Designs Test
__Borderline visual-motor problem__

Bender Visual-Motor
Gestalt Test__Borderline__

Illinois Test of Psycholinguistic
Abilities (See ITPA Profile)
Total Language__5-9__
Scaled Score_____

Hiskey-Nebraska Test

Bead Pattern_____	Visual Attention Span_____
Memory for Colors_____	Block Patterns_____
Picture Identification_____	Completion of Drawings_____
Picture Association_____	Memory for Digits_____
Paper Folding_____	Puzzle Analogies_____
	Spatial Reasoning_____

Other Tests:

Name _____ CASE of GINGER _____ Age __6-9__ Birthdate _____

ILLINOIS TEST OF PSYCHOLINGUISTIC ABILITIES

(Experimental Edition, 1961)

	REPRESENTATIONAL LEVEL						AUTOMATIC-SEQUENTIAL LEVEL		
	DECODING		ASSOCIATIONAL		ENCODING		AUTOMATIC	SEQUENTIAL	
	Auditory	Visual	Auditory-Vocal	Visual-Motor	Vocal	Motor	Auditory-Vocal	Auditory-Vocal	Visual-Motor
	1	2	3	4	5	6	7	8	9
Description	Comprehension of spoken word.	Comprehension of picture and written word.	Ability to relate spoken words in a meaningful way (auditory symbols)	Ability to relate visual symbols in a meaningful way	Ability to express ideas in spoken words	Ability to express ideas in gestures	Ability to predict future linguistic events from past experiences	Memory of auditory symbols	Memory of visual symbols
Score	5-5	5-2	6-1	5-9	5-1	6-4	5-9	6-3	6-4

Language Age scale: 9-0, 8-6, 8-0, 7-6, 7-0, 6-6, 6-0, 5-6, 5-0, 4-6, 4-0, 3-6, 3-0, 2-6

CA: (dashed line at 6-6)

11. Case of EGL. *Auditory problem: specific dyslexia.*

The parents requested that the boy's specific weaknesses be determined.

NAME: EGL   EXAMINER: Jane Doe

DATE OF
DATE OF BIRTH: EXAMINATION: C.A. 11–3

EVALUATION FOR LEARNING DISABILITIES

BEHAVIOR AND APPEARANCE

EGL, a nice-looking boy with ash-blond hair and light brown eyes, appeared physiologically normal. He was very friendly and outgoing, and he could relate in a warm way. The activities seemed to interest EGL, as he readily responded to each situation. Thus the testing progressed smoothly without any obstacles.

TEST RESULTS

See Psychometric Summary.

SUMMARY

Examination of EGL found him to be functioning in the normal range of intellectual ability with a WISC Full Scale I.Q. of 110. His above average score on the *Peabody Picture Vocabulary Test* is comparable to the vocabulary scaled score of 12 on the WISC. The DAP reveals a weakness in memory for detail, but it also suggests a poor self-concept.

The scatter of WISC scores is not severe except in one case, that of the digit span subtest. For these scaled scores, ten is normal, but on this subtest his score fell to five. This shows a poor memory for auditory symbols and may suggest mild anxiety. The slightly lowered score on the information test substantiates the fact that his memory problem influences his intellectual functioning. The verbal area scores show that he has normal comprehension, reasoning, vocabulary, and ability to associate ideas. The performance area scores reveal that he has normal spatial ability in discriminating between essential and nonessential detail. In other words, since he can recognize essential parts of common objects, a visual-motor problem would not necessarily affect his ability to recognize and discriminate objects that he comprehends. The picture arrangement test shows also that EGL is capable of adequate planning and of anticipating the results of that planning in a social situation. The object assembly test likewise shows good visual-motor organization of familiar objects.

EGL's visual-motor function as discussed above is normal or above normal. But at the point of separation between *familiar objects* and *symbols,* there exists a serious problem. The coding test reveals a slow psychomotor speed and also difficulty when working in situations that deal with the symbolic. Since EGL shows normal intelligence, it is his inability to recognize the unfamiliar that suggests a learning problem.

Since the WRAT shows that EGL is achieving far below expectancy for his I.Q., these tests, as compared to those of the WISC, reveal that EGL fully qualifies on the basis of Jastak's five criteria for dyslexia. Therefore, his learning disorder can be identified as dyslexia; namely, his difficulty lies in recognizing and remembering symbols.

Further examination revealed that there is some language problem in addition to the kind of reading problem described above. An error score of $X = 4/30$ and $Y = 0/10$ on the auditory discrimination test shows that EGL misses some of his auditory cues. The *Illinois Test of Psycholinguistic Abilities* (1961 edition), which revealed a lowered score on two auditory scales, substantiates this problem. Although EGL is too old for this test, it was administered to determine whether or not he would fall below the nine-year level in any area.

The Memory-For-Designs difference score of 11 places his perceptual-motor problem, as related to memory, in the critical area. The Bender-Gestalt shows a fairly normal record; yet the scores on several designs deviated enough to reveal that EGL makes some mistakes even though he has learned to compensate to a degree when he is allowed to copy the designs. Of course, his school record shows that he has had a persistent reading problem.

Auditory training techniques and memory techniques with emphasis on learning to overachievement are recommended. Oral rather than written examinations should be administered, and a reading tutor should be provided.

———————————————

Consultant

PSYCHOMETRIC SUMMARY

Intelligence Tests:

Wechsler Intelligence Scales

_____WPPSI   ___√___WISC   _____WAIS

WPPSI Scaled Scores

Verbal		Performance	
Information		Animal House	
Comprehension		Picture Completion	
Arithmetic		Mazes	
Similarities		Geometric Design	
Vocabulary		Block Design	
(Sentences)		Animal House (Retest)	

WISC and WAIS Scaled Scores

Verbal		Performance	
Information	9	Picture Completion	14
Comprehension	11	Picture Arrangement	13
Arithmetic	10	Block Design	11
Similarities	12	Object Assembly	15
Vocabulary	12	Coding or Digit Symbol	7
Digit Span	5	Mazes	6

Verbal Scale I.Q. ____105____
Performance Scale I.Q. ___114___
Full Scale I.Q. ___110___

Stanford-Binet (Form L-M)	Draw-A-Person Test	Peabody Picture Vocabulary
C.A._____	C.A. _11-3_	C.A. _11-3_
M.A._____	M.A. _8-3_	M.A. _14-8_
I.Q._____	I.Q. _ − _	I.Q. _120_

Wide Range Achievement Test

Reading Grade Level	2.5	Standard Score	73	Percentile____
Spelling Grade Level	2.2	Standard Score	71	Percentile____
Arithmetic Grade Level	3.9	Standard Score	84	Percentile____

Purdue Perceptual-Motor
Survey_____

Wepman Auditory Discrimination
Test_ X = 4/30   Y = 0/10 _

Children's Apperception
Test_____

Memory-For-Designs Test
Dif. Score = 11 (Critical problem area for visual-motor functions),

Bender Visual-Motor
Gestalt Test_ Atypical Record _

Illinois Test of Psycholinguistic
Abilities (See ITPA Profile)
Total Language_ AN _
Scaled Score_____

Hiskey-Nebraska Test

Bead Pattern_____	Visual Attention Span_____
Memory for Colors_____	Block Patterns_____
Picture Identification_____	Completion of Drawings_____
Picture Association_____	Memory for Digits_____
Paper Folding_____	Puzzle Analogies_____
	Spatial Reasoning_____

Other Tests:

Name __CASE OF E GL__ Age __11-3__ Birthdate _____

ILLINOIS TEST OF PSYCHOLINGUISTIC ABILITIES

(Experimental Edition, 1961)

CA: 11-3

	DECODING		ASSOCIATIONAL			ENCODING		AUTOMATIC	SEQUENTIAL	
	Auditory	Visual	Auditory	Vocal	Visual-Motor	Vocal	Motor	Auditory	Vocal	AuditoryVocal	Visual-Motor
	1	2	3		4	5	6	7	8	9
	Comprehension of spoken word.	Comprehension of picture and written word.	Ability to relate spoken words in a meaningful way (auditory symbols)		Ability to relate visual symbols in a meaningful way	Ability to express ideas in spoken words	Ability to express ideas in gestures	Ability to predict future linguistic events from past experiences	Memory of auditory symbols	Memory of visual symbols
	AN	AN	AN		AN	AN	AN	8-0	9-4	AN

Language Age: 9-0, 8-6, 8-0, 7-6, 7-0, 6-6, 6-0, 5-6, 5-0, 4-6, 4-0, 3-6, 3-0, 2-6

12.   Case of BS.   *Visual-motor problem.*

Referral was made by the parents to determine reasons for the child's academic failures.

NAME: BS   EXAMINER: Jane Doe

DATE OF BIRTH: DATE OF
                                         EXAMINATION: C.A. 12–7

EVALUATION FOR LEARNING DISABILITIES

BEHAVIOR AND APPEARANCE

BS had ash-blond hair and blue eyes, and his height and weight were normal for the age of 12 years 7 months. Dressed in good, casual school clothing, he was clean and neat. Throughout the period, BS was very polite and obedient. He was also very quiet and reserved, rarely volunteering any extraneous remarks. When he did speak, his remarks were related specifically to his work. The testing progressed naturally with very few obstacles, the performance tasks holding a greater interest for him than the verbal tasks.

TEST RESULTS

See Psychometric Summary.

SUMMARY

Examination found BS to be functioning in the normal range of intellectual ability with a Full Scale WISC I.Q. of 98 and a PPVT I.Q. of 95. Some minor scatter suggestive of his weaknesses and strengths appeared, but there were no extremes.

In the verbal area his information, comprehension, and vocabulary abilities were inferior to his normal memory for digits and reasoning abilities and his above average ability to associate ideas presented to him orally. The performance area scores give evidence that BS has a low normal ability to discriminate essential from nonessential detail and a low normal psychomotor speed as well as an average to above average ability to organize and manipulate three-dimensional visual-motor activities, such as those using blocks and puzzles.

However, this above average score was not achieved without problems. BS rotated two block designs by 90° but attempted to control this tendency after his errors were pointed out. His normal score on the object assembly test would have been higher had he not inverted a puzzle piece in two of the patterns. Even extra time and encouragement to correct these failed to make him aware of his mistakes. A similar approach to the picture completion test resulted in his missing enough of the detail to achieve only a low normal score.

The ITPA performance provides further evidence of this kind of error. Although the norms for the ITPA (1961 edition) do not extend beyond nine years of age, the test was administered to determine whether or not BS has any weaknesses that would fall to this age level. Most of the subtests revealed scores above the nine-year level, but the visual-motor association test revealed a language age of 8–7, and the visual decoding (visual reception) test revealed a raw score just one point higher than the last norm of eight years and nine months. (His raw score was 18; the raw score for eight years and nine months is 17.) Thus BS also has a significant weakness in visual decoding. Although his visual-motor sequencing (visual memory) score of 27 is above the nine-year level, his actual level of achievement is indefinite; and since his responses revealed some scatter (he missed some of the easy sequences and passed some of the hard ones), the suggestion is strong that his specific reading problem is that of missing *visual cues.*

The WRAT reading and spelling achievements at grades 3.7 and 3.9 substantiate this reading problem. Although his arithmetic achievement at grade 5.3 was higher, it also fell below his expectancy. This lowered arithmetic score can probably be attributed to his confusion of visual cues; for example, he inverted and rotated numbers that caused their numerical values to change. BS has established foot and hand dominance on the right, but his choice of eye dominance seems to fluctuate between the left and right.

Whatever the basic cause, BS has been an unsuccessful reader. Since the test data suggests that his problem lies in the visual-motor channel rather than in the auditory channel, BS should be guided through a structured visual perception program. The Grace Fernald kinesthetic techniques are also recommended in order to facilitate his perception. BS should be trained to practice daily techniques such as those suggested in *Aid to Psycholinguistic Teaching* (Bush & Giles, 1969). Tutorial services are advisable.

Consultant

Intelligence Tests:

Wechsler Intelligence Scales

_____WPPSI   √WISC   _____WAIS

WPPSI Scaled Scores

Verbal		Performance	
Information_____		Animal House_____	
Comprehension_____		Picture Completion_____	
Arithmetic_____		Mazes_____	
Similarities_____		Geometric Design_____	
Vocabulary_____		Block Design_____	
(Sentences)_____		Animal House	
		(Retest)_____	

WISC and WAIS Scaled Scores

Verbal		Performance	
Information____7____		Picture Completion____8____	
Comprehension____7____		Picture Arrangement____13____	
Arithmetic____10____		Block Design____12____	
Similarities____14____		Object Assembly____10____	
Vocabulary____7____		Coding or Digit Symbol____9____	
Digit Span____10____		Mazes____9____	

Verbal Scale I.Q.____94____
Performance Scale I.Q.____103____
Full Scale I.Q.____98____

Stanford-Binet (Form L-M)	Draw-A-Person Test	Peabody Picture Vocabulary
C.A._____	C.A._____	C.A.__12-7__
M.A._____	M.A._____	M.A.__12-5__
I.Q._____	I.Q._____	I.Q.__95__

Wide Range Achievement Test

Reading Grade Level____3.9____	Standard Score____75____	Percentile_____
Spelling Grade Level____3.7____	Standard Score____74____	Percentile_____
Arithmetic Grade Level____5.3____	Standard Score____84____	Percentile_____

Purdue Perceptual-Motor
Survey_____

Wepman Auditory Discrimination
Test_____

Children's Apperception
Test_____

Memory-For-Designs Test
__Atypical Record (visual-motor
problem)

Bender Visual-Motor
Gestalt Test__Atypical Record__
(visual-motor problem)

Illinois Test of Psycholinguistic
Abilities (See ITPA Profile)
Total Language____AN____
Scaled Score_____

Hiskey-Nebraska Test

Bead Pattern_____	Visual Attention Span_____
Memory for Colors_____	Block Patterns_____
Picture Identification_____	Completion of Drawings_____
Picture Association_____	Memory for Digits_____
Paper Folding_____	Puzzle Analogies_____
	Spatial Reasoning_____

Other Tests:

Name __CASE of BS__   Age __12-7__   Birthdate _____

ILLINOIS TEST OF PSYCHOLINGUISTIC ABILITIES

(Experimental Edition, 1961)

CA: 12-7

Language Age	REPRESENTATIONAL LEVEL						AUTOMATIC-SEQUENTIAL LEVEL			Language Age
	DECODING		ASSOCIATIONAL		ENCODING		AUTOMATIC	SEQUENTIAL		
	Auditory	Visual	Auditory-Vocal	Visual-Motor	Vocal	Motor	Auditory-Vocal	Auditory-Vocal	Visual-Motor	
	1	2	3	4	5	6	7	8	9	
9-0										9-0
8-6										8-6
8-0										8-0
7-6										7-6
7-0										7-0
6-6										6-6
6-0										6-0
5-6										5-6
5-0										5-0
4-6										4-6
4-0										4-0
3-6										3-6
3-0										3-0
2-6										2-6
	9-0	AN	AN	8-7	AN	AN	AN	AN	AN	

Column descriptions:
1. Comprehension of spoken word.
2. Comprehension of picture and written word.
3. Ability to relate spoken words in a meaningful way (auditory symbols)
4. Ability to relate visual symbols in a meaningful way
5. Ability to express ideas in spoken words
6. Ability to express ideas in gestures
7. Ability to predict future linguistic events from past experiences
8. Memory of auditory symbols
9. Memory of visual symbols

13.   Case of Melva.   *Language deficit: auditory problem.*

Referral was made by the principal of the child's elementary school
to help determine school placement.

NAME <u>Melva</u>   EXAMINER <u>Jane Doe</u>

                            DATE OF
DATE OF BIRTH<u>   </u>   EXAMINATION<u>   </u>   C.A. <u>9–9</u>

EVALUATION FOR LEARNING DISABILITIES

BEHAVIOR AND APPEARANCE

Melva was a very nice-looking child, normal in height and weight
for her nine years and nine months. Her good school clothing was clean
and neat. Her speech was noticeably slow, and she was very quiet and
reserved. But she related in a warm way and participated in all the
tasks. Thus the testing progressed smoothly, although her slowness in
reponding required more time than usual.

TEST RESULTS

See Psychometric Summary.

SUMMARY

Examination of Melva found her to be functioning in the dull range
of intellectual ability with a Full Scale WISC I.Q. of 83, a PPVT I.Q.
of 84, and a DAP I.Q. of 73. Some scatter among the subtest scores
suggests that she has both strengths and weaknesses in the verbal and
performance areas.

Substantiated by the ITPA language age of 7, Melva's weaker area
is verbal. According to the WISC, she functioned in the dull range on
the information, comprehension, arithmetical reasoning, and memory
for digits subtests. Her vocabulary was borderline retarded, while her
concept formation (abstract or associative thinking) fell within the
normal range.

The performance-scaled scores reveal normal ability in discriminating
essential from nonessential detail and also normal perceptual organization and visual imagery. Also she achieved normal visual sequencing
relative to social procedure and to geometric symbols (see ITPA, Scale
No. 9).

Melva apparently has difficulty learning through the auditory channel. The ITPA (1961 edition) revealed lower language ages on the auditory tests than on the visual tests. Also a lowered score on the vocal encoding (verbal expression) test suggests a weakness in the expression of ideas.

In reading, spelling, and arithmetic, Melva is achieving at the first- and second-grade levels — levels of expectancy for a child of her age and I.Q. However, her many normal abilities suggest that her achievement could be somewhat higher. Placement for a child whose primary mental abilities are half normal and half below normal is difficult, because the regular classroom presents challenges that progress too fast and the special education classroom directs its activities according to the progress of the retarded child.

Melva needs a very enriched language program in which she is encouraged to talk a great deal. This feedback along with other listening tasks can help to improve her reading. Because Melva shows a normal visual retention span but not a normal auditory retention span, her reading difficulty is perhaps the result of her inability to recall the names of the symbols she sees. Special reading classes with emphasis on language development are necessary for Melva. Planning should also include vocational training as early as possible in the school program.

_____

Consultant

Intelligence Tests:

Wechsler Intelligence Scales

_____WPPSI   __✓__WISC   _____WAIS

WPPSI Scaled Scores

Verbal	Performance
Information_____	Animal House_____
Comprehension_____	Picture Completion_____
Arithmetic_____	Mazes_____
Similarities_____	Geometric Design_____
Vocabulary_____	Block Design_____
(Sentences)_____	Animal House
	(Retest)_____

WISC and WAIS Scaled Scores

Verbal		Performance	
Information	6	Picture Completion	10
Comprehension	6	Picture Arrangement	11
Arithmetic	6	Block Design	7
Similarities	9	Object Assembly	9
Vocabulary	5	Coding or Digit Symbol	7
Digit Span	6	Mazes	

Verbal Scale I.Q._____77_____
Performance Scale I.Q.__92_____
Full Scale I.Q._____83_____

Stanford-Binet (Form L-M)	Draw-A-Person Test	Peabody Picture Vocabulary
C.A._____	C.A._9-9_	C.A._9-9_
M.A._____	M.A._8-3_	M.A._8-3_
I.Q._____	I.Q._84_	I.Q._84_

Wide Range Achievement Test

Reading Grade Level	1.7	Standard Score 74	Percentile_____
Spelling Grade Level	2.0	Standard Score 77	Percentile_____
Arithmetic Grade Level	2.6	Standard Score 82	Percentile_____

Purdue Perceptual-Motor
Survey_____

Wepman Auditory Discrimination
Test_____

Children's Apperception
Test_____

Memory-For-Designs Test
_Normal   Record_____

Bender Visual-Motor
Gestalt Test_Normal Record_____

Illinois Test of Psycholinguistic
Abilities (See ITPA Profile)
Total Language____7-0_____
Scaled Score_____

Hiskey-Nebraska Test

Bead Pattern_____	Visual Attention Span_____
Memory for Colors_____	Block Patterns_____
Picture Identification_____	Completion of Drawings_____
Picture Association_____	Memory for Digits_____
Paper Folding_____	Puzzle Analogies_____
	Spatial Reasoning_____

Other Tests:

Name __CASE of MELVA__ Age __9-9__ Birthdate _____

ILLINOIS TEST OF PSYCHOLINGUISTIC ABILITIES

(Experimental Edition, 1961)

CA: 9-9

	REPRESENTATIONAL LEVEL						AUTOMATIC-SEQUENTIAL LEVEL		
	DECODING		ASSOCIATIONAL		ENCODING		AUTOMATIC	SEQUENTIAL	
Language Age	Auditory	Visual	AuditoryVocal	Visual-Motor	Vocal	Motor	AuditoryVocal	AuditoryVocal	Visual-Motor
	1	2	3	4	5	6	7	8	9
	Comprehension of spoken word.	Comprehension of picture and written word.	Ability to relate spoken words in a meaningful way (auditory symbols)	Ability to relate visual symbols in a meaningful way	Ability to express ideas in spoken words	Ability to express ideas in gestures	Ability to predict future linguistic events from past experiences	Memory of auditory symbols	Memory of visual symbols
Score	7-1	7-10	5-10	8-7	6-7	AN	3-10	5-4	AN

Age scale: 9-0, 8-6, 8-0, 7-6, 7-0, 6-6, 6-0, 5-6, 5-0, 4-6, 4-0, 3-6, 3-0, 2-6

14.   Case of CD.   *Minimal brain injury with both language and motor*
problems.

Referral was made by the mother to determine the best means for
remediation.

NAME CD   EXAMINER Jane Doe

                                    DATE OF
DATE OF BIRTH   EXAMINATION   C.A. 6–4

EVALUATION FOR LEARNING DISABILITIES

BEHAVIOR AND APPEARANCE

CD appeared normal in all physiological aspects. Dressed comfortably in casual summer clothes, he was neat, clean, and quite handsome.
Separating him from his mother caused no problem, since he was willing
to enter the testing room without her. Although his compliance allowed
the testing to progress very smoothly, CD began to tire after about two
hours. Despite his fatigue, he apparently would have continued to respond upon request; however, part of the testing was postponed until a
later date.

TEST RESULTS

See Psychometric Summary.

SUMMARY

CD had a wide discrepancy between verbal and performance with
some erraticism in each. Although his Full Scale WISC I.Q. was 82,
his WISC verbal I.Q. of 74 revealed achievement typical of a border
line retarded child. His range of information, memory, and vocabulary
are his greatest weaknesses, the vocabulary weakness reflected particularly in the PPVT I.Q. of 65. In addition, his comprehension, reasoning, and concept formation all fell within the dull range. Consequently
his language or verbal abilities reflect an obvious problem area.

CD's performance abilities indicate a more normal intelligence, but
here again there was some erratic functioning. Two scores of 13 reveal
his above average performances in forming designs with blocks and
in managing puzzles. The picture completion and picture arrangement
scaled scores both reflect normal functioning, but at the low normal level,
suggesting that his spatial ability to discriminate essential from non-

essential detail and his ability to plan and anticipate social procedure are both low normal. Handling a pen or pencil for making the small symbols on the coding test and for completing the *Goodenough Draw-A-Person Test* proved difficult for CD because of his severe weakness in fine motor functioning. Yet in spite of this difficulty on the DAP, he achieved an I.Q. of 86 because the body parts of his drawing could easily be identified. This DAP I.Q. correlates with an even higher WISC performance I.Q. of 93. The Bender and the Memory-For-Designs Tests, both administered on a later date, show a severe weakness in fine motor coordination. However, emphasis should be placed on the fact that this weakness is not evident when CD works with blocks or puzzles. Because the WRAT scores show that he is achieving at the kindergarten level in reading, spelling, and arithmetic, CD is not yet ready for the first grade, although he may be ready for a special education class such as a public school MBI room.

The scores on the ITPA (1961 edition) reflect CD's severe language weakness, and his responses to both visual understanding and auditory understanding tasks suggest that he will benefit by remediation techniques in both areas.

Psycholinguistic training should follow, but a prompt administration of the *Purdue Perceptual-Motor Survey* is first recommended.

Consultant

ADDENDUM

The *Purdue Perceptual-Motor Survey,* administered at a later date, found that CD was having difficulty with hypertension, ocular pursuit, and differentiation. Exercises found in *Motoric Aids to Learning* (Chaney & Kephart, 1968) are recommended to aid the development of a kinesthetic, auditory match, to provide relaxation exercises, and to aid in the differentiation of his legs.

PSYCHOMETRIC SUMMARY

Intelligence Tests:

Wechsler Intelligence Scales

_____WPPSI   √ WISC   _____WAIS

WPPSI Scaled Scores

Verbal   Performance
Information_____   Animal House_____
Comprehension_____   Picture Completion_____
Arithmetic_____   Mazes_____
Similarities_____   Geometric Design_____
Vocabulary_____   Block Design_____
(Sentences)_____   Animal House
                                        (Retest)_____

WISC and WAIS Scaled Scores

Verbal   Performance
Information___5_____   Picture Completion_____9_____
Comprehension___6_____   Picture Arrangement____8_____
Arithmetic___7_____   Block Design_____13_____
Similarities___6_____   Object Assembly____13_____
Vocabulary___5_____   Coding or Digit Symbol___3____
Digit Span___5_____   Mazes_____

Verbal Scale I.Q.____74____
Performance Scale I.Q.___94____
Full Scale I.Q.____82____

Stanford-Binet (Form L-M)   Draw-A-Person Test   Peabody Picture Vocabulary
C.A._____   C.A._6-4_ (21 Days)   C.A._6-4_
M.A._____   M.A._5-6_   M.A._4-2_
I.Q._____   I.Q._87_   I.Q._65_

Wide Range Achievement Test

Reading Grade Level___Kg .1___Standard Score__72__Percentile_____
Spelling Grade Level___Kg .6___Standard Score__81__Percentile_____
Arithmetic Grade Level___Kg .7___Standard Score__83__Percentile_____

Purdue Perceptual-Motor   Wepman Auditory Discrimination
Survey___Atypical Record___   Test_____

Children's Apperception   Memory-For-Designs Test
Test_____   _Critical visual-motor problem_

Bender Visual-Motor   Illinois Test of Psycholinguistic
Gestalt Test__Critical visual-__   Abilities (See ITPA Profile)
            motor problem   Total Language___4-6___
                                    Scaled Score_____

Hiskey-Nebraska Test

Bead Pattern_____   Visual Attention Span_____
Memory for Colors_____   Block Patterns_____
Picture Identification_____   Completion of Drawings_____
Picture Association_____   Memory for Digits_____
Paper Folding_____   Puzzle Analogies_____
                                    Spatial Reasoning_____

Other Tests:

221

Name __CASE OF CD__ Age __6-4__ Birthdate _____

ILLINOIS TEST OF PSYCHOLINGUISTIC ABILITIES

(Experimental Edition, 1961)

	REPRESENTATIONAL LEVEL						AUTOMATIC-SEQUENTIAL LEVEL		
	DECODING		ASSOCIATIONAL		ENCODING		AUTOMATIC	SEQUENTIAL	
	Auditory	Visual	Auditory Vocal	Visual-Motor	Vocal	Motor	Auditory Vocal	Auditory Vocal	Visual-Motor
	1	2	3	4	5	6	7	8	9
Description	Comprehension of spoken word.	Comprehension of picture and written word.	Ability to relate spoken words in a meaningful way (auditory symbols)	Ability to relate visual symbols in a meaningful way	Ability to express ideas in spoken words	Ability to express ideas in gestures	Ability to predict future linguistic events from past experiences	Memory of auditory symbols	Memory of visual symbols
Language Age	4-7	3-8	4-5	4-4	5-1	3-10	2-9	6-3	4-7

Language Age scale: 9-0, 8-6, 8-0, 7-6, 7-0, 6-6, 6-0, 5-6, 5-0, 4-6, 4-0, 3-6, 3-0, 2-6

CA:

VERBAL AND PERFORMANCE
FUNCTIONS AT SAME LEVEL

15. Case of Brad. *Sequencing and memory problems.*

Referral was made by the mother to determine aids for remediation.

NAME Brad   EXAMINER Jane Doe

DATE OF BIRTH   DATE OF EXAMINATION   C.A. 12–4

EVALUATION FOR LEARNING DISABILITIES

BEHAVIOR AND APPEARANCE

With ash-blond hair and blue eyes, Brad was normal in height and weight for his 12 years 4 months. He appeared very neat and clean in his good school clothes. He was quiet and reserved but normally responsive. Although Brad exhibited some hesitant and apprehensive behavior at the beginning, he became more assured and his responses more normal as the testing progressed. Turning his paper to get a better perspective and erasing often in an attempt to make correct copies of the designs revealed that Brad was experiencing a visual-motor problem.

TEST RESULTS

See Psychometric Summary.

SUMMARY

Examination of Brad found him functioning in the normal range of intellectual ability with a WISC I.Q. of 96 and a PPVT I.Q. of 99. The scatter of scores occurring in both the verbal and the performance areas reveals his greatest weaknesses.

The significant verbal scatter evident in the very low arithmetic and digit span subtest scores not only suggests a lack of ability to concentrate but also a memory and reasoning weakness. His vocabulary and range of information were mildly low, while his comprehension and concept formation were high average.

The significant performance scatter occurred in the very low coding and picture arrangement subtest scores, showing that Brad has a slow psychomotor speed and that he is slow in sequencing meaningful picture activities. Brad has no major discrimination problem when working with three-dimensional objects such as blocks or puzzles, for he is able to work fast and accurately with these. Conversely he used an atypical approach to the Memory-For Designs drawings and the Bender figures. On the MFD his work revealed a figure foreground problem, while on both tests he exhibited unusual difficulty in completing the designs. He made slight rotations and did a lot of sketching, even after erasing.

The WRAT reveals that Brad is achieving at the second-grade level in reading, spelling, and arithmetic. This critically low level suggests the level of a retarded child, whereas Brad has normal intelligence. The Hiskey-Nebraska scales provide some evidence that he has linguistic problems in recalling visual sequence and in associating visual stimuli, yet his spatial ability appears normal. Therefore, Brad's major problems concern sequencing, memory, and motor output. Remediation requires a highly structured program in motor activities and kinesthetic techniques. Brad should practice these daily in connection with his school assignments.

―――――――――――――

Consultant

PSYCHOMETRIC SUMMARY

Intelligence Tests:

Wechsler Intelligence Scales

_____WPPSI   __√__WISC   _____WAIS

WPPSI Scaled Scores

Verbal	Performance
Information_____	Animal House_____
Comprehension_____	Picture Completion_____
Arithmetic_____	Mazes_____
Similarities_____	Geometric Design_____
Vocabulary_____	Block Design_____
(Sentences)_____	Animal House
	(Retest)_____

WISC and WAIS Scaled Scores

Verbal		Performance	
Information	9	Picture Completion	12
Comprehension	11	Picture Arrangement	17
Arithmetic	6	Block Design	11
Similarities	11	Object Assembly	15
Vocabulary	8	Coding or Digit Symbol	4
Digit Span	7	Mazes	

Verbal Scale I.Q._____94_____
Performance Scale I.Q._____99_____
Full Scale I.Q._____96_____

Stanford-Binet (Form L-M)	Draw-A-Person Test	Peabody Picture Vocabulary
C.A._____	C.A._____	C.A. _12-4_
M.A._____	M.A._____	M.A. _11-9_
I.Q._____	I.Q._____	I.Q. _99_

Wide Range Achievement Test

Reading Grade Level	2.4	Standard Score 66	Percentile_____
Spelling Grade Level	2.6	Standard Score 68	Percentile_____
Arithmetic Grade Level	2.9	Standard Score 70	Percentile_____

Purdue Perceptual-Motor
Survey_____

Wepman Auditory Discrimination
Test $X = 2/30$ $Y = 1/10$

Children's Apperception
Test_____

Memory-For-Designs Test
_____Atypical Record_____

Bender Visual-Motor
Gestalt Test__Atypical Record__

Illinois Test of Psycholinguistic
Abilities (See ITPA Profile)
Total Language_____A N_____
Scaled Score_____

Hiskey-Nebraska Test

Bead Pattern_____	Visual Attention Span	5-0
Memory for Colors_____	Block Patterns_____	
Picture Identification_____	Completion of Drawings	Above Average
Picture Association_____	Memory for Digits_____	
Paper Folding_____	Puzzle Analogies	8-0
	Spatial Reasoning	13-0

Other Tests:

Name _____ CASE OF BRAD _____ Age _12-4_ Birthdate _____

ILLINOIS TEST OF PSYCHOLINGUISTIC ABILITIES

(Experimental Edition, 1961)

CA = 12-4

	Language Age			REPRESENTATIONAL LEVEL								AUTOMATIC-SEQUENTIAL LEVEL			
		DECODING		ASSOCIATIONAL		ENCODING			AUTOMATIC	SEQUENTIAL	
		Auditory	Visual	Auditory Vocal	Visual-Motor	Vocal	Motor		Auditory Vocal	Auditory Vocal	Visual-Motor
		1	2	3	4	5	6	7	8	9
		Comprehension of spoken word.	Comprehension of picture and written word.	Ability to relate spoken words in a meaningful way (auditory symbols)	Ability to relate visual symbols in a meaningful way	Ability to express ideas in spoken words	Ability to express ideas in gestures	Ability to predict future linguistic events from past experiences	Memory of auditory symbols	Memory of visual symbols
	9-0									
	8-6									
	8-0									
	7-6									
	7-0									
	6-6									
	6-0									
	5-6									
	5-0									
	4-6									
	4-0									
	3-6									
	3-0									
	2-6									
		AN	AN	AN	9-7	AN	AN	AN	9-6	8-6

16. Case of Kim. *Hyperactive and basic perceptual-motor problems.*

Referral was from the school to determine aids to help Kim "settle down" in the classroom. His mother brought him to the testing situation but did not report his gun accident until a later conference.

NAME Kim   EXAMINER Jane Doe

                                           DATE OF

DATE OF BIRTH_____EXAMINATION_____ C.A. 8–3

EVALUATION FOR LEARNING DISABILITIES

BEHAVIOR AND APPEARANCE

Kim had brown hair and blue eyes, and his height and weight were normal for his eight years and three months. Dressed in good school clothes, he was clean and neat. Kim's mild hyperactivity was immediately detected and observed from the beginning. Before the testing began, he was across the room handling the typewriter and other objects sitting on the table. When the activities started, however, he cooperated fully, participating in all the tasks. It was necessary to ask him to be seated many times, but in each instance he obediently resumed the activities. Kim also needed reassurance about the length of time for testing.

TEST RESULTS

See Psychometric Summary.

SUMMARY

Examination found Kim functioning in the normal range of intellectual ability, but at a level below the mean of his age group. His Full Scale WISC I.Q. and PPVT I.Q. were both 92, but his DAP I.Q. was 73, a score reflecting his general immaturity of self-concept and his poor perception of human figure detail but not his global intellectual function.

The test data shows normal rather than dull or low normal performance of five of the tasks: comprehension, vocabulary, memory for digits, discriminative ability relative to environmental essentials, and the ability to plan and participate in social procedures. Other test item responses suggest a difficulty in visual-motor performance; that is, he exhibits slow psychomotor speed, poor alignment ability (eye-hand coordination), and poor visual imagery. In the verbal area Kim's achievements in concept formation and range of information were dull normal.

Kim's irregular drawings of the Bender figures suggest that he needs guidelines and other aids when performing visual-motor tasks. The MFD difference score of 12 places him in the critical area relative to such visual-motor problems. The ITPA (1968 edition) shows that he does not communicate easily through either the auditory or the visual channel. Although he is readily talkative, he is slow to express ideas. Thus he needs psycholinguistic remediation. Recalling auditory sequence presents no problem for him. However, he misses some auditory associations, some word meanings, and some grammatical structures. The ITPA profile locates Kim's weak areas for which a program can be structured based on remediation techniques according to Kirk, Bush and Giles, and Valett (see Appendix B). The Frostig program specifically as well as Kephart's routine exercises are also recommended.

_____

Consultant

ADDENDUM

A follow-up on this case resulted from the teacher's request for a conference. Kim had been the victim of a gun accident, and a bullet had been removed from his brain. However, the neurosurgeon had reported no brain damage. Before withdrawing Kim from the classroom, several attempts were made to counteract his hyperactivity. At first he was placed in isolation. Then his desk was placed in a corner of the classroom where he would not be distracted by the other children. But this situation was satisfactory for only a day or two. Because his basic visual-motor problem was so severe, any fine motor activities depleted his energy after only a short while. Administration of the PMS by the physical education instructor revealed that development of a kinesthetic-auditory match would prevent Kim from having to depend solely upon his eyes for accurate perception. He was placed in an MBI room where competition was less severe. Last report of Kim showed satisfactory progress in the MBI room and a reduction in his hyperactivity.

Intelligence Tests:

Wechsler Intelligence Scales

_____WPPSI   ✓ WISC   _____WAIS

WPPSI Scaled Scores

Verbal		Performance	
Information		Animal House	
Comprehension		Picture Completion	
Arithmetic		Mazes	
Similarities		Geometric Design	
Vocabulary		Block Design	
(Sentences)		Animal House (Retest)	

WISC and WAIS Scaled Scores

Verbal		Performance	
Information	7	Picture Completion	11
Comprehension	11	Picture Arrangement	10
Arithmetic	9	Block Design	9
Similarities	7	Object Assembly	7
Vocabulary	11	Coding or Digit Symbol	7
Digit Span	11	Mazes	

Verbal Scale I.Q. ___94___
Performance Scale I.Q. ___92___
Full Scale I.Q. ___92___

Stanford-Binet (Form L-M)	Draw-A-Person Test	Peabody Picture Vocabulary
C.A.	C.A. 8-3	C.A. 8-3
M.A.	M.A. 6-0	M.A. 7-1
I.Q.	I.Q. 73	I.Q. 92

Wide Range Achievement Test

Reading Grade Level ___1.9___ Standard Score __85__ Percentile_____
Spelling Grade Level ___2.0___ Standard Score __86__ Percentile_____
Arithmetic Grade Level ___2.6___ Standard Score __92__ Percentile_____

Purdue Perceptual-Motor
Survey ___See Summary___

Wepman Auditory Discrimination
Test _____

Children's Appreciation
Test _____

Memory-For-Designs Test
___Critical visual-motor problem___

Bender Visual-Motor
Gestalt Test ___Borderline visual-motor problem___

Illinois Test of Psycholinguistic
Abilities (See ITPA Profile)
Total Language ___6-10___
Scaled Score _____

Hiskey-Nebraska Test

Bead Pattern	Visual Attention Span
Memory for Colors	Block Patterns
Picture Identification	Completion of Drawings
Picture Association	Memory for Digits
Paper Folding	Puzzle Analogies
	Spatial Reasoning

Other Tests:

Date of Examination _____ Name ___CASE of Kim___ Age ___8-3___

PROFILE OF ABILITIES   Mean Scaled Score = 36   Standard Deviation = 6

ITPA SCORES

	Representational Level								Automatic Level				
	Reception		Association		Expression		Closure		Sequential Memory		Supplemental Tests	
Scaled Scores	Auditory	Visual	Auditory	Visual	Verbal	Manual	Grammatic	Visual	Auditory	Visual	Auditory Closure	Sound Blending
	Comprehension of spoken word.	Comprehension of picture and written word.	Ability to relate spoken words in a meaningful way.	Ability to relate visual symbols in a meaningful way.	Ability to express ideas in spoken words.	Ability to express ideas in gestures.	Ability to use correct grammar.	Ability to perceive objects in incomplete form.	Memory of auditory symbols in sequence.	Memory for visual symbols in sequence.	Automatic function to understand difficult and incomplete speech.	Automatic function in synthesizing parts of words.
64												
60												
56												
52												
48												
44												
40												
36												
32												
28												
24												
20												
16												
12												
8												
4												
	7-6	6-5	5-7	7-2	5-8	8-4	6-8	6-1	AN	5-7		

230

17. Case of OM. *Memory problem and dyslexia.*

Referral was made by the mother to determine specific problem areas.

NAME OM   EXAMINER Jane Doe

                                      DATE OF
DATE OF BIRTH   EXAMINATION   C.A. 7–10

EVALUATION FOR LEARNING DISABILITIES

BEHAVIOR AND APPEARANCE

OM was an attractive blond-haired, blue-eyed boy with nice facial features and a display of freckles. He appeared to be slightly small in height and weight for his seven years and ten months, yet his stature was within normal limits.

He held his pencil in a tight grasp with his left hand as he worked at the written activities. There was a mildly impulsive approach to the tasks with which he appeared to be familiar. When presented with new material, however, he appeared to be more observing and was noticeably slower as he coordinated the eye-hand movements. He was also noted to have a minor speech defect; he did not pronounce the *r* sounds consistently.

During the last hour of the test he was "wiggly," but he remained at the tasks without coercion.

TEST RESULTS

See Psychometric Summary.

SUMMARY

OM was examined and found to be functioning in the dull normal range of intellectual ability. His Full Scale WISC I.Q. and his PPVT I.Q. (form B) were both found to be 85. His performance I.Q. of 89 and his verbal I.Q. of 85 being at approximately the same position substantiates the thesis that OM, in general ability, performs about the same in both verbal and performance tasks, even though there were strengths and weaknesses in both areas.

In the verbal area his greatest strength, concept formation or abstract thinking, was found to be normal. His comprehension, arithmetical reasoning, vocabulary, and memory for digits was found to be low normal, while his memory for general information was found to be borderline retarded.

The performance scores showed the same range as found in the verbal area. His eye-hand coordination and motor speed were found to be borderline retarded and his visual-spatial ability, in contrast, was found to be at the low normal position. His greatest strength in the performance area was his ability to discriminate essential from nonessential detail. This was in the high average range. The eye-hand coordination tasks, when not timed, showed expectancy function for dull-normal ability. Both the Bender and the MFD drawings, while somewhat immature, were commensurate with his general level of intelligence. It is apparent that when OM is given extra time with his fine motor tasks, he will perform more accurately.

The ITPA scores revealed that OM has both visual and auditory perceptual problems (mildly so), but that the processes of closure and memory functions, regardless of the sensory channel, are his greatest input weaknesses. His scores on expression subtests showed that he is also slow in output functions, particularly in verbal expression, and that he has an ideational fluency problem; i.e., OM has difficulty in expressing ideas about things.

According to the Guilford construct of intelligence (SOI), as it relates to the tests in this battery, OM is below his expected ability in memory and cognition of systems, units, and relations, both semantic and symbolic. This is more specifically explained by adding that he has no trouble knowing and remembering meaningful objects such as furniture, toys, and vehicles, but he has difficulty recognizing and knowing some semantic and symbolic units as letters, numbers, and signs. He was also found to be slow in the process of evaluating differences among geometric designs (units) and in problem solving.

The WRAT shows a typical dyslexia profile, with his reading achievement at Kindergarten 0.4, spelling at grade 1.2, and arithmetic at grade 1.9. Both the reading and spelling are below expectancy, but the arithmetic achievement is commensurate with his general ability as noted by the WISC I.Q. scores. Specifically he does not remember how to spell and he does not know all of the letters of the alphabet. He missed the following letters consistently: R, Q, E, P, and U. There may be others that he does not know, but not all were covered in the test. Although his arithmetic achievement was the highest of the three, he did make some mistakes which should be noted. He confused *41* with *14* and he thought that 28 was more than 42. He also overlooked the arithmetic signs for addition and subtraction. It therefore appears that OM needs remediation beginning with the initial basic skills.

Recommendations include kinesthetic approaches to visual and auditory tasks with a structured routine of perceptual-motor activities designed to aid in the process of memory. These activities will be discussed with the parents and with the remediation clinician.

_____

Consultant

Intelligence Tests:

Wechsler Intelligence Scales

_____WPPSI   ✓ WISC   _____WAIS

WPPSI Scaled Scores

Verbal		Performance	
Information_____		Animal House_____	
Comprehension_____		Picture Completion_____	
Arithmetic_____		Mazes_____	
Similarities_____		Geometric Design_____	
Vocabulary_____		Block Design_____	
(Sentences)_____		Animal House	
		(Retest)	

WISC and WAIS Scaled Scores

Verbal		Performance	
Information **5**		Picture Completion **12**	
Comprehension **7**		Picture Arrangement **7**	
Arithmetic **8**		Block Design **9**	
Similarities **10**		Object Assembly **9**	
Vocabulary **8**		Coding or Digit Symbol **5**	
Digit Span **(8)**		Mazes	

Verbal Scale I.Q. **85**
Performance Scale I.Q. **89**
Full Scale I.Q. **85**

Stanford-Binet (Form L-M)	Draw-A-Person Test	Peabody Picture Vocabulary
C.A._____	C.A. **7-10**	C.A. **7-10**
M.A._____	M.A. **7-3**	M.A. **6-4**
I.Q._____	I.Q._____	I.Q. **85**

Wide Range Achievement Test

Reading Grade Level **Kg. .4**_____Standard Score_____Percentile_____
Spelling Grade Level____**1.2**_____Standard Score_____Percentile_____
Arithmetic Grade Level____**1.9**_____Standard Score_____Percentile_____

Purdue Perceptual Motor Survey____▬____	Wepman Auditory Discrimination Test_____
Children's Apperception Test_____	Memory-For-Designs Test ____**NORMAL**____
Bender Visual-Motor Gestalt Test____**NORMAL**____	Illinois Test of Psycholinguistic Abilities (See ITPA Profile) Total Language **6-3** Scaled Score_____

Hiskey-Nebraska Test

Bead Pattern_____	Visual Attention Span_____
Memory for Colors_____	Block Patterns_____
Picture Identification_____	Completion of Drawings_____
Picture Association_____	Memory for Digits_____
Paper Folding_____	Puzzle Analogies_____
	Spatial Reasoning_____

Other Tests:

Date of Examination _____ Name **OM** _____ Age **7—10**

PROFILE OF ABILITIES Mean Scaled Score = 36 Standard Deviation = 6

ITPA SCORES

Level	Category	Subtest	Description	Score
Representational Level	Reception	Auditory	Comprehension of spoken word.	6-5
		Visual	Comprehension of picture and written word.	6-7
	Association	Auditory	Ability to relate spoken words in a meaningful way.	6-2
		Visual	Ability to relate visual symbols in a meaningful way.	6-10
	Expression	Verbal	Ability to express ideas in spoken words.	5-10
		Manual	Ability to express ideas in gestures.	6-5
Automatic Level	Closure	Grammatic	Ability to use correct grammar.	5-4
		Visual	Ability to perceive objects in incomplete form.	6-9
	Sequential Memory	Auditory	Memory of auditory symbols in sequence.	6-0
		Visual	Memory for visual symbols in sequence.	5-10
	Auditory Closure		Automatic function to understand difficult and incomplete speech.	5-9
	Sound Blending		Automatic function in synthesizing parts of words.	8-7

Scaled Scores: 64 60 56 52 48 44 40 36 32 28 24 20 16 12 8 4

235

SOI Test Profile Information

OM
School _____
Age 7-10

Information	Meeker Text pp. 137–138	WISC			
MMU _3_	(_3_)	**Picture Completion**			
MMR _2_	(_3_)	CFU _10_	(_8_)		
MSS _2_	(_1_)	CFS _10_	(_8_)		
CMU ___	(___)	**Picture Arrangement**			
MMS _2_	(_1_)	EMR _3_	(_5_)		
NMR ___	(___)	NMS _3_	(_5_)		
NMU ___	(___)	**Block Design**			
EMR ___	(___)	CFR _3_	(_3_)		
Comprehension		EFR _3_	(_3_)		
EMI ___	(_4_)	**Object Assembly**			
Arithmetic		CFS _2_	(_2_)		
MSI _5_	(_6_)	CFT _2_	(_2_)		
CMS _5_	(_6_)	EFR _2_	(_2_)		
Similarities		**Coding**			
EMR _4_	(_4_)	NFU _19_	(_38_)	C _34_ (_34_)	100%
CMT ___	(_2_)	EFU _19_	(_38_)		
Vocabulary		NSU ___	(___)	M _17_ (_21_)	80%
CMU _10_	(_11_)	ESU ___	(___)		
Digits		**Mazes**			
MSS-F _4_	(_5_)	CFI ___	(___)	E _46_ (_64_)	71%
mss-B _3_	(_3_)			N _21_ (_43_)	46%

(Right margin vertical labels: Total Obtained · Total Expectancy · Percentage)

ITPA   DETROIT

Strengths (Tests)	SOI	Weaknesses (Tests)	SOI	Strengths (Tests)	SOI	Weaknesses (Tests)	SOI
Sd. Blding.	CFU-A	Verbal Exp.	DMU				
" "	NMU-A	Gram. Closure	CMU and MMR				
		Vis. Seq. Mem.	MPS-V				
		Aud. Clos.	CFU-A and NMU-A				

SLOSSON (from 2–0)

Correct		Incorrect	Correct		Incorrect
___	CMU	___	___	MMU	___
___	CMS	___	___	EFU	___
___	CMC	___	___	EMR	___
___	CMI	___	___	NFU	___
___	CMR	___	___	NMR	___
___	MSU	___	___	NMI	___
___	MMS	___	___	NMU	___
___	MSI	___			
___	MSS	___			

From Mary N. Meeker, *The Structure of Intellect* (Columbus: Charles E. Merrill, 1969).
Adapted by Marjorie Rives, Educational Diagnostician, Eastern Panhandle Cooperative,
Shamrock, Texas.

236

Use different colors to represent different tests.

		Figural	Symbolic	Semantic	Behavioral
Units	C	CFU-Aud.		CMU	
	M				
	E				
	N			NMU-aud.	
	D			DMU	
Classes	C				
	M				
	E				
	N				
	D				
Relations	C				
	M			MMR	
	E				
	N				
	D				
Systems	C				
	M	MFS-Visual			
	E				
	N				
	D				
Transformations	C				
	M				
	E				
	N				
	D				
Implications	C				
	M				
	E				
	N				
	D				

Other Information

From Mary N. Meeker, *The Structure of Intellect* (Columbus: Charles E. Merrill, 1969). Adapted by Marjorie Rives, Educational Diagnostician, Eastern Panhandle Cooperative, Shamrock, Texas.

JUNIOR HIGH SCHOOL

18.   Case of Don.   *Figure-ground visual-motor problem.*

Referred by the mother because of concern over a possible reading problem.

NAME Don   EXAMINER Jane Doe

DATE OF BIRTH_____ DATE OF EXAMINATION_____ C.A. 12–11

EVALUATION FOR LEARNING DISABILITIES

BEHAVIOR AND APPEARANCE

Don, a very nice-looking boy with ash-blond hair and blue eyes, appeared physiologically normal. He was dressed in very good school clothing, and he was clean and neat. Apparently happy and assured as he performed the tasks, Don displayed a very warm, outgoing, and friendly personality. If a task was too difficult for him, he made no apologies as though he understood that performance on all the activities was not expected of him. Don made many extraneous remarks, all of which were appropriate, and there was no evidence of anxiety as a result of the testing situation.

TEST RESULTS

See Psychometric Summary.

SUMMARY

Examination found Don functioning in the superior level of intellectual ability with a Full Scale WISC I.Q. of 123. The PPVT I.Q. of 112, reflecting his high average ability in vocabulary, does not account for his superior achievements in memory for ideas, comprehension, and concept formation. A drop to the normal level in memory for digits functioning may be attributed to the tension of a testing situation, but his relaxed behavior belied such a state.

The performance area shows a similar scatter with scaled scores ranging between 7 and 17. Because Don has difficulty in forming an accurate picture image of common objects, he could not satisfactorily complete the picture puzzles. His slowness and frustration in working with blocks netted him a score lower than most of the other visual-motor task scores; he had difficulty matching and aligning design patterns. Unlike this function of finding correct matching situations, the motor speed function did not cause him any trouble.

On the Bender Test Don reproduced some designs accurately, although he had to erase more often than normal. Design 7 of the MFD showed serious distortion of a simple pattern because he failed to visualize the foreground as it actually appeared. Therefore, Don was instructed to redraw the designs on background interference paper according to the Canter revision of the Bender.* This interference, which caused him difficulty in drawing the sinusoidal curves of design 6, emphasizes that Don's most critical problem is that of determining the foreground of visual stimuli.

Parts of the ITPA (1961 edition) and the Hiskey-Nebraska were administered to reveal Don's marginal problems in visual association (see scores on psychometric data sheet). The lowered learning age and language age scores substantiate these problems. The ITPA also suggests a mild memory problem involving both visual and auditory sequencing. Dominance appears to be well established on the right side, and there is no finger agnosia.

The WRAT shows underachievement when compared to Don's I.Q. That is, his reading level of 8.3, spelling level of 6.8, and arithmetic level of 7.1 are below expectancy for a 13-year-old (twelve years and eleven months) with an I.Q. of 123. That his specific problems of foreground relationships and visual memory imagery are causing him to underproduce can be assumed. Don should spend time daily in remediation techniques for figure foreground problems as prescribed by the Frostig Visual Perception Program and the ITPA handbooks.

Consultant

ADDENDUM

The *Durrell-Sullivan Reading Capacity and Achievement Test* was administered the following week to gain more information on Don's read-

---

*Canter has made an important contribution to the field of learning disabilities in his revision of the Bender Visual-Motor Gestalt Test, although his original objective was to discriminate the brain injured. See Arthur Canter, "A Background Interference Procedure to Increase Sensitivity of the Bender-Gestalt Test to Organic Brain Disorder," in *Journal of Consulting and Clinical Psychology* 30, no. 2 (April 1966), pp. 91–97.

ing abilities. His word meaning was above grade 7.1 (the highest norm), his paragraph meaning at grade 7.1, his spelling at grade 6.9, and his written recall rated "fair." Therefore, the reading levels that Don had achieved on the WRAT were substantiated by those achieved on the Durrell-Sullivan tests. Because these levels are below his capacity, his mother was told that Don should be tutored according to structured visual perception programs to help him reach his expectancy level.

PSYCHOMETRIC SUMMARY

Intelligence Tests:

Wechsler Intelligence Scales

_____WPPSI   __✓__WISC   _____WAIS

WPPSI Scaled Scores

Verbal	Performance
Information_____	Animal House_____
Comprehension_____	Picture Completion_____
Arithmetic_____	Mazes_____
Similarities_____	Geometric Design_____
Vocabulary_____	Block Design_____
(Sentences)_____	Animal House
	(Retest)_____

WISC and WAIS Scaled Scores

Verbal	Performance
Information____15	Picture Completion____13
Comprehension____13	Picture Arrangement____17
Arithmetic____13	Block Design____10
Similarities____17	Object Assembly____7
Vocabulary____11	Coding or Digit Symbol____15
Digit Span____10	Mazes____8

Verbal Scale I.Q.____124
Performance Scale I.Q.____117
Full Scale I.Q.____123

Stanford-Binet (Form L-M)	Draw-A-Person Test	Peabody Picture Vocabulary
C.A._____	C.A.__12-11	C.A.__12-11
M.A._____	M.A.__12-0	M.A.__15-3
I.Q._____	I.Q.__—	I.Q.__112

Wide Range Achievement Test

Reading Grade Level____8.3	Standard Score__103	Percentile_____
Spelling Grade Level____6.8	Standard Score__94	Percentile_____
Arithmetic Grade Level____7.1	Standard Score__96	Percentile_____

Purdue Perceptual-Motor
  Survey_____

Wepman Auditory Discrimination
  Test_____

Children's Apperception
  Test_____

Memory-For-Designs Test
  ____Atypical Record

Bender Visual-Motor
  Gestalt Test____Atypical Record

Illinois Test of Psycholinguistic
  Abilities (See ITPA Profile)
  Total Language____AN
  Scaled Score_____

Hiskey-Nebraska Test

Bead Pattern_____	Visual Attention Span_____
Memory for Colors_____	Block Patterns_____
Picture Identification_____	Completion of Drawings_____
Picture Association_____	Memory for Digits_____
Paper Folding_____	Puzzle Analogies____12-0
	Spatial Reasoning____8-0

Other Tests:

Name _____ Age _12 - 11_ Birthdate _____

CASE OF DON

CA : 12-11

ILLINOIS TEST OF PSYCHOLINGUISTIC ABILITIES

(Experimental Edition, 1961)

	REPRESENTATIONAL LEVEL						AUTOMATIC-SEQUENTIAL LEVEL			
	DECODING		ASSOCIATIONAL		ENCODING		AUTOMATIC	SEQUENTIAL		
Language Age	Auditory 1	Visual 2	AuditoryVocal 3	Visual-Motor 4	Vocal 5	Motor 6	AuditoryVocal 7	AuditoryVocal 8	Visual-Motor 9	
	Comprehension of spoken word.	Comprehension of picture and written word.	Ability to relate spoken words in a meaningful way (auditory symbols)	Ability to relate visual symbols in a meaningful way	Ability to express ideas in spoken words	Ability to express ideas in gestures	Ability to predict future linguistic events from past experiences	Memory of auditory symbols	Memory of visual symbols	
9-0										
8-6										
8-0										
7-6										
7-0										
6-6										
6-0										
5-6										
5-0										
4-6										
4-0										
3-6										
3-0										
2-6										

Handwritten: *Questionable Problem Area* (under Visual, column 2)

Handwritten: *Questionable Problem Area* (under Memory of auditory symbols, column 8)

19. Case of HS. *Underproducer.*

Referral was made by the mother to determine why HS lacked motivation.

NAME HS   EXAMINER Jane Doe

                                         DATE OF
DATE OF BIRTH   EXAMINATION   C.A. 15–4

EVALUATION FOR LEARNING DISABILITIES

BEHAVIOR AND APPEARANCE

Normal in height and weight for his 15 years and 4 months, HS appeared comfortably groomed in a clean sport shirt, jeans, and cowboy boots. He drew meticulously but held his pencil oddly and rather tightly. His thumb rested above the forefinger with the thumb joint extended to such a position that the pressure depended more on it than on the forefinger. Therefore, his thumb guided his writing.

While mildly reserved, HS was responsive to all the tasks, and he showed no tendency to terminate any of them early. His perseverance allowed the testing to progress very smoothly.

TEST RESULTS

See Psychometric Summary.

SUMMARY

Examination of HS found him functioning in the superior range of intellectual ability with a Full Scale WISC I.Q. of 122 and a PPVT I.Q. of 130. His verbal abilities, showing some mild scatter, are superior to his performance abilities.

His greatest verbal strengths lie in vocabulary, range of information, comprehension, and concept formation. Arithmetic ability and memory for digits, although weaker than the other abilities, both show normal functioning. Because these lowered scores may be attributed to the effect of distractibility on concentration, they imply that his performance was rather characteristic of his working behavior.

The performance I.Q. of 114, showing a slight drop below the full scale and verbal I.Q.'s, reveals slower visual-motor functioning. His discriminative ability, visual-motor organization, and coordination, although all at the normal level, are low for one with a verbal I.Q. of 125.

HS drew the MFD test patterns with normal accuracy, but his plan of organization was rather unusual. He drew the Bender figures in a similarly disorganized manner, even to the point of allowing the designs to overlap. And his substitution of small circles for dots, suggesting a perceptual problem, reveals further atypical performance. The Canter background interference paper (BIP), used with the Bender designs for a second drawing at the end of the test, interfered with his otherwise normal performance and increased his Z-score from 47 on the standard drawing to 64 on the BIP drawing, an increase which strengthens the perceptual problem diagnosis.

The Hiskey-Nebraska (as well as the Bender) substantiates a problem of poor visual orientation and perceptual disorganization. His scores reveal unpredictable performance on visual and/or motor tasks.

A discrepency is revealed between classroom performance and test performance. In the school situation, HS is not producing according to capacity, yet on the WRAT, he achieved and maintained his expectancy level. His arithmetic achievement, the lowest of the three at 10.8, is commensurate with his scaled score of 11 on the WISC arithmetic subtest, and his achievements at grades 12 on spelling and 13 on reading reach the expectancy level of his superior verbal I.Q.

Reason for his lack of motivation cannot be determined by the test results alone. Further counseling with the parents is recommended.

_____

Consultant

ADDENDUM

A follow-up counseling session was held with the mother who revealed that HS was inconsistent in his study habits and that his inconsistency may have been the result of a lack of motivation. In a later counseling session with HS, he learned of and was surprised by his intellectual level. He showed great concern over his possible perceptual problem, but his understanding of it apparently gave him confidence. A six weeks' progress report showed that HS had raised all his grades, even math. The parents probably used better judgment thereafter in their handling of him.

PSYCHOMETRIC SUMMARY

Intelligence Tests:

Wechsler Intelligence Scales

_____WPPSI   __√__WISC   _____WAIS

WPPSI Scaled Scores

Verbal

Information_____
Comprehension_____
Arithmetic_____
Similarities_____
Vocabulary_____
(Sentences)_____

Performance

Animal House_____
Picture Completion_____
Mazes_____
Geometric Design_____
Block Design_____
Animal House
(Retest)_____

WISC and WAIS Scaled Scores

Verbal

Information____16____
Comprehension____14____
Arithmetic____11____
Similarities____14____
Vocabulary____15____
Digit Span____11____

Performance

Picture Completion____11____
Picture Arrangement____12____
Block Design____14____
Object Assembly____12____
Coding or Digit Symbol____11____
Mazes_____

Verbal Scale I.Q.____125____
Performance Scale I.Q.____114____
Full Scale I.Q.____112____

Stanford-Binet (Form L-M)
C.A._____
M.A._____
I.Q._____

Draw-A-Person Test
C.A._____
M.A._____
I.Q._____

Peabody Picture Vocabulary
C.A.__15-4__
M.A.__18+__
I.Q.__130__

Wide Range Achievement Test

Reading Grade Level__13.0__ Standard Score__121__ Percentile_____
Spelling Grade Level__12.0__ Standard Score__115__ Percentile_____
Arithmetic Grade Level__10.8__ Standard Score__108__ Percentile_____

Purdue Perceptual-Motor
Survey_____

Wepman Auditory Discrimination
Test__Perfect Score__

Children's Apperception
Test_____

Memory-For-Designs Test
__Normal Record__

Bender Visual-Motor
Gestalt Test__Normal Record__

Illinois Test of Psycholinguistic
Abilities (See ITPA Profile)
Total Language_____
Scaled Score_____

Hiskey-Nebraska Test

Bead Pattern_____
Memory for Colors_____
Picture Identification_____
Picture Association_____
Paper Folding_____

Visual Attention Span__12-6__
Block Patterns_____
Completion of Drawings__17-6__
Memory for Digits_____
Puzzle Analogies__16-6__
Spatial Reasoning__15-6__

Other Tests: Canter BIP Edition : Atypical Record

20.   Case of KR.   *Mild visual-motor and memory sequencing*
problems.

The parents referred KR because they wished to have an understanding of her tendency toward failure.

NAME KR   EXAMINER Jane Doe

                                    DATE OF
DATE OF BIRTH   EXAMINATION   C.A. 14–2

EVALUATION FOR LEARNING DISABILITIES

BEHAVIOR AND APPEARANCE

Normal in height and weight for a fourteen-year-old, KR was a very
attractive young lady with dark hair. Dressed appropriately in very
good clothing, she was well-groomed, clean, and neat.

KR was pleasant and friendly, yet quiet and reserved. For the most
part she worked normally with the test materials, but she needed more
time than usual to study and choose between stimulus figures. The
testing progressed rather smoothly.

TEST RESULTS

See Psychometric Summary.

SUMMARY

Examination found KR functioning in the normal range of intellectual
ability with a Full Scale WISC I.Q. of 109 and a PPVT I.Q. of 112.
Her verbal and performance abilities differ significantly. While her verbal
I.Q. of 100 is at the mean normal level, her performance I.Q. of 117
ranges into the very bright level. Scatter in both areas show weaknesses
as well as strengths.

In the verbal area her weaknesses were reflected in range of information, vocabulary, and memory for digits, all of which were at the low
normal level. This kind of achievement pattern is common for those
who do not read a great deal. In contrast, KR reached the high average
level in comprehension and concept formation and the mean normal
level in arithmetical reasoning. On the arithmetic test she missed one
response because she was pressed for time; however, her reasoning was
correct.

The block design score was the only performance score that fell below normal. KR became confused with one design and continued to repeat the same mistakes. This low score may have occurred by chance even though it fell significantly below the coding and picture completion scores. But when KR has to organize and coordinate new visual-motor tasks, she does not perform as accurately and consistently as she does when discriminating differences or copying previously practiced eye-hand coordination tasks. On these latter tasks her functioning was superior.

The WRAT reveals slight underachievement with a reading level of grade 7.3, a spelling level of grade 6.7, and an arithmetic level of grade 8.0. According to KR's I.Q. she should be achieving more consistently at the middle eighth-grade level and above.

The Bender-Gestalt test recorded atypical behavior. (No quantitative score could be established for her because she is too old for the Koppitz scoring system and too young for the Pascall and Suttel scoring system.) In spite of her above average abilities in the performance area, KR has an apparent visual-motor problem, for she made small circles instead of dots on designs 1, 3, and 5, and she erased more than usual. She had to work slowly and carefully in order to reproduce the designs as well as she did. KR's more normal achievement on the MFD suggests that she can perform visual-motor functions more easily when she reproduces designs from memory rather than copies them from the original. In other words, when the visual stimulus is present, the integration of visual and motor functions may be disruptive to her working behavior.

The ITPA (1961 edition) and the Hiskey-Nebraska scales provide further reasons for KR's underachievement, although there are no norms above nine years on the ITPA. Because of poor association at the representational level she missed some of her visual cues (see Scale 4, ITPA Profile), and she scored only one point above the top norm of 8–6 at the automatic-sequential level, suggesting that she has difficulty remembering the sequence of auditory symbols. Although her visual-motor sequential score was above the norm of nine years, those mistakes that she made suggesting a weakness in this area reveal that KR is having trouble with the recall of symbol sequences, which is a common factor influencing the achievement of reading and spelling. The Hiskey picture analogies subtest, locating KR's learning age at 14–0, further substantiates her poor association at the representational level, yet on the spatial reasoning subtest she scored above normal. It thus appears that KR is experiencing some visual-motor problems in making associations and in memory for proper symbol sequences. There is no evidence that these weaknesses are severe, but they could be considered possible causes for her underachievement.

Remediation techniques for such weaknesses can be found in *Aids to Psycholinguistic Teaching* (Bush & Giles, 1969). KR can practice some of these tasks daily, particularly those which deal with kinesthetic approaches such as writing spelling words in the air or on textured materials to get the *feel* of the word. Some supervision should be provided to assure accurate reproduction of letters. In addition KR should memorize difficult word spellings the night before she uses them in English themes. Overlearning is always necessary when a memory problem is involved. KR's problem is one that could relate to any academic weakness.

Consultant

PSYCHOMETRIC SUMMARY

Intelligence Tests:

Wechsler Intelligence Scales

_____WPPSI   _✓_WISC   _____WAIS

WPPSI Scaled Scores

Verbal	Performance
Information_____	Animal House_____
Comprehension_____	Picture Completion_____
Arithmetic_____	Mazes_____
Similarities_____	Geometric Design_____
Vocabulary_____	Block Design_____
(Sentences)_____	Animal House (Retest)_____

WISC and WAIS Scaled Scores

Verbal		Performance	
Information	7	Picture Completion	14
Comprehension	12	Picture Arrangement	12
Arithmetic	10	Block Design	9
Similarities	12	Object Assembly	12
Vocabulary	9	Coding or Digit Symbol	15
Digit Span	8	Mazes	

Verbal Scale I.Q._____100_____
Performance Scale I.Q.__117_____
Full Scale I.Q._____109_____

Stanford-Binet (Form L-M)	Draw-A-Person Test	Peabody Picture Vocabulary
C.A._____	C.A._____	C.A._14-2_
M.A._____	M.A._____	M.A._15-3_
I.Q._____	I.Q._____	I.Q._106_

Wide Range Achievement Test

Reading Grade Level_7.5_	Standard Score_93_	Percentile_____
Spelling Grade Level_6.7_	Standard Score_88_	Percentile_____
Arithmetic Grade Level_8.0_	Standard Score_95_	Percentile_____

Purdue Perceptual-Motor Survey_____

Wepman Auditory Discrimination Test_____

Children's Apperception Test_____

Memory-For-Designs Test
_____Normal_____

Bender Visual-Motor Gestalt Test____Atypical____

Illinois Test of Psycholinguistic Abilities (See ITPA Profile)
Total Language_____
Scaled Score_____

Hiskey-Nebraska Test

Bead Pattern_____	Visual Attention Span_____
Memory for Colors_____	Block Patterns_____
Picture Identification_____	Completion of Drawings_____
Picture Association_____	Memory for Digits_____
Paper Folding_____	Puzzle Analogies_14-0_
	Spatial Reasoning_14-6_

Other Tests:

Name _____ CASE OF KR _____ Age 14-2 _____ Birthdate _____

ILLINOIS TEST OF PSYCHOLINGUISTIC ABILITIES
(Experimental Edition, 1961)

CA: 14-2

	REPRESENTATIONAL LEVEL						AUTOMATIC-SEQUENTIAL LEVEL		
	DECODING		ASSOCIATIONAL		ENCODING		AUTOMATIC	SEQUENTIAL	
Language Age	Auditory	Visual	Auditory-Vocal	Visual-Motor	Vocal	Motor	Auditory-Vocal	Auditory-Vocal	Visual-Motor
	1	2	3	4	5	6	7	8	9
9-0									
8-6									
8-0									
7-6									
7-0									
6-6									
6-0									
5-6									
5-0									
4-6									
4-0									
3-6									
3-0									
2-6									
	AN	AN	AN	9-3	AN	AN	AN	8-10	AN
	Comprehension of spoken word.	Comprehension of picture and written word.	Ability to relate spoken words in a meaningful way (auditory symbols)	Ability to relate visual symbols in a meaningful way	Ability to express ideas in spoken words	Ability to express ideas in gestures	Ability to predict future linguistic events from past experiences	Memory of auditory symbols	Memory of visual symbols

21. Case of GR. *Slow learner, auditory and kinesthetic (dyspraxia) deficiences.*

This case was referred to recheck intellectual and learning disability status.

NAME   **GR**   EXAMINER   Jane Doe

DATE OF BIRTH   DATE OF EXAMINATION   C.A. 12–9

EVALUATION FOR LEARNING DISABILITIES

BEHAVIOR AND APPEARANCE

GR was a nice-looking young adolescent who appeared to be normal in physiological growth and development for his 12 years and 9 months. He wore heavy bangs with a relatively short hair cut and he was dressed casually in good school clothes.

At the outset he was quiet and somewhat shy and throughout the testing he maintained this manner of response. He did, however, answer all questions and was obediently compliant.

One other overt behaviorism was his manner of speech. It was difficult to discriminate his "muffled" words each time he spoke. He did not project his speech articulation distinctly, and often it was necessary to ask him to repeat his answers.

RESULTS

See Psychometric Summary.

SUMMARY

GR was examined and found to be functioning in the dull normal range of intellectual ability. His WISC-R Full Scale I.Q. was found to be 84, his verbal I.Q. 81, and his performance I.Q. 88. A vocabulary I.Q. of 84 was obtained on the PPVT. In comparison to his scores at C.A. 9–4, GR has shown an increase in his global verbal ability. His Stanford Binet I.Q. at that age was found to be 73; however, the normal level of function found in his picture vocabulary ability was not found in the present battery. There was a slight drop in score on the PPVT.

Though the present I.Q. scores suggest a level of intellectual function in the dull normal range, the scatter of abilities in the test reflect some strengths in the normal area of function. The verbal subtests showed normal comprehension but low normal ability in memory for range of information, and borderline retardation in arithmetical reasoning, vocabulary, memory for digits, and abstract thinking. The weaknesses found here were also found in the *Detroit Tests of Learning Aptitude,* with the auditory problem detected earlier still a major problem at the present time. It seems apparent that there has been an auditory perceptual deficiency throughout his life.

Whereas visual perception is not seen to be consistently at the normal level, there are many tasks found to be normal. His ability to visually discriminate essential from nonessential details and to visually organize and sequence pictures in proper meaningful order were all found to be normal. His visual-motor speed, however, was found to be somewhat slower in function. The DTLA motor speed test also reflected this latter weakness. Both the Bender and the MFD figures suggested that GR has a mild eye-hand coordination problem. His visual spatial ability, while apparently normal, differs from his eye-hand coordination. When he was required to make motor responses to visual tasks, as in pencil manipulation and speech, GR found it difficult to produce adequate results.

The SOI factors from the DTLA emphasized some memory weaknesses, kinesthetic disturbance in fine-motor tasks, and weaknesses in knowledge of social comprehension. This added emphasis seems to depict the global learning problem that GR has had to deal with throughout his elementary grades. However, GR's greatest deficiencies still appear to be in the auditory channel and in his lack of ability to control purposeful movements (dyspraxia).

The WRAT showed that he is achieving at grade 4.4 in reading, grade 3.0 in spelling, and at grade 2.9 in arithmetic. These levels are slightly below expectancy for GR.

There is an apparent weakness in arithmetical reasoning as shown by the WISC-R arithmetic subtest and the WRAT. He missed all of the division and multiplication problems (WRAT) and even missed one subtraction problem. It seems evident that he needs to review basic math facts. In reading and spelling he lacked phonetic skills in his approach, which possibly (with his memory deficiencies in both auditory and visual tasks) accounts for his low achievement in these subjects.

Since there are perceptive deficiencies of long duration with verbal weaknesses still evident (though somewhat improved), it is recommended that GR be placed in language/learning disability training at the junior high level. It would also appear wise to direct him toward a vocational curriculum, since he would have great difficulty in regular math and language at the secondary level.

—————————————
Consultant

DETROIT TEST OF LEARNING APTITUDE PROFILE
Ages 9–13 years

Name _____   C.A._____

Observations

	Code	06	07	08	09	10	11	12	13	14	15	16	17	18	Years
2. Verbal Absurdities	RC,VA														
4. Verbal Opposites	VA														
5. Motor Speed and Precision	PJ,MA														
6. Auditory Attention Span for Unrelated Words	AAA														
8. Social Adjustments	RC														
9. Visual Attention Span for Objects	VAA														
10. Orientation	RC,PJ,TSR														
11. Free Association	VA														
12. Memory for Designs	TSR,VAA,MA														
13. Auditory Attention Span for Related Syllables	AAA														
15. Social Adjustment	RC														
16. Visual Attention Span for Letters															
17. Disarranged Pictures	RC,TSR,VAA														
18. Oral Directions	PJ,AAA,VAA,MA														
19. Likenesses and Differences	VA														

Code Legend

RC:	Reading and Comprehension	NA:	Number Ability
PJ:	Practical Judgment	AAA:	Auditory Attentive Ability
VA:	Verbal Ability	VAA:	Visual Attentive Ability
TSR:	Time and Space Relationships	MA:	Motor Ability

253

PSYCHOMETRIC SUMMARY

Intelligence Tests:

Wechsler Intelligence Scales

_____WPPSI   ✓ WISC   _____WAIS

WPPSI Scaled Scores

Verbal   Performance

Information_____   Animal House_____
Comprehension_____   Picture Completion_____
Arithmetic_____   Mazes_____
Similarities_____   Geometric Design_____
Vocabulary_____   Block Design_____
(Sentences)_____   Animal House
                                              (Retest)

WISC and WAIS Scaled Scores

Verbal   Performance

Information__ *8*_____   Picture Completion___ *12*_____
Comprehension__ *6*_____   Picture Arrangement___ *9*____
Arithmetic__ *5*_____   Block Design____ *7*_____
Similarities__ *5*_____   Object Assembly___ *10*_____
Vocabulary__ *11*_____   Coding or Digit Symbol_ *4*___
Digit Span__ *6*_____   Mazes

Verbal Scale I.Q.___ *81*_____
Performance Scale I.Q.__ *88*___
Full Scale I.Q.____ *84*_____

Stanford-Binet (Form L-M)   Draw-A-Person Test   Peabody Picture Vocabulary
C.A._____   C.A._ *12-9*___   C.A._ *12-9*___
M.A._____   M.A._ *6-9*____   M.A._ *10-5*___
I.Q._____   I.Q._____—____   I.Q._ *84*_____

Wide Range Achievement Test

Reading Grade Level__ *4.4*_____Standard Score__ *78*___Percentile_____
Spelling Grade Level___ *3.0*_____Standard Score__ *69*___Percentile_____
Arithmetic Grade Level__ *2.9*_____Standard Score__ *69*___Percentile_____

Purdue Perceptual Motor   Wepman Auditory Discrimination
   Survey_____   Test__ *X=7/30 Y=1/10*____

Children's Apperception   Memory-For-Designs Test
   Test_____   *Below Average*

Bender Visual-Motor   Illinois Test of Psycholinguistic
   Gestalt Test___ *Below Average*___   Abilities (See ITPA Profile)
                                     Total Language____ *(MED) 9-0*____
                                     Scaled Score_____

Hiskey-Nebraska Test

Bead Pattern_____   Visual Attention Span_____
Memory for Colors_____   Block Patterns_____
Picture Identification_____   Completion of Drawings_____
Picture Association_____   Memory for Digits_____
Paper Folding_____   Puzzle Analogies_____
                                       Spatial Reasoning_____

Other Tests:

Name __GR__

School _____

Age __12__

Information	Meeker Text pp. 137–138	WISC

Picture Completion

MMU _____	(_____)	CFU _____ (_____)
MMR _____	(_____)	CFS _____ (_____)
MSS _____	(_____)	Picture Arrangement
CMU _____	(_____)	EMR _____ (_____)
MMS _____	(_____)	NMS _____ (_____)
NMR _____	(_____)	Block Design
NMU _____	(_____)	CFR _____ (_____)
EMR _____	(_____)	EFR _____ (_____)

Comprehension

EMI _____	(_____)	Object Assembly
Arithmetic		CFS _____ (_____)
MSI _____	(_____)	CFT _____ (_____)
CMS _____	(_____)	EFR _____ (_____)
Similarities		Coding
EMR _____	(_____)	NFU _____ (_____)
CMT _____	(_____)	EFU _____ (_____)
Vocabulary		NSU _____ (_____)
CMU _____	(_____)	ESU _____ (_____)
Digits		Mazes
MSS-F _____	(_____)	CFI _____ (_____)

(WISC-R)

(No norms for the revised WISC)

C _____ (___) _____

M _____ (___) _____

E _____ (___) _____

N _____ (___) _____

ITPA

Strengths (Tests)	SOI	Weaknesses (Tests)	SOI
_____	_____	_____	_____
_____	_____	_____	_____
_____	_____	_____	_____
_____	_____	_____	_____
_____	_____	_____	_____
_____	_____	_____	_____
_____	_____	_____	_____

DETROIT

Strengths (Tests)	SOI	Weaknesses (Tests)	SOI
_____	_____	Verbal DPP	CMR-NMR, DMS
_____	_____	Motor Speed	NFU-KIN
_____	_____	Aud Att Un Wds	MMU
_____	_____	Vis Att Obj	MFU-VIS
_____	_____	Aud Att Sub	MMS
_____	_____	Soc Adj B	CMU
_____	_____	Vis Att Let	MSU-VIS

SLOSSON (from 2–0)

Correct		Incorrect	Correct		Incorrect
_____	CMU	_____	_____	MMU	_____
_____	CMS	_____	_____	EFU	_____
_____	CMC	_____	_____	EMR	_____
_____	CMI	_____	_____	NFU	_____
_____	CMR	_____	_____	NMR	_____
_____	MSU	_____	_____	NMI	_____
_____	MMS	_____	_____	NMU	_____
_____	MSI	_____	_____		_____
_____	MSS	_____	_____		_____

From Mary N. Meeker, *The Structure of Intellect* (Columbus: Charles E. Merrill, 1969). Adapted by Marjorie Rives, Educational Diagnostician, Eastern Panhandle Cooperative, Shamrock, Texas.

		Figural	Symbolic	Semantic	Behavioral
Units	C			*cmU*	
	M	*mFU-Vis*	*msu Vis*	*mmU*	
	E				
	N	*NFU*			
	D				
Classes	C				
	M				
	E				
	N				
	D				
Relations	C			*cmR*	
	M				
	E				
	N			*NmR*	
	D				
Systems	C				
	M			*mms*	
	E				
	N				
	D			*Oms*	
Transformations	C				
	M				
	E				
	N				
	D				
Implications	C				
	M				
	E				
	N				
	D				

Other Information

From Mary N. Meeker, *The Structure of Intellect* (Columbus: Charles E. Merrill, 1969). Adapted by Marjorie Rives, Educational Diagnostician, Eastern Panhandle Cooperative, Shamrock, Texas.

SENIOR HIGH SCHOOL

At the high school level, most students have learned how to compensate for their learning problems without counseling. For this reason perhaps there are fewer referrals at this level. Students are usually referred either because parents are concerned about college potential or because parents desire evaluations of interest, temperament, and aptitude in situations concerning dropouts or potential dropouts. Case 22 in particular was referred for these reasons.

The following three cases all suggest visual-motor problems, but only one reveals auditory impairment. Subtle auditory problems, which can be detected by tests in the younger years, are difficult to discover in youth of high school age and even more difficult to detect in some adults. But modern testing instruments have made it much easier to detect visual-motor problems.

22. Case of Brent. *Potential dropout with a visual-motor problem.*

This case was referred by the parents to try to keep Brent in school.

NAME __Brent_____ EXAMINER __Jane Doe_____

DATE OF BIRTH _____ DATE OF EXAMINATION_____ C.A. __16–3__

EVALUATION FOR LEARNING DISABILITIES

BEHAVIOR AND APPEARANCE

Brent had light brown hair and brown eyes, and he was normal in height and weight for a sixteen-year-old. His hair was very curly and tousled, his face sprinkled with a number of pimples, and his ruffled western shirt was open at the neck. Brent was right-handed, and his writing habits were normal except that he often gripped the pencil too tightly. His cooperation allowed the testing to progress smoothly, even though he displayed a mild shyness.

TEST RESULTS

See Psychometric Summary.

SUMMARY

Examination of Brent found him functioning in the normal range of intellectual ability with a WAIS Full Scale I.Q. of 102 and a PPVT

I.Q. of 108. No variance between the verbal and performance scores occurred on the WAIS, but scatter within each area suggests significant weaknesses in his ability to function academically.

In the verbal area his vocabulary, reasoning, and concept formation show normal achievement, while his range of information and comprehension, although still normal, show a lag. The digit span score of six suggests a significant weakness in memory or immediate recall of digits. This kind of verbal score pattern is typical for cases in which anxiety and/or poor memory influence the ability to function.

The performance area also reveals both strengths and weaknesses. The test pattern scores and Brent's approach to the tasks suggest that he is missing too many visual cues. His failure to see such cues as water not flowing from a tilted water pitcher and the missing handle on a car door provides evidence of a mild visual discrimination problem. On the MFD he made a few mistakes, but for the most part his performance was normal. The Bender-Gestalt, however, reveals one significant feature common to visual-motor problems — Brent drew small circles instead of dots, indicating slight imperception even though his global score was normal. His multiplying instead of adding on the arithmetic test also indicates this mild perceptual problem. Evidently he mistook the plus symbol for a multiplication sign.

The WRAT shows achievement below expectancy. His seventh and eighth grade performances in reading, spelling, and arithmetic show that Brent is strongly influenced by a visual-motor problem and/or possible psychological problems.

Brent's shyness may suggest insecurity. If further information can substantiate psychogenic problems, he should undergo psychological treatment. The family physician should be consulted in this regard.

Brent's mild visual-motor problem may have been an influencing factor throughout his schooling, and because of lack of help his achievement may have become progressively worse. However, he shows the capacity to compete normally, a capacity of which he should be informed. Counseling will also recommend some remedial aids. These will be elementary, but if Brent is willing, he can probably show a measurable learning increase in his academic work. Every effort should be made to keep him in school.

The elementary remedial techniques should include a series of perceptual-motor exercises with a structured developmental visual perception program. A trained reading specialist should work with him, and his counseling should continue.

_____

Consultant

PSYCHOMETRIC SUMMARY

Intelligence Tests:

Wechsler Intelligence Scales

_____WPPSI   _____WISC   _√_WAIS

WPPSI Scaled Scores

Verbal		Performance	
Information_____		Animal House_____	
Comprehension_____		Picture Completion_____	
Arithmetic_____		Mazes_____	
Similarities_____		Geometric Design_____	
Vocabulary_____		Block Design_____	
(Sentences)_____		Animal House	
		(Retest)_____	

WISC and WAIS Scaled Scores

Verbal		Performance	
Information	9	Picture Completion	8
Comprehension	9	Picture Arrangement	15
Arithmetic	11	Block Design	9
Similarities	12	Object Assembly	8
Vocabulary	10	Coding or Digit Symbol	10
Digit Span	6	Mazes	

Verbal Scale I.Q. ___102___
Performance Scale I.Q. ___102___
Full Scale I.Q. ___102___

Stanford-Binet (Form L-M)	Draw-A-Person Test	Peabody Picture Vocabulary
C.A._____	C.A._____	C.A. _16-3_
M.A._____	M.A._____	M.A. _18-0_
I.Q._____	I.Q._____	I.Q. _108_

Wide Range Achievement Test

Reading Grade Level___8.1___ Standard Score_92_Percentile_____
Spelling Grade Level___7.6___ Standard Score_89_Percentile_____
Arithmetic Grade Level___7.4___ Standard Score_88_Percentile_____

Purdue Perceptual-Motor
Survey_____

Wepman Auditory Discrimination
Test_____

Children's Apperception
Test_____

Memory-For-Designs Test
Normal Range

Bender Visual-Motor
Gestalt Test_Normal Range_

Illinois Test of Psycholinguistic
Abilities (See ITPA Profile)
Total Language_____
Scaled Score_____

Hiskey-Nebraska Test

Bead Pattern_____		Visual Attention Span_____	
Memory for Colors_____		Block Patterns_____	
Picture Identification_____		Completion of Drawings_____	
Picture Association_____		Memory for Digits_____	
Paper Folding_____		Puzzle Analogies_____	
		Spatial Reasoning_____	

Other Tests:

23.   Case of Sam.   *Slow visual-motor function.*

Referral was made by the mother to help determine future planning as it concerns college potential and vocational aptitude.

NAME   Sam   EXAMINER   Jane Doe

	DATE OF	
DATE OF BIRTH	EXAMINATION	C.A. 17–0

EVALUATION FOR LEARNING DISABILITIES

BEHAVIOR AND APPEARANCE

Sam was a nice-looking seventeen-year-old with ash-blond hair and hazel eyes. He was appropriately and stylishly dressed, and he was neat and clean.

Observation found Sam using a cautious approach to many of the tasks as though he were planning rather than working on impulse. Because he cooperated fully, the testing progressed quite well.

TEST RESULTS

See Psychometric Summary.

SUMMARY

Examination of Sam found him functioning in the normal range of intellectual ability with a Full Scale WAIS I.Q. of 105 and a PPVT I.Q. of 104. Some extreme scatter reveals that he has strengths ranging into the superior level and weaknesses falling to the low normal level. His range of information, reasoning, vocabulary, and visual-motor abilities all fell at the low normal level; his visual discrimination, memory, and concept formation all fell at the normal level; and his comprehension reached the superior level.

The Wide Range Achievement Test showed grade level placements of 11.6 in reading, 9.6 in spelling, and 10.1 in arithmetic. His reading level, suggesting adequate word recognition, is commensurate with his I.Q. His spelling and arithmetic levels are commensurate with some aspects of the WAIS such as low normal reasoning and low normal visual-motor abilities. These low scores on the WAIS suggest the possibility of a perceptual-motor problem which could have caused the drop in academic achievement. Sam will likely continue to experience difficulty when confronted with visual-motor tasks, but his cautious approach will probably prevent any serious difficulty. His careful work with the Bender figures and with the MFD designs shows how he has been compensating, for his achievements on these were normal. The WAIS indicates that Sam has slow visual-motor responses, although his spatial ability alone does not seem to be a problem.

Aptitude test scores reveal Sam's inclinations toward clerical routine, computation, and general sales. (Computation is not the same as arithmetical reasoning.) In clerical routine and computation he should be able to perform better than any 94 out of 100 people, whereas he should be able to handle general sales better than any 59 out of 100 people.

Sam shows a stronger interest in general sales than in clerical routine; however, it is not unusual for interests to change, particularly those of young people. This test of interests also shows the fact that Sam is average in his power-seeking need and that he has a desire for self-aggrandizement. Although he works at a cautious and deliberate pace, he shows a normal attitude toward vigorous activities. His social interests and emotional stability also are normal.

Sam has a normal global intelligence with some erratic functioning, which suggests that he has always had a mild learning disorder. His lowered vocabulary and reasoning abilities could hinder his performance at the college level, but his strengths suggest that he may be able to counteract these weaknesses. A business career in general sales should be given consideration in planning for the future.

_____

Consultant

PSYCHOMETRIC SUMMARY

Intelligence Tests:

Wechsler Intelligence Scales

_____WPPSI _____WISC __✓__WAIS

WPPSI Scaled Scores

Verbal	Performance
Information_____	Animal House_____
Comprehension_____	Picture Completion_____
Arithmetic_____	Mazes_____
Similarities_____	Geometric Design_____
Vocabulary_____	Block Design_____
(Sentences)_____	Animal House
	(Retest)_____

WISC and WAIS Scaled Scores

Verbal		Performance	
Information	9	Picture Completion	11
Comprehension	18	Picture Arrangement	9
Arithmetic	8	Block Design	8
Similarities	12	Object Assembly	9
Vocabulary	9	Coding or Digit Symbol	8
Digit Span	11	Mazes	

Verbal Scale I.Q.___112___
Performance Scale I.Q.__95___
Full Scale I.Q.___105___

Stanford-Binet (Form L-M)	Draw-A-Person Test	Peabody Picture Vocabulary
C.A._____	C.A._____	C.A. 17-0
M.A._____	M.A._____	M.A. 18-0
I.Q._____	I.Q._____	I.Q. 104

Wide Range Achievement Test

Reading Grade Level___11.6_____Standard Score_____Percentile_____
Spelling Grade Level___9.6_____Standard Score_____Percentile_____
Arithmetic Grade Level__10.1_____Standard Score_____Percentile_____

Purdue Perceptual-Motor
Survey_____

Wepman Auditory Discrimination
Test_____

Children's Apperception
Test_____

Memory-For-Designs Test
Normal Range

Bender Visual-Motor
Gestalt Test_Normal Range_

Illinois Test of Psycholinguistic
Abilities (See ITPA Profile)
Total Language_____
Scaled Score_____

Hiskey-Nebraska Test

Bead Pattern_____	Visual Attention Span_____
Memory for Colors_____	Block Patterns_____
Picture Identification_____	Completion of Drawings_____
Picture Association_____	Memory for Digits_____
Paper Folding_____	Puzzle Analogies_____
	Spatial Reasoning_____

Other Tests: How Well Do You Know Your Interests
Thurstone Temperament
Aptitude Tests for Occupations

262

24.   Case of CJ.   *Visual-motor and auditory reception problems.*

Referral was made by the parents to determine what procedure to follow in order to keep CJ in school.

NAME __CJ_____   EXAMINER __Jane Doe_____

DATE OF BIRTH_____   DATE OF
                                EXAMINATION_____   C.A. __17–11__

EVALUATION FOR LEARNING DISABILITIES

BEHAVIOR AND APPEARANCE

CJ had blond hair and blue eyes, and he was tall and thin. His dress was casual yet appropriate, and he wore very modified bangs. He was pleasant and friendly though reticent, and he spoke with a drawl. As he worked, he kept his mouth open slightly; his breathing was loud, but he seemed unaware of it. He mentioned that he had a sore throat.

CJ's full cooperation allowed the testing to progress very smoothly. He made many extraneous remarks, associating what he was doing with some of his other experiences. He related warmly, and he did not appear to be apprehensive or insecure.

TEST RESULTS

See Psychometric Summary.

SUMMARY

Examination found CJ functioning on the borderline of mild retardation with a PPVT I.Q. of 74 and a WAIS I.Q. of 79. The WAIS verbal I.Q. of 82 suggests dull verbal ability, but this is misleading, as are the PPVT and WAIS I.Q.'s, since CJ shows extreme scatter with some subtests revealing normal scores.

In the verbal area he achieved normal comprehension and normal concept formation. His reasoning, vocabulary, and range of information were mildly retarded, while his memory for digits was severely retarded.

In the performance area CJ's perceptual ability to discriminate essential from nonessential detail fell at the low normal level, and his visual organization at the dull level. Because the other visual-motor tasks ranged only slightly below these, the performance area reflects a more stable functioning in the dull range.

The WRAT scores reveal levels of achievement between the fourth and fifth grades in reading, spelling, and arithmetic. These achievements are commensurate with his capacity except that they do not reflect his greater strengths in comprehension and concept formation. The weakness in memory for digits or symbols possibly limits the help that these strengths may give him; he cannot depend on memory as an aid.

The Bender-Gestalt record shows a Z-score of 66, which is at a borderline position outside the normal range, suggesting poor visual-motor coordination. The MFD difference score of -2 places him in the normal range when compared to individuals with visual-motor problems. The discrepancy between the two scores on the Bender-Gestalt and the MFD suggests his motor coordination is improved if he does not look at the design to be copied as he draws. The normal MFD score, in contrast to the digit span score of 2 on the WAIS, suggests that CJ has no difficulty remembering very simple visual symbols but great difficulty recalling auditory symbols. The digit symbol score of 5 suggests a slow psychomotor speed.

That CJ has often experienced failure is understandable, and were he not in a small high school that offers individual help, he would not have been able to compete as successfully as he has. To expect more from him without highly specialized tutoring is unrealistic. He should undergo remediation in the form of kinesthetic, auditory, and visual perception aids. Difficult lessons recorded on tape for him to hear repeatedly may help him to develop a greater sense of achievement. Vocational training through the public school is also suggested.

_____

Consultant

PSYCHOMETRIC SUMMARY

Intelligence Tests:

Wechsler Intelligence Scales

_____WPPSI   _____WISC   _√_WAIS

WPPSI Scaled Scores

Verbal	Performance
Information_____	Animal House_____
Comprehension_____	Picture Completion_____
Arithmetic_____	Mazes_____
Similarities_____	Geometric Design_____
Vocabulary_____	Block Design_____
(Sentences)_____	Animal House
	(Retest)_____

WISC and WAIS Scaled Scores

Verbal		Performance	
Information	_5_	Picture Completion	_8_
Comprehension	_9_	Picture Arrangement	_6_
Arithmetic	_5_	Block Design	_7_
Similarities	_10_	Object Assembly	_6_
Vocabulary	_5_	Coding or Digit Symbol	_5_
Digit Span	_2_	Mazes	

Verbal Scale I.Q.____82____
Performance Scale I.Q. _78____
Full Scale I.Q.___ _79____

Stanford-Binet (Form L-M)	Draw-A-Person Test	Peabody Picture Vocabulary
C.A._____	C.A._____	C.A._17-11_
M.A._____	M.A._____	M.A._11-7_
I.Q._____	I.Q._____	I.Q._74_

Wide Range Achievement Test

Reading Grade Level_____4.6____Standard Score_74____Percentile_____
Spelling Grade Level_____5.5____Standard Score_79____Percentile_____
Arithmetic Grade Level____4.4____Standard Score_73____Percentile_____

Purdue Perceptual-Motor
Survey_____

Wepman Auditory Discrimination
Test_____

Children's Apperception
Test_____

Memory-For-Designs Test
_-2_

Bender Visual-Motor
Gestalt Test_____Z- score = 66____

Illinois Test of Psycholinguistic
Abilities (See ITPA Profile)
Total Language_____
Scaled Score_____

Hiskey-Nebraska Test

Bead Pattern_____	Visual Attention Span_____
Memory for Colors_____	Block Patterns_____
Picture Identification_____	Completion of Drawings_____
Picture Association_____	Memory for Digits_____
Paper Folding_____	Puzzle Analogies_____
	Spatial Reasoning_____

Other Tests:

Appendix

A. Stanford Binet Worksheet
B. Recommended Resources
C. Tests Useful in Evaluating Learning Disorders
D. Worksheet—Detroit Test of Learning Aptitude
    Profile-Ages 3-6
E. Worksheet—Detroit Test of Learning Aptitude
    Profile-Ages 7-8; 13
F. Worksheet—Detroit Test of Learning Aptitude
    Profile-Ages 9-12
G. Worksheet—Detroit Test of Learning Aptitude
    Profile-Age 14
H. Worksheet—Stanford Binet and Structure of Intellect
I. Structure of Intellect Definitions and Model
J. Structure of Intellect with Emphasis in Content and
    Products
K. Structure of Intellect Profile (Stanford Binet)
L. SOI Test Profile Information
M. SOI Deficiency Areas Profile
N. WISC-R Profile

A. STANFORD BINET WORKSHEET

Ceiling _____
Base _____

C.A. _____
M.A. _____
I.Q. _____

Year of Tests	2	2-6	3	3-6	4	4-6	5	6	7	8	9	10	11	12	13	14	AA	SAI	SA II	SA III
Language	3, 5, 6, A	1, 2, 3, 4	2		1, 4	A	3	1		1	4, A	1, 3, 5	3	1, 5, 6	2, 5	1	1, 3, 8	1, 3, 5	1	1
Meaningful (Memory)					2, A	5				2			4	4	3			4	6	6
Nonmeaningful (Memory)		5	A						6, A		6	6								
Visual (Memory)			4								3		1	A	6					
Conceptual Thinking					3	2		2, 5	2, 5	4			6			6	5, 7	6, A		2, 3, A
Verbal (Reasoning)	2									3	2	A	2	2	4	3			2, A	5
Nonverbal (Reasoning)				1, 2, 3, 5, A	5	3	5, 6	3							1	5	6			
Numerical (Reasoning)								4			5	2				2, 4, A	2, 4	2	4	4
Visual-Motor	1, 4	A	1, 3, 5, 6			1, 4, 6	1, 2, 4, A	6	3		1				A		A			
Social Intelligence		6		4, 6	6			A	1, 4	5, 6, A		4	5, A	3						

Factors

269

B. RECOMMENDED RESOURCES

AUDITORY PERCEPTION

Books:

Bereiter, C., & Englemann, S. *Language Learning Activities,* 1966. Anti-Defamation League of B'nai B'rith, 315 Lexington Avenue, New York, New York, 10016.

Hegge, T.G., Kirk, Winifred D., & Kirk, Samuel A. *Remedial Reading Drills.* Ann Arbor, Mi.: George Wahr Publishing Co., 1965.

Johnson, D., & Myklebust, H. *Children with Learning Disabilities.* New York: Grune and Stratton, 1967.

Miller, J.G. *Phonics First.* 4611 Cole Street, Amarillo, Tx., 79106, 1966.

Myklebust, H. *Progress in Learning Disabilities.* Vol. 1. New York: Grune and Stratton, 1967.

Programmed Activities:

Gillingham, A., & Stillman, B. *Remedial Training for Children with Specific Disability in Reading, Spelling, and Penmanship.* Cambridge, Ma.: Educators Publishing Service, 1960.

Sullivan Series for Reading. *Programmed Reading.* St. Louis, Mo.: Webster Division, McGraw-Hill Book Co., 1968.

Distar Program, Science Research Associates, Chicago, Il.

VISUAL PERCEPTION

Books:

Money, J. *Reading Disability.* Baltimore: John Hopkins Press, 1962.

Programmed Activities:

Frostig Visual Perception Program. Follett Publishing Co., 201 N. Wells Street, Chicago, Il., 60606.

Visual Perception Programs from Teaching Resources. 100 Boylston Street, Boston, Ma., 02116.
   a.   Ruth Cheeves Program
   b.   Dubnoff School Program

c. Pathway School Program
d. Fairbanks Robinson Program
e. Erie Program

PERCEPTUAL-MOTOR

Books:

Kephart, N.C. (Ed.) *The Slow Learner Series.* Columbus: Charles E. Merrill Publishing Co.
  a. Benyon, S.D. *Intensive Programming for Slow Learners,* 1968.
  b. Chaney, C.M., & Kephart, N.C. *Motoric Aids to Perceptual Training,* 1968.
  c. Ebersole, M., Kephart, N.C., & Ebersole, J. *Steps to Achievement for the Slow Learner,* 1968.
  d. Ismail, A.H. & Gruber, J.J. *Motor Aptitude and Intellectual Performance,* 1967.
  e. Kephart, N.C. *The Slow Learner in the Classroom,* 1960.
  f. Simpson, D. M. *Learning to Learn,* 1968.
  g. Nunn, N., & Jones, C. *The Learning Pyramid: Potential Through Perception,* 1973.

Barsch, R.H. *Achieving Perceptual-Motor Efficiency.* Seattle, Washington: Special Child Publications, 1967.

Cratty, B.J. *Developmental Sequences of Perceptual-Motor Tasks.* Freeport, L.I., N.Y.: Educational Activities, 1967.

PSYCHOLINGUISTIC AIDS

Bush, W.J., & Giles, M.T. *Aids to Psycholinguistic Teaching.* Columbus: Charles E. Merrill, 1969.

Kirk, S.A. *Diagnostic Remediation of Psycholinguistics.* Urbana, Il.: University of Illinois Press, 1966.

Mills, RE. *The Teaching of Word Recognition,* The Mills Center, 1512 E. Broward Blvd., Ft. Lauderdale, Fl.

Valett, R.E. *The Remediation of Learning Disabilities.* Palo Alto, Ca.: Fearon Publishers, 1968.

Wedemeyer, A., & Cejka, J. *Instructional Activities,* Love Publishing, 6635 East Villanova Place, Denver, 80222.

| Arithmetic Instructional Activities | 1972 |
| Creative Ideas for Exceptional Children | 1975 |

Language Instructional Activities   1972
Learning Games for Exceptional Children 1971

KINESTHETIC AIDS

Books:

Fernald, G. *Remedial Techniques in Basic School Subjects.* Manchester, Mo.: McGraw-Hill, 1943.

STRUCTURE OF INTELLECT AIDS (SOI)

Meeker, M. *SOI Abilities Workbooks.* SOI Institute, 214 Main, El Segundo, Ca., 90245.

MANUAL AND VERBAL EXPRESSIVE AIDS

Bates, E. *How to Make Puppets.* Canyon, Tx.: West Texas State University Press, 1975.
Bates, Enid, and Lowes, Ruth. *Potpourri of Puppetry.* Belmont, Ca.: Fearon Publishers/Lear Siegler Inc., 1976.

C. TESTS USEFUL IN EVALUATING LEARNING DISORDERS

INTELLIGENCE (CAPACITY)

1. *Arthur Point Scale of Performance Tests,* Revised Form II. Psychological Corp., 304 East 45th Street, New York, New York. 1943.
2. *Columbia Mental Maturity Scale,* (Rev. ed.) Harcourt Brace Jovanovich, 757 3rd Avenue, New York, New York. 1959.
3. *Draw-A-Person,* Harcourt Brace Jovanovich, 757 3rd Avenue, New York, New York. 1954.
4. *Full Range Picture Vocabulary Test.* Psychological Test Specialists, Missoula, Mt. 1948.
5. *Goodenough-Harris Drawing Test.* Harcourt Brace Jovanovich, 757 3rd Avenue, New York, New York. 1963.
6. *Hiskey-Nebraska Test of Learning Aptitude.* University of Nebraska, Lincoln, Ne. 1966.
7. *Leiter International Performance Scale.* Western Psychological Services, 12035 Wilshire Boulevard, Los Angeles, Ca. 1948.
8. *McCarthy Scale of Children's Abilities.* The Psychological Corporation, 757 3rd Avenue, New York, New York, 10017.
9. *Minnesota Pre-School Scale.* American Guidance Service, Publishers' Building, Circle Pines, Mn. 1940.
10. *Peabody Picture Vocabulary Test* (PPVT). American Guidance Service, Publishers' Building, Circle Pines, Mn. 1959.
11. *Pictorial Test of Intelligence.* Houghton Mifflin, 110 Tremont Street, Boston, Ma. 1964.
12. *Raven Progressive Matrices.* Psychological Corp., 304 East 45th Street, New York, New York. 1947.
13. *Slosson Intelligence Test* (SIT). Slosson Educational Publication, 140 Pine Street, E. Aurora, N.Y.
14. *Stanford-Binet Intelligence Scale.* Combined L-M Form. Houghton Mifflin, 110 Tremont Street, Boston, Ma. 1960.
15. *Wechsler Intelligence Scale for Adults* (WISC). Psychological Corp., 304 East 45th Street, New York, New York. 1949.
16. *Wechsler Intelligence Scale for Children* (WISC). Psychological Corp., 304 East 45th Street, New York, New York. 1949.

VISUAL-MOTOR PROBLEMS

1. *Ayres Test.* Western Psychological Services, 12031 Wilshire Blvd., Los Angeles, Ca., 90025.
   a. *Southern California Sensory Integration Tests*

    b. *Sensory Integration and Learning Disorders*
    c. *Southern California Test Battery for Assessment of Motor and Sensory Dysfunction*
    d. *Ayres Space Test*
    e. *Southern California Kinesthesia And Tactile Perception Tests*
    f. *Southern California Figure-Ground Visual Perception Test*
    g. *Southern California Motor Accuracy Test*
    h. *Southern California Perceptual-Motor Tests*

2. *Bender Visual-Motor Gestalt Test.* Psychological Corp., 304 East 45th Street, New York, New York. 1962.

3. *Benton Revised Visual Retention Test.* Psychological Corp., 304 East 45th Street, New York, New York. 1955.

4. *Goodenough-Harris Drawing Test.* Harcourt Brace Jovanovich, 757 3rd Avenue, New York, New York. 1963.

5. *Frostig Developmental Test of Visual Perception.* Consulting Psychological Press, Palo Alto, Ca. 1961.

6. *Lincoln-Oseretsky Motor Development Scale.* Western Psychological Services, 12035 Wilshire Blvd., Los Angeles, Ca. 1955.

7. *Memory-For-Designs Test.* Psychological Test Specialists, Box 1441, Missoula, Mt. 1960.

8. *Minnesota Percepto-Diagnostic Test.* Western Psychological Services, 12034 Wilshire Blvd., Los Angeles, Ca. 1964.

9. Perceptual Rating Survey Scale. In Kephart, N.C. *Slow Learner in the Classroom.* Columbus: Charles E. Merrill, 1960.

10. Purdue Perceptual-Motor Survey. Columbus: Charles E. Merrill, 1966.

11. *Visual-Motor Integration.* Follett Educational Corp., 1010 West Washington Blvd., Chicago, Il. 1967.

SELECTED READING TESTS (LEVEL AND ANALYTIC)

1. *Auditory Blending Test.* Essay Press, Box 5, Planetarium Station, New York, New York. 1963.

2. *California Reading Test.* California Test Bureau, Del Monte Research Park, Monterey, Ca. 1957 edition, 1963 norms.

3. *Diagnostic Reading Test of Word Analysis Skills.* Essay Press, Box 5, Planetarium Station, New York, New York. 1959.

4. *Durrell Analysis of Reading Difficulty.* Harcourt Brace Jovanovich, 750 3rd Avenue, New York, New York. 1955.

5. (a) *Gates Primary Reading* (1st and 2nd grades); (b) *Gates Advanced Primary* (2nd and 3rd grades); (c) *Gates Reading Survey* (3rd–10th). Bureau of Publications, Columbia University, New York, New York. 1958.

6. *Gray Oral Reading Test.* Bobbs-Merrill, 1720 East 38th Street, Indianapolis, In. 1963.

7. *Iota Word Recognition.* In Monroe, M. *Diagnostic Reading Examination.* C.H. Stoelting Co., 424 North Homan Avenue, Chicago, Il. 1931.

8. *Spache Diagnostic Reading Scales.* California Test Bureau, Del Monte Research Park, Monterey, Ca. 1963.

9. *Word Discrimination.* In Monroe, M. *Diagnostic Reading Examination.* C.H. Stoelting Co. 424 Homan Avenue, Chicago, Il. 1931.

DEVELOPMENTAL LANGUAGE TESTS

1. *Illinois Test of Psycholinguistic Abilities.* University of Illinois Press, 4300 62nd St., Urbana, Il. 1968.

2. *Detroit Tests of Learning Aptitude.* Bobbs-Merrill, Inc. Indianapolis, In., 46206. 1955.

3. *Picture Story Language Test.* Grune and Stratton, 1965.

AUDITORY PERCEPTION

1. *Wepman's Auditory Discrimination Test.* Language Research Associates, 950 East 59th Street, Chicago, Il. 1958.

2. *Goldman-Fristoe-Woodcock-Test of Auditory Discrimination.* American Guidance Service Publishers Building, Circle Pine, Mn., 55015.

ACHIEVEMENT TESTS

1. *California Achievement Test* CTB/McGraw-Hill. Del Monte Research Park, Monterey, Ca., 93940.

2. *Keymath Diagnostic Arithmetic Test.* American Guidance Service Inc. Publisher's Building, Circle Pines, Mn., 55014.

3. *Peabody Individual Achievement Test.* American Guidance Service Inc. Publisher's Building, Circle Pines, Mn., 55014.

4. *Wide Range Achievement Test.* Psychological Corp., 304 East 45th Street, New York, New York. 1965.

CRITERION-REFERENCED TESTS

1. *Basic Schools Skills Inventory* (BSSI). Follett Publishing Co. 201 N. Wells St., Chicago, Il., 60606.

2. *Early Learning System.* SPECO Educational Systems, Inc. 1244 Security Drive, Dallas, Tx., 75247.

3. *Behavioral Characteristic Progression.* Santa Cruz County Office of Education, 701 Ocean Street, Room 200, Santa Cruz, Ca., 95060.

4. *Individual Criterion-referenced Tests* (ICRT). Educational Development Corporation, Tulsa, Ok.

5. *Prescriptive Reading Inventory* (PRI), CTB/McGraw-Hill. Del Monte Research Park, Monterey, Ca., 93940.

SOCIAL MATURITY SCALES

Preschool Attainment Record. American Guidance Service Inc., Publisher's Building, Circle Pines, Mn., 55014.

Vineland Social Maturity Scale. American Guidance Service Inc., Publisher's Building, Circle Pines, Mn., 55014.

TEACHER CHECKLIST AND SCREENING INSTRUMENTS

1. Clements, S.D. *Minimal Brain Dysfunction in Children.* U.S. Department of Health, Education and Welfare, Washington, D.C.

2. Giles, M.T. *Individual Learning Disabilities Classroom Screening Instrument: Pre-school, Kindergarten/Adolescent Levels.* Learning Pathways, Inc., P.O. Box 1407, Evergreen, Co., 80439.

3. Jansky, J. *The Jansky Screening Index.* 120 E. 89th St., New York, New York, 10028.

4. *L/D Screen Syllabication Test and Behavior Rating Scale.* Region X, Education Service Center, Richardson, Tx.

5. *Meeker-Cromwell Behavior Rating Scale.* SOI Institute, 214 Main, El Segundo, Ca., 90245. (Language progression and personality development-affective)

6. Meier, J.H., Cazier, V.O., & Giles, M.T. *Individual Learning Disabilities Classroom Screening Instrument.* Learning Pathways, Inc., P.O. Box 1407, Evergreen, Co., 80439.

7. Mills, R.E. *Learning Methods Test* (Rev. ed.) The Mills School, Inc., 1512 E. Broward Boulevard, Fort Lauderdale, Fl.

8. Slingerland, B.H., *Screening Tests for Identifying Children With Specific Learning Disabilities.* Educators Publishing Service, Cambridge, Ma., 02139.

9. Zevely, C.R., *Survey of Spelling Skills.* West Texas State University, Canyon, Tx., 79016.

D. WORKSHEET

DETROIT TESTS OF LEARNING APTITUDE PROFILE

Ages 3–6 years

Name _____   Birthdate _____

Observations

	3-0	3-3	3-6	3-9	4-0	4-3	4-6	4-9	5-0	5-3	5-6	5-9	6-0	6-3	6-6	6-9	7-0	7-3	7-6	7-9	8-0	8-3	8-6	8-9	9-0	9-3	9-6	10	11	12
1. Pictorial Absurdities RC VAA																														
3. Pictorial Orientation VAA																														
5. Motor Speed and Precision																														
6. Auditory Attention AAA Span for Unrelated Words																														
7. Oral Commissions PJ NA,AAA,MA																														
8. Social Adjustments RC																														
9. Visual Attention Span for Objects VAA																														
10. Orientation RC PJ,TSR																														
11. Free Association VA																														
12. Memory for Designs TSR VAA,MA																														
13. Auditory Attention AAA Span for Related Syllables																														
14. Number Ability NA																														
15. Social Adjustment B RC																														

Code Legend

RC:	Reading and Comprehension	NA:	Number Ability
PJ:	Practical Judgment	VAA:	Visual Attentive Ability
VA:	Verbal Ability	AAA:	Auditory Attentive Ability
TSR:	Time and Space Relationships	MA:	Motor Ability

E. WORKSHEET

DETROIT TESTS OF LEARNING APTITUDE
PROFILE for ages 7–8 and age 13

Choose at least 9 subtests covering
the 8 mental faculties—
See DTLA Manual, p. 4

Name_____   Birthdate _____

Age _____   Date of Exam_____

	05	06	07	08	09	10	11	12	13	14	15	16	17	18	19	Learning Age
1. Pictorial Absurdities																
2. Verbal Absurdities																
3. Pictorial Opposites																
4. Verbal Opposites																
5. Motor Speed and Precision																
6. Auditory Attention Span for Unrelated Words																
7. Oral Commissions																
8. Social Adjustment A																
9. Visual Attention Span for Objects																
10. Orientation																
11. Free Association																
12. Memory for Designs																
13. Auditory Attention Span for Related Syllables																
14. Number Ability																
15. Social Adjustment B																
16. Visual Attention Span for Letters																
17. Disarranged Pictures																
18. Oral Directions																
19. Likenesses and Differences																

Refer to mental
faculties measured,
page ii, Manual.

F. WORKSHEET

Name _____   Birthdate _____

	Code		06	07	08	09	10	11	12	13	14	15	16	17	18	Years
2.	Verbal Absurdities	RC,VA														
4.	Verbal Opposites	VA														
5.	Motor Speed and Precision	PJ,MA														
6.	Auditory Attention Span for Unrelated Words	AAA														
9.	Visual Attention Span for Objects	VAA														
10.	Orientation	RC,PJ,TSR														
11.	Free Association	VA														
12.	Memory for Designs	TSR,VAA,MA														
13.	Auditory Attention Span for Related Syllables	AAA														
15.	Social Adjustment	RC														
16.	Visual Attention Span for Letters															
17.	Disarranged Pictures	RC,TSR,VAA														
18.	Oral Directions	PJ,AAA,VAA,MA														
19.	Likenesses and Differences	VA														

Code Legend   Observations

RC:	Reading and Comprehension
PJ:	Practical Judgment
VA:	Verbal Ability
TSR:	Time and Space Relationships
NA:	Number Ability
AAA:	Auditory Attentive Ability
VAA:	Visual Attentive Ability
MA:	Motor Ability

G. WORKSHEET

DETROIT TEST OF LEARNING APTITUDE PROFILE
Ages 14 years or older

Name _____   Birthdate _____

Code Measure		06	07	08	09	10	11	12	13	14	15	16	17	18	Years
2. Verbal Absurdities	RC,VA														
4. Verbal Opposites	VA														
5. Motor Speed and Precision	PJ,MA														
6. Auditory Attention Span for Unrelated Words	AAA														
9. Visual Attention Span for Objects	VAA														
11. Free Association	VA														
12. Memory for Designs	TSR,VAA,MA														
13. Auditory Attention Span for Related Syllables	AAA														
15. Social Adjustment B	RC														
16. Visual Attention Span for Letters	VAA														
17. Disarranged Pictures	RC,TSR,VAA														
18. Oral Directions	PJ,AAA,VAA,MA														
19. Likenesses and Differences	VA														

Code Legend

RC:	Reading and Comprehension
PJ:	Practical Judgment
VA:	Verbal Ability
TSR:	Time and Space Relationships
NA:	Number Ability
AAA:	Auditory Attentive Ability
VAA:	Visual Attentive Ability
MA:	Motor Ability

Observations

H. WORKSHEET

STANFORD BINET AND STRUCTURE OF INTELLECT
Test Numbers, Levels and SOI Code Letters

Emphasizing the Face of Operations

Cognition

Stanford Binet Yr. and Mo.	CFU	CFC	CFR	CFS	CFT	CFI	CSC	CSR	CSS	CMU	CMC	CMR	CMS	CMT	CMI	For Tallying and Observation
2–0	A			4						5	3					
2–6	3				A					4	2		6			
3–0			1	1.3						2						
3–6	2	3		2	2						4				6	
4–0		5								1		3			4,6	
4–6		3								3		2	6	4	A,4,6	
5–0	1	5		6	2,6,A					3						
6–0	3									1	A	5		2		
7–0						2,6	2					5		2		
8–0										1				4	4	
9–0					1											
10–0						2				1,3					4	
11–0										3				6	5,A	
12–0						1				1,5		6				
13–0				5	A					2					4	
14–0							4,A		2	1						
AA				6	A		2		1,3,7,8			3	4	7	5	
SA–I										1,5		3		6		
SA–II							4	A		1,5		A	6	5	2,3	
SA–III				4						1,3,A		3,A	6		2	

Adapted from Mary Meeker, *Structure of Intellect*, (Columbus: Charles E. Merrill, 1969).

H. WORKSHEET

Emphasizing the Face of Operations

STANFORD BINET AND STRUCTURE OF INTELLECT
Test Numbers, Levels and SOI Code Letters

MEMORY AND EVALUATION

St. Binet Yr. and Mo.	MFU	MFS	MFT	MSU	MSS	MSI	MMU	MMR	MMS	EFU	EFR	EFS	EFI	ESR	EMU	EMR	EMS	EMT	For Tallying and Observation
2-0		2										4							
2-6				5	5			6											
3-0	4			A						4						4			
3-6										3	1, A					6			
4-0	2, 4								A	5									
4-6	A								5	3		1							
5-0										5		4							
6-0						3, 4										5, A			
7-0				6, A	A							3				A	1	4	
8-0							2	2, 6									3	5	
9-0	3, 6				6	5			6					1		4, A	2		
10-0				6				4								4, A	A		
11-0	1							A	4							2, A	2		
12-0	A			4	4								3			2, 6	2, 3		
13-0		6							3							4			
14-0		5			3										3				
AA		6				4										7			
SA-I			2	4	2, 4	2										3			
SA-II								2, 6								2, 5			
SA-III		4				5		6						5					

Adapted from Mary Meeker, *Structure of Intellect* (Columbus: Charles E. Merrill, 1969).

H. WORKSHEET

STANFORD BINET AND STRUCTURE OF INTELLECT

Emphasizing the Face of Operations

CONVERGENT PRODUCTION and DIVERGENT PRODUCTION

Test Numbers, Levels and SOI Code Numbers

St. Binet Yr. and Mo.	NFU	NFC	NFR	NFS	NFI	NSR	NSS	NSI	NMU	NMC	NMR	NMS	NMT	NMI	DFC	DSU	DST	DMU	DMR	DMS	DMT	DMI
2–0	1, 4								5		6											
2–6	1, 3, 5, 6		A						4, 3		1											
3–0				3					2													
3–6		5																				
4–0													2									
4–6									1		3, 4									3		
5–0	4		2, A		1						2, A									2		
6–0										2	4											2
7–0	3										5			4								4
8–0														4,5A								5
9–0							5												4, A			
10–0					2						4				2			4				4
11–0										6						5						A
12–0														6								
13–0				6					6		5	5										
14–0			5				4	4, A					6	3			4, A				4, A	
AA			6			2		2					5	3			2		5	5	2	
SA–I			6					4	6				6, A									
SA–II						A					2	5	3					2				
SA–III			4				5	6, A			3		2				4	3, A		3	4	2

Adapted from Mary Meeker, *Structure of Intellect* (Columbus, Charles E. Merrill, 1969).

*For age expectancies the reader is referred to the Stanford Binet SOI accumulated total sheets available from SOI Institute, 214 Main, El Segundo, Calif. 90245.

I. DEFINITIONS AND MODEL

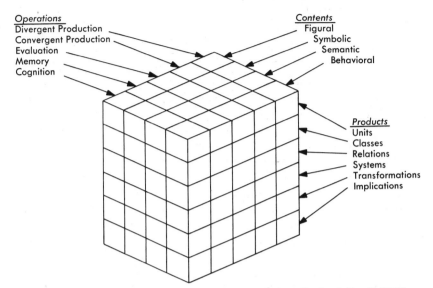

Adapted from Mary Meeker, *Structure of Intellect* (Columbus: Charles E. Merrill, 1969).

Basic kind of process or operation performed
- (a) Cognition   (c)
- (b) Memory   (m)
- (c) Convergent thinking   (n)
- (d) Divergent thinking   (d)
- (e) Evaluation   (e)

- (a) Cognition means discovery of rediscovery or recognition.
- (b) Memory means retention of what is cognized.
- (c) Convergent thinking is a kind of productive-thinking operation that generates new information from known information and remembered information. In this case the information leads to one acceptable answer.
- (d) In divergent thinking we think in different directions, sometimes searching, sometimes seeking variety.
- (e) In evaluation we reach decisions as to goodness, correctness, suitability, or adequacy of what we know, what we remember, and what to produce in productive thinking.

Basic kind of material or content involved
- (a) Figural   (f)

(b) Symbolic (s)
(c) Semantic (m)
(d) Behavioral (b)

(a) Figural content is concrete material such as is perceived through the senses. It does not represent anything except itself. Visual material has properties such as size, form, color, location, or texture. Things we hear or feel provide other examples of figural material.
(b) Symbolic content is composed of letters, digits, and other conventional signs, usually organized in general systems, such as the alphabet or the number system.
(c) Semantic content is in the form of verbal meanings or ideas, for which no examples are necessary.
(d) Behavioral aspect is not material or content but is included on the construct and evidently refers to the function of the content material.

Basic kinds of products of the *operations* and *content*
(a) Units
(b) Classes
(c) Relations
(d) Systems
(e) Transformations
(f) Implications

As far as factor analysis has offered help, these are the only kinds of products that we can know. There is enough evidence available to suggest that, regardless of the combinations of operations and content, the same six kinds of products may be found associated. These may serve as basic classes into which one might fit all kinds of information psychologically.

J. STRUCTURE OF INTELLECT WITH EMPHASIS ON CONTENT AND PRODUCTS

This is designed to aid diagnostician to think in terms of the two faces Content and Products.

Content
Units
Classes
Relations
System
Transformations
Implications

Products
Figural
Symbolic
Semantic
Behavioral

Operations
Cognition
Memory
Evaluation
Convergent Production
Divergent Production

UNITS	CLASSES	RELATIONS
Figural	*Figural*	*Figural*
CFU-V — Ability to recognize classes of figural items of information	CFC — Ability to recognize classes of figural items or information	CFR — Ability to recognize figural relations between forms
CFU-A — Ability to perceive auditory figural units-sounds		
MFU — Ability to remember given figural objects		
EFU — Ability to judge units of figural information as being similar or different	EFC — Ability to classify units specified in some way	EFR — Ability to recognize change in lines of forms or figures; selection of next form to follow

Structure of Intellect, Contents and Products (cont.)

UNITS	CLASSES	RELATIONS
	NFC — Ability to classify, uniquely or conventionally, items of figural information	
DFU — Ability to produce many figures conforming to simple specifications	DFC — Ability to gauge figural information in different ways	
Symbolic	*Symbolic*	*Symbolic*
CSU-V — Ability to recognize graphic symbolic units such as words	CSC — Ability to recognize common properties in sets of symbolic information	CSR — Ability to see relations between items of symbolic information
CSU-A — Ability to decode auditory information in the form of language symbols		
MSU — Ability to remember isolated items of symbolic information, such as syllables in words.	MSC — Ability to remember symbolic class properties	MSR — Ability to remember definitive connections between units of symbolic information
ESU — Ability to make rapid decisions regarding the identification of letter or number sets	ESC — Ability to judge applicability of class properties of symbolic information; i.e., judging of a class in which to place numbers, letters or signs.	ESR — Ability to make choices among symbolic relationships of similarity and consistency in given letters or numerals

Structure of Intellect, Contents and Products (cont.)

UNITS	CLASSES	RELATIONS
NSU	**NSC** Ability to uniquely classify items of symbolic information	**NSR** Ability to complete specified symbolic relationship
DSU Ability to produce many symbolic units which conform to simple specifications, not involving meanings	**DSC** Ability to group items of symbolic information in different ways	**DSR** Ability to relate letters or numbers in many different ways
Semantic	*Semantic*	*Semantic*
CMU Ability to comprehend the meanings of words or ideas	**CMC** Ability to recognize common properties of words, ideas, objects	**CMR** Ability to see relations between ideas or meanings of words
MMU Ability to remember isolated ideas or word meanings	**MMC** Ability to remember verbal or ideational class properties	**MMR** Ability to remember meaningful connections between items of verbal information
EMU Ability to make judgments about the suitability or adequacy of ideas and word meanings in terms of meeting certain given criteria	**EMC** Ability to judge applicability of class properties of semantic information	**EMR** Ability to make choices among semantic relationships based on the similarity and consistency of the meanings

289

Structure of Intellect, Contents and Products (cont.)

UNITS

NMU — Ability to converge on an appropriate name (or summarizing word) for any given information

DMU — Ability to produce many elementary ideas appropriate to given requirements

Behavioral

CBU — Ability to understand units of expression such as facial expression

SYSTEMS

Figural

CFS — Ability to comprehend arangements and positions of visual objects in space

CLASSES

NMC — Ability to produce verbally meaningful classes under specific conditions and restrictions

DMC — Ability to produce many categories of ideas appropriate in meaning to a given idea

Behavioral

CBC — Ability to see similarity of behavioral information in different expressional modes

TRANSFORMATIONS

Figural

CFT — Ability to visualize how a given figure or object will appear after given changes such as unfolding or rotation

RELATIONS

NMR — Ability to produce a word or idea that conforms to specific relationship requirements

DMR — Ability to produce many relationships appropriate in meaning to a given idea

Behavioral

CBR — Ability to understand social relationships

IMPLICATIONS

Figural

CFI — Ability to forsee the consequences involved in figural problems

Structure of Intellect, Contents and Products (cont.)

	SYSTEMS		TRANSFORMATIONS		IMPLICATIONS
MFS-V	Ability to remember the spatial order or placement of visual information				
MFS-A	Ability to remember auditory or rhythm or melody				
DFS	Ability to produce composites of figural information in many ways	DFT	Ability to process figural information in revised ways	DFI	Ability to elaborate on figural information
Symbolic		*Symbolic*		*Symbolic*	
CSS	Ability to understand the systematic interrelatedness of symbols within an organized set			CSI	Ability to foresee or be sensitive to consequences in a symbolic problem
MSS	Ability to remember the order of symbolic information	MST	Ability to remember changes in symbolic information	MSI	Ability to remember arbitrary connections between symbols
ESS	Ability to estimate appropriateness of aspects of a symbolic system	EST	Ability to judge whether or not an ordering of substitutive symbols is adequate	ESI	Ability to judge whether there is consistency of, probability of, or inferences from given symbolic information

Structure of Intellect, Contents and Products (cont.)

SYSTEMS	TRANSFORMATIONS	IMPLICATIONS
NSS Ability to produce a fully determined order or sequence of symbols.	NST Ability to produce new symbolic items of information by revising given items	NSI Ability to produce a completely determined symbolic deduction from given symbolic information, where implication has not been practiced as such
DSS Ability to organize sets of symbolic information into different systematic arrangements		DSI Ability to produce varied implications from given symbolic information
Semantic	*Semantic*	*Semantic*
CMS Ability to comprehend relatively complex ideas	CMT Ability to see potential changes of interpretation of objects and situations	CMI Ability to anticipate or be sensitive to the needs of others or understand a given situation in meaningful terms
MMS Ability to remember meaningfully ordered verbal information	MMT Ability to remember changes in meaning or redefinitions	MMI Ability to remember arbitrary connections between pairs of meaningful elements of information

Structure of Intellect, Contents and Products (cont.)

SYSTEMS	TRANSFORMATIONS	IMPLICATIONS
EMS Ability to judge the internal consistency of a complex of meaningful information	**EMT** Ability to judge which objects or ideas could best be transformed or redefined in order to meet new requirements	**EMI** Ability to judge adequacy of meaningful deduction
NMS Ability to order information into a verbally meaningful sequence	**NMT** Ability to produce uses for objects by taking them out of their given context and redefining them	**NMI** Ability to deduce meaningful information implicit in the given information
DMS Ability to organize words in various meaningful complex ideas	**DMT** Ability to produce unusual, remote or clever responses involving reinterpretation or new emphasis on some aspects of an object or situation	**DMI** Ability to produce many antecedents, concurrents or consequences of given information
Behavioral **CBS** Ability to comprehend a social situation or sequence of social events	*Behavioral* **CBT** Ability to interpret either a facial gesture, a statement expression, a whole social situation so that its behavioral significance is changed	*Behavioral* **CBI** Ability to draw implications or make predictions about what will happen following a given social situation

From Mary N. Meeker, *The Structure of Intellect*. Columbus: Charles E. Merrill, 1969. Adapted by Avaril Wedemeyer.

K. TALLY SHEET FOR STANFORD BINET (LM) TEMPLATES

STRUCTURE OF INTELLECT PROFILE
With a Flow Diagram of the Processes*

Tally Sheet for Stanford Binet (LM) Templates

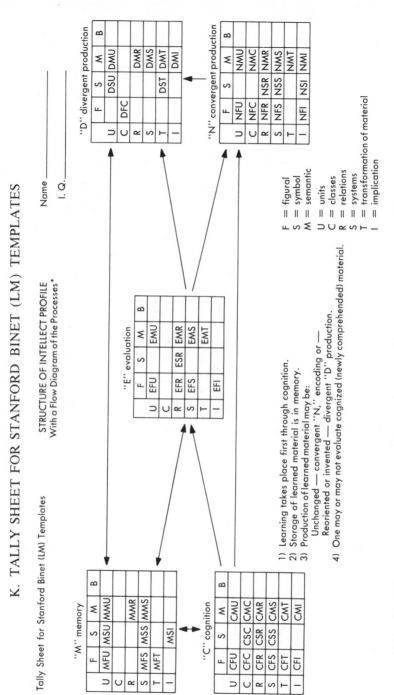

"M" memory

	F	S	M	B
U	MFU	MSU	MMU	
C				
R			MMR	
S	MFS	MSS	MMS	
T	MFT			
I		MSI		

"C" cognition

	F	S	M	B
U	CFU	CSU	CMU	
C	CFC	CSC	CMC	
R	CFR	CSR	CMR	
S	CFS	CSS	CMS	
T	CFT		CMT	
I	CFI		CMI	

"E" evaluation

	F	S	M	B
U	EFU		EMU	
C				
R	EFR	ESR	EMR	
S	EFS		EMS	
T			EMT	
I	EFI			

"D" divergent production

	F	S	M	B
U		DSU	DMU	
C	DFC			
R			DMR	
S			DMS	
T		DST	DMT	
I			DMI	

"N" convergent production

	F	S	M	B
U	NFU	NSU	NMU	
C	NFC		NMC	
R	NFR	NSR	NMR	
S	NFS	NSS	NMS	
T			NMT	
I	NFI	NSI	NMI	

1) Learning takes place first through cognition.
2) Storage of learned material is in memory.
3) Production of learned material may be:
   Unchanged — convergent "N," encoding or —
   Reoriented or invented — divergent "D" production.
4) One may or may not evaluate cognized (newly comprehended) material.

F = figural
S = symbol
M = semantic

U = units
C = classes
R = relations
S = systems
T = transformation of material
I = implication

*Adapted by Mary Meeker, *Structure of Intellect* (Columbus: Charles E. Merrill, 1969).

L. SOI—TEST PROFILE INFORMATION

SOI Test Profile Information

Name _____

School _____

Age _____

Information	Meeker Text pp. 137–138	WISC _____
MMU _____	(_____)	**Picture Completion**
MMR _____	(_____)	CFU _____ (_____)
MSS _____	(_____)	CFS _____ (_____)
CMU _____	(_____)	**Picture Arrangement**
MMS _____	(_____)	EMR _____ (_____)
NMR _____	(_____)	NMS _____ (_____)
NMU _____	(_____)	**Block Design**
EMR _____	(_____)	CFR _____ (_____)
Comprehension		EFR _____ (_____)
EMI _____	(_____)	**Object Assembly**
Arithmetic		CFS _____ (_____)
MSI _____	(_____)	CFT _____ (_____)
CMS _____	(_____)	EFR _____ (_____)
Similarities		**Coding**
EMR _____	(_____)	NFU _____ (_____) C ____ (__) ____
CMT _____	(_____)	EFU _____ (_____)
Vocabulary		NSU _____ (_____) M ____ (__) ____
CMU _____	(_____)	ESU _____ (_____)
Digits		**Mazes** E ____ (__) ____
MSS-F _____	(_____)	CFI _____ (_____) N ____ (__) ____

ITPA

Strengths (Tests)	SOI	Weaknesses (Tests)	SOI
_____	_____	_____	_____
_____	_____	_____	_____
_____	_____	_____	_____
_____	_____	_____	_____
_____	_____	_____	_____
_____	_____	_____	_____
_____	_____	_____	_____

DETROIT

Strengths (Tests)	SOI	Weaknesses (Tests)	SOI
_____	_____	_____	_____
_____	_____	_____	_____
_____	_____	_____	_____
_____	_____	_____	_____
_____	_____	_____	_____
_____	_____	_____	_____
_____	_____	_____	_____

SLOSSON (from 2–0)

Correct		Incorrect	Correct		Incorrect
_____	CMU	_____	_____	MMU	_____
_____	CMS	_____	_____	EFU	_____
_____	CMC	_____	_____	EMR	_____
_____	CMI	_____	_____	NFU	_____
_____	CMR	_____	_____	NMR	_____
_____	MSU	_____	_____	NMI	_____
_____	MMS	_____	_____	NMU	_____
_____	MSI	_____			
_____	MSS	_____			

From Mary N. Meeker, *The Structure of Intellect* (Columbus: Charles E. Merrill, 1969). Adapted by Marjorie Rives, Educational Diagnostician, Eastern Panhandle Cooperative, Shamrock, Texas.

M. SOI DEFICIENCY AREAS

Use different colors to represent different tests.		Figural	Symbolic	Semantic	Behavioral
Units	C				
	M				
	E				
	N				
	D				
Classes	C				
	M				
	E				
	N				
	D				
Relations	C				
	M				
	E				
	N				
	D				
Systems	C				
	M				
	E				
	N				
	D				
Transformations	C				
	M				
	E				
	N				
	D				
Implications	C				
	M				
	E				
	N				
	D				

Other Information

From Mary N. Meeker, *The Structure of Intellect* (Columbus: Charles E. Merrill, 1969). Adapted by Marjorie Rives, Educational Diagnostician, Eastern Panhandle Cooperative, Shamrock, Texas.

N. WISC-R PROFILE

WISC-R PROFILE

Raw Score Equivalents for Test Ages

Name _____ Birthdate _____

Age _____

School _____

Date of Test _____ Examiner _____

| | | | | | Age Equivalents and Raw Scores* | | | | | | | |
Tests	6½	7½	8½	9½	10½	11½	12½	13½	14½	15½	16½	Abilities Measured
VERBAL												
Inform.	6	8	11	12.5	14	16	17.5	18.5	19.5	21	22.5	Information from experience and education
Simil.	7	8.5	10	11.5	13.5	15	16.5	18	19.2	20	21	Logical and abstract thinking ability
Arith.	6	8	9.5	11	12	13	13.5	14	—	15	15.5	Concentration and arithmetic reasoning
Vocab.	15-16	19-20	24	27	30-31	34	37	39.4	42	45	48	Word knowledge from experience and education
Comp.	8-9	11	13	15	17	20	22	23.5	25	26	27	Practical knowledge and social judgment
Di. Span.	7	9	10	10.8	11.5	12	13	13.6	14.2	14.9	15.5	Attention and rote memory
PERFORMANCE												
P. Compl.	12	14	16	17	18	19	20	20.9	21.5	21.9	22.5	Visual alertness and visual memory
P. Arrang.	11-13	17	20	23	26	28	29.5	30.9	31.9	32.9	34	Interpretation of social situations
B. Design	8-9	12-13	16-17	22	26-27	31	35	38	41	43	46	Analysis in formation of abstracts
O. Assem.	12	15	17.5	19.5	21.5	22.5	22.9	24.5	25.2	26	27	Putting together of concrete forms
Code A	31-34	39-40										Speed of learning and writing symbols
Code B			32	36-37	41	46	50-51	54-55	58-59	62	66-67	
Mazes	13	16	18.5	20	21	22.3	23.3	23.9	24.4	24.9	26	Planning and following a visual pattern

*The numbers (raw scores) with decimals are approximations.

O. WECHSLER INTELLIGENCE SCALE FOR CHILDREN

WECHSLER INTELLIGENCE SCALE FOR CHILDREN

NAME _____ SEX _____ DATE _____

I.Q. VERBAL _____ PERFORMANCE _____ FULL SCALE _____

VERBAL SCALED SCORES

Information	0 1 2 3 4 5 6 7 8 9 10 11 12 13 14 15 16 17 18 19 20
General Knowledge—Long Term Memory From Experience—Education	
Comprehension	0 1 2 3 4 5 6.7 8 9 10 11 12 13 14 15 16 17 18 19 20
Practical Knowledge and Social Judgment—Reasoning—Logical Solutions	
Arithmetic	0 1 2 3 4 5 6 7 8 9 10 11 12 13 14 15 16 17 18 19 20
Concentration, Enumerating—Arithmetic Reasoning—Sequencing	
Similarities	0 1 2 3 4 5 6 7 8 9 10 11 12 13 14 15 16 17 18 19 20
Relationship & Abstract Thinking—Association of Abstract Ideas	
Vocabulary	0 1 2 3 4 5 6 7 8 9 10 11 12 13 14 15 16 17 18 19 20
Word Knowledge—Verbal Fluency—Expressive Vocabulary	
Digit Span	0 1 2 3 4 5 6 7 8 9 10 11 12 13 14 15 16 17 18 19 20
Attention, Concentration, Rote & Immediate Memory—Sequencing	
Verbal I.Q.	44 50 56 62 69 75 81 87 94 100 106 113 119 123 131 138 144 150 156

PERFORMANCE SCALED SCORES

Picture Completion	0 1 2 3 4 5 6 7 8 9 10 11 12 13 14 15 16 17 18 19 20
Visual Memory & Alertness to Details	
Picture Arrangement	0 1 2 3 4 5 6 7 8 9 10 11 12 13 14 15 16 17 18 19 20
Interpretation of Social Situation—Sequencing—Visual Alertness	
Block Design	0 1 2 3 4 5 6 7 8 9 10 11 12 13 14 15 16 17 18 19 20
Reproduce Abstract Design from Pattern—Visual Perception	
Object Assembly	0 1 2 3 4 5 6 7 8 9 10 11 12 13 14 15 16 17 18 19 20
Reproduce Familiar Forms from Memory—Visual Retention—Visual Organization	
Coding	0 1 2 3 4 5 6 7 8 9 10 11 12 13 14 15 16 17 18 19 20
Speed and Accuracy of Learning Meaningless Symbols—Immediate Visual Memory—Motor Control	
Mazes	0 1 2 3 4 5 6 7 8 9 10 11 12 13 14 15 16 17 18 19 20
Planning & Following Visual Pattern—Motor Control	
Performance I.Q.	− 44 51 58 65 72 79 86 93 100 107 114 121 128 135 142 149 156
Full Scale I.Q.	− 46 49 56 64 71 78 85 93 100 107 115 122 129 138 144 151 154
Percentile Rank	− 1 3 8 13 33 50 67 81 92 97 99+

RETARDED			AVERAGE		SUPERIOR
Trainable	Educable	Slow Learner	Low Average	Bright Average	Adapted by Wilma Jo Bush, Ed D. and Chas. R. Jones, Ed. D., 1971

298

P. KNOW THE CHILD TO TEACH THE CHILD

Psychological Date_____C.A._____M.A._____I.Q._____

G Good	S Satisfactory	P Poor
AA Above average	A Average	BA Below average

RECEPTION ORALLY

Understanding of spoken language
_____ Discrimination skills
_____ Follows directions
_____ Understands what others read
_____ Retention

Level of Achievement

_____ AA _____ A _____ BA

RECEPTION VISUALLY

Understanding of printed language
_____ Discrimination skills
_____ Follows directions
_____ Understands what he reads
_____ Retention

Level of Achievement

_____ AA _____ A _____ BA

EXPRESSIVE ORALLY

Spoken language
_____ Speaks clearly (except for some pronunciation)
_____ Speaks in sentences
_____ Tells story in sequence
_____ Retention
_____ Speed of answering

Level of Achievement

_____ AA _____ A _____ BA

EXPRESSIVE VISUALLY

Written language
From visual model
_____ On board
_____ On paper
_____ From oral dictation
_____ Formation of letters
_____ Writes sentences
_____ Writes stories
_____ Retention or revisualization
_____ Speed of writing

Level of Achievement

_____ AA _____ A _____ BA

AWARENESS OF CONCEPTS

_____ At concrete level
_____ At abstract level

BEHAVIOR

_____ Finishes assignment
_____ Moves often
_____ Gets along with peers

VISUAL RECEPTION

_____ Identification of single picture
_____ Identification of picture (scene)
_____ Difference in forms
_____ Likenesses in forms

Reading (recall of sound name from visual symbol)

_____ Consonants
_____ Vowels
_____ Blends
_____ Digraphs, dipthongs

Recall (similar words)

_____ Beginning letter
_____ Middle letter
_____ End letter
_____ Similar meaning
_____ Reversals
_____ Nouns
_____ Pronouns
_____ Verbs
_____ Adverbs
_____ Functional words
_____ Omission of letters
_____ Omission of words
_____ Omission of lines

Comprehension

_____ Silent Reading
_____ Retention

Level of Achievement

_____ AA _____ A _____ BA

AUDITORY RECEPTION

_____ Identification of sounds in
        environment
_____ Listening and recall

Single letter

_____ Consonants
   _____ initial
   _____ medial
   _____ ending
_____ Vowels

Two or more letters

_____ Blends
_____ Digraphs-dipthongs
_____ Familiar word parts

Words

_____ Blends sounds to make words
_____ Repeats nonsense syllables
_____ Repeats words
_____ Repeats sentence
_____ Rhymes

Comprehension

_____ Follows directions (orally)
_____ Must repeat direction
_____ Understands when directions
        given individually
_____ Distracted by extraneous
        noises
_____ Makes noises
_____ Verbalizes
_____ Retention
_____ From own oral reading
_____ From others reading

Level of Achievement

_____ AA _____ A _____ BA

VISUAL EXPRESSION

_____ Formation
_____ Reversals
_____ Can't stay between lines
_____ From board
_____ From model on paper
_____ Labored writing

Level of Achievement

_____ AA _____ A _____ BA

WRITTEN LANGUAGE

Recall oral dictation

_____ _____ Letters
_____ _____ Nouns
_____ _____ Pronouns
_____ _____ Verbs
_____ _____ Functional words
_____ _____ Sentences
_____ _____ Retention

FACIAL EXPRESSION

_____ Inappropriate
_____ Seldom uses facial
expressions
_____ Does not use appropriate
noises for play

AUDITORY EXPRESSION

*Oral Lanuague (deletes parts
of speech)*

_____ Nouns
_____ Pronouns
_____ Verbs
_____ Adverbs
_____ Functional words

Oral reading

_____ Intonation
_____ Word-reader
_____ Disregard of punctuation

Level of Achievement

_____ AA _____ A _____ BA

NONVERBAL

Math

_____ Understands relationship of
symbols to amount

_____ Needs concrete objects to
count and compute
_____ Can't recall number facts
_____ Unable to organize problems
on paper
_____ Computation good; reading
problem poor
_____ Fails to understand opera-
tions
_____ Difficulty telling time
_____ Count
_____ Add
_____ Subtract
_____ Multiply
_____ Divide
_____ Retention

Level of Achievement

_____ AA _____ A _____ BA

BEHAVIOR

_____ Adjustment to peers
_____ Adjustment to adults
_____ Self-concept
_____ Ability to finish assignments
_____ Reaction to change
_____ Reaction to music
_____ Eye-hand coordination

Noted excessive movement

Yes _____ No _____

Noted perservation

Yes _____ No _____

Dominance   *(Left)*   *(Right)*

Hand   _____   _____
Eye   _____   _____
Leg   _____   _____

Confuses left and right—

Yes _____ No _____

Memory

_____ Long term

_____ Short term

Association

_____ Difficulty understanding
abstract ideas given
verbally

_____ Difficulty understanding
abstract ideas given
visually

_____ Has conceptualization
problem

_____ Difficulty realizing
consequences

_____ Difficulty with inferences

From M. Serio, "Know the Child to Teach the Child," *Academic Theory,* V (3), 1970.

Q. IDENTIFICATION OF EARLIER CATEGORIES

The earlier attempts at classification of learning disabilities show that terms have grown out of medical reports and special education. These classifications are broad in nature, each having unique characteristics. However, there are similar symptoms and characteristics found within 12 groups.

Though these broad categories offer little measureable help in determining a style of learning or a specific deficiency in learning, they do in some cases identify global classifications that can ultimately be used in securing legislative action for the provision of funds.

The purpose of adding these 12 categories is to provide the reader a brief resource to examine an important historical approach to identifying learning problems.

1. Minimal brain injury (MBI), or minimal brain dysfunction (MBD)
2. Aphasia or dysphasia
3. Dyslexia (not to be confused with alexia)
4. Perceptual impairment or perceptual-motor impairment
5. Specific language disability
6. Neurological impairment
7. Word blindness
8. Strephosymbolia
9. Hyperkinesia
10. Hypokinesia
11. Dyspraxia
12. Educational retardation

MINIMAL BRAIN DYSFUNCTION

Minimal brain dysfunction is used to designate a condition in children in which the neurological impairment is "minimal"; behavior and learning are affected without lowering the general intellectual capacity. This dysfunction may manifest itself in various combinations of impairment of perception, conceptualization, language, memory, and the control of attention, impulse, or motor function. This term also has been widely used as a result of the work of Alfred A. Strauss and has been adopted by several states to designate what special education facilities are needed for hyperactive children who have learning problems. In addition to Strauss's work (1955, 1947), Kephart (1960), Cruickshank (1958), Clements and Lehtimen (1964), Birch (1964), Penfield (1939), Johnson and Myklebust (1967), and Bortner (1967) have offered effective curricula for these children.

Although symptoms are present during the preschool years, the typical child does not show severe characteristics until beginning school. Here such a child first experiences the pressure of being required to perform according to specifications. Hampered by deficiencies, the minimally brain-damaged child gradually falls behind because underlying problems have not been detected.

Minimally brain damaged children may exhibit any number of the symptoms. They may find it difficult to keep up with class in reading, spelling, and arithmetic. Their penmanship may be illegible. They may have trouble grasping concrete and abstract concepts. Their performance may be erratic—high in some areas, low in others. They may appear to be in perpetual motion, spending more time under the seat than in it. They may be easily distracted, shifting their attention for no apparent reason and being able to concentrate for only short periods of time. Usually they are emotionally unstable. Moods change rapidly from one extreme to another, and any frustration or disappointment may cause tantrums, crying spells, or hostility.

Clements (1966) offers some very specific symptoms of minimal brain dysfunction:

Test performance indicators

1. Spotty or patchy intellectual deficiencies; achievement low in some areas, high in others
2. Below mental age level on drawing tests (man, house, etc.)
3. Geometric figure drawings poor for age and measured intelligence
4. Poor performance on block design and marble board tests
5. Poor showing on group tests (intelligence and achievement) and on daily classroom examinations that require reading
6. Characteristic subtest patterns on the *Wechsler Intelligence Scale for Children,* including "scatter" with both verbal and performance scales: high verbal — low performance; low verbal — high performance

Impairments of perception and concept formation

1. Impaired discrimination of size
2. Impaired discrimination of right-left and up-down

3. Impaired tactile discriminations
4. Poor spatial orientation
5. Impaired orientation in time
6. Distorted concept of body image
7. Impaired judgment of distance
8. Impaired discrimination of figure-ground
9. Impaired discrimination of part-whole
10. Frequent perceptual reversals in reading and in writing letters and numbers
11. Poor perceptual integration; unable to fuse sensory impressions into meaningful entities

Specific neurologic indicators

1. Few, if any, apparent gross abnormalities
2. Many "soft" equivocal or borderline findings
3. Reflex asymmetry frequent
4. Frequency of mild visual or hearing impairments
5. Strabismus
6. Nystagmus
7. High incidence of left and mixed laterality, and confused perception of laterality
8. Hyperkinesis
9. Hypokinesis
10. General awkwardness
11. Poor fine visual-motor coordination

Disorders of speech and communication

1. Impaired discrimination of auditory stimuli
2. Various categories of aphasia
3. Slow language development
4. Frequent mild hearing loss
5. Frequent mild speech irregularities

Disorders of motor function

1. Frequent athetoid, choreiform, tremulous or rigid movements of hands
2. Frequent delayed motor milestones
3. Frequent tics and grimaces
4. Hyperactivity
5. Hypoactivity

Academic achievement and adjustment (chief complaints about the child by his parents and teachers)

1. Reading disabilities
2. Arithmetic disabilities
3. Spelling disabilities
4. Poor writing, printing, or drawing ability
5. Variability in performance from day to day or even hour to hour
6. Poor ability to organize work
7. Slowness in finishing work
8. Frequent confusion about instructions, yet success with verbal tasks

Disorders of thinking processes

1. Poor ability for abstract reasoning
2. Thinking generally concrete
3. Difficulties in concept formation
4. Thinking frequently disorganized
5. Poor short-term and long-term memory
6. Thinking sometimes autistic
7. Frequent thought perseveration

Physical characteristics

1. Excessive drooling in the young child
2. Thumb-sucking, nail-biting, head-banging, and teeth-grinding in the young child
3. Food habits often peculiar
4. Slow to toilet train
5. Easy fatigability
6. High frequency of enuresis
7. Encopresis

Emotional characteristics

1. Impulsive
2. Explosive
3. Poor emotional and impulse control
4. Low tolerance for frustration
5. Reckless and uninhibited; impulsive, then remorseful

Sleep Characteristics

1. Body or head rocking before falling into sleep
2. Irregular sleep patterns in the young child
3. Excessive movement during sleep
4. Sleep abnormally light or deep
5. Resistance to naps and early bedtime, i.e., seems to require less sleep than the average child

Relationship capacities

1. Peer group relationships generally poor
2. Overexcitable in normal play with other children
3. Better adjustment when playmates are limited to one or two
4. Frequently poor judgment in social and interpersonal situations
5. Socially bold and aggressive
6. Inappropriate, unselective, and often excessive displays of affection
7. Easy acceptance of others alternating with withdrawal and shyness
8. Excessive need to touch, cling, and hold on to others

Variations of physical development

1. Frequent lags in developmental milestones; e.g., motor, language, etc.
2. Generalized maturational lag during early school years
3. Physically immature; or
4. Physical development normal or advanced for age

Characteristics of social behavior

1. Social competence frequently below average for age and measured intelligence
2. Behavior often inappropriate for situation and consequence apparently not foreseen
3. Possibly negative and aggressive to authority
4. Possibly antisocial behavior

Variations of personality

1. Overly gullible and easily led by peers and older youngsters
2. Frequent rage reactions and tantrums when crossed

3. Very sensitive to others
4. Excessive variation in mood and responsiveness from day to day and even hour to hour
5. Poor adjustment to environmental changes
6. Sweet and even-tempered, cooperative and friendly (most commonly the so-called hypokinetic child)

Disorders of attention and concentration

1. Short attention span for age
2. Overly distractible for age
3. Impaired concentration ability

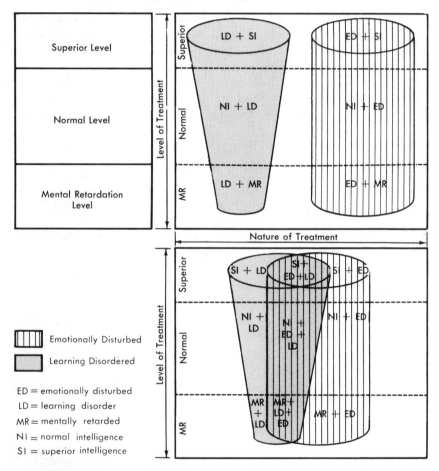

FIGURE A. 1.   Intellectual Level and Problem Areas of the MBI.

4. Motor or verbal perservation
5. Impaired ability to make decisions, particularly from many choices

Such an array of symptoms leaves little for other learning-disorder categories. Though they are symptoms that accompany the minimally brain-injured child, they cannot be confined to this singular kind of disorder. They do overlap with the symptoms in all other learning-disorder categories, and they can be found at any level of development from the severely retarded to the intellectually superior.

It is with this last point that some authorities disagree in regard to learning disorders. The brain-damaged syndrome, which was really the prototype for the learning-disorder syndrome, is now considered to be at the normal intelligence level. However, the consultant must understand the wide fluctuation of abilities typical of the MBI child, even though their condition seems to limit them to the average range of intellectual ability. The I.Q. of the MBI can show: (1) a retarded level of mental development; (2) a normal level of mental development; (3) a superior level of mental development; (4) a high performance intelligence over verbal intelligence; and (5) a high verbal intelligence over performance intelligence. In addition, there is likely to be a wide scattering of abilities that fall erratically into all levels of development. Furthermore, the problem can easily be compounded by an emotional disturbance that may cause the MBI syndrome to overlap into another category. Figure A.1 shows the involvement that can be expected of the minimally brain-injured child.

APHASIA

Aphasia refers to a condition in which a child fails to acquire meaningful spoken language by the age of three or three and one-half. This inability to speak cannot be explained by deafness, mental retardation, speech organ defects, or environmental factors. Inconsistent audiograms and observations that the child sometimes hears more than others or that he ignores very loud sounds are all suggestive of aphasia. (The consultant or school psychologist probably will not be confronted with severe cases, and the cases mild enough for public school placement are likely to be placed in rooms for the minimally brain injured.)

Aphasia exists in many forms, with symptoms as multiple as the many kinds of atypical behavior it effects. A short, representative list of symptoms for three of the major categories of this condition follows:

Receptive aphasia

1. Cannot identify what is heard
2. Cannot carry out directions
3. Poor vocabulary
4. Does not understand what is happening in pictures
5. Does not understand what he/she reads

Expressive aphasia

1. Seldom talks in class
2. Has trouble imitating children
3. May talk but not express coherent ideas
4. Seldom uses gestures
5. Drawing and writing are poor

Inner aphasia

1. Does not make associations; therefore, abstract reasoning is difficult
2. Will respond inappropriately when called upon
3. Slow to respond

DYSLEXIA

Dyslexia, a reading disability, is another type of learning disorder. The term has been used in the field of medicine for about eight decades, but because of the lack of understanding and the lack of academic pressure on the masses of children, it was not generally accepted by educators until recently. It is now becoming more widely used to identify children with normal intelligence who are having difficulty competing with other students in the public schools.

Dyslexia, as compared with other reading difficulties, concerns primarily word perception. *Dorland's Medical Dictionary* (1965) gives the following: (1) an inability to read understandingly due to a central lesion, and (2) a condition in which reading is possible but is attended with fatigue and disagreeable sensations. Some authorities refer to *specific dyslexia,* while others refer to *developmental dyslexia.* The former makes reference to some organic pathology, while the latter refers to the possibility of a lag in growth and development. Most authorities use the term specific dyslexia to mean a specific reading disability in children who have some neurological involvement. McGlannan differentiates *genetic dyslexia* from other types and defines it as ". . . one demonstrable effect of a basic genetic anomaly manifested essentially by inconstancy of spatial and temporal relations. This inconsistency results in inadequate association and integration of symbols with attendant language disabilities. Concurrent and customary presenting symptoms are ambilaterality, directional confusion, and maturational lags" (McGlannan, 1968, p. 185).

Although authorities suggest that the physical factor has some connection with dyslexia, they propose different factors for the origin of the disorder. In spite of this disagreement, all of them concur that dyslexia is nothing more than a specific reading problem. Therefore, it describes only one part of the comprehensive field of learning disorders.

Symptoms

1. Impairment in right-left orientation
2. Tendency to read words backwards, such as "was" for "saw"
3. Lack of finger dexterity
4. Difficulty with mental arithmetic, dyscalculia, sometimes known to accompany dyslexia
5. Memory (immediate recall) may be impaired
6. Auditory difficulties may occur — may not be able to sound back words and sounds that are heard
7. Visual memory — may not be able to revisualize objects, words, or letters
8. In reading aloud the child may not be able to convert visual symbols into their auditory equivalents to pronounce words correctly

PERCEPTUAL IMPAIRMENT OR PERCEPTUAL–MOTOR IMPAIRMENT

The terms *perceptual impairment* and *perceptual-motor impairment,* which are particularly emphasized by Kephart, Barsch, Money, and Cratty to describe learning disabilities, are really not one and the same, yet they do identify similar problems. The consultant should be aware that perception can be identified without the motor counterpart. Perception per se assumes discrimination or the function of distinguishing between sensory stimuli. These stimuli, in turn, must be organized into a meaningful pattern. The child discriminates and interprets an object as a whole. But when perceptual-motor impairment occurs, the integration between perception and the motor movement patterns is disrupted. The child who does not perceive adequately cannot translate through the motor pathway. Conversely, the child who has an initial lack of motor control cannot adequately perceive. It follows therefore that the perceptual-motor match is not completed, and for that reason the child is not able to see or to hear normally. Obviously, a child with this problem would have difficulty in understanding and expressing ideas. Studies on the growth and development of the child (Sherrington, 1951; Gesell, 1940; and Piaget, 1967) give the motor data priority, since motor movement patterns precede awareness. This sequence of motor movement before perception describes the problems underlying learning disabilities and suggests operative methods of remediation that can be used by both the parent and the teacher.

Symptoms

1. Poor visual-motor coordination
2. Poor body balance while walking forward, backward, or sideways
3. Lack of skill in jumping and skipping
4. Difficulty in perceiving self in time and space
   (a) Will not be able to tell time at the appropriate growth period (Chancey and Kephart, 1968; Bateman, 1968)
   (b) Will not know readily the parts of the body
   (c) Will be clumsy in relation to other children
   (d) Will not readily respond to directions of right and left — a laterality problem
5. Difficulty in making normal rhythmical movements in writing and may tend to increase or decrease the size, shape, color, or brightness
6. An uneven or jerky ocular movement
7. Trouble with object constancy — with size, shape, color, or brightness
   (a) Letters may become reversed — a *d* becomes a *b,* for example
   (b) Difficulty in establishing consistent responses; that is, may know how to spell or read a word on one day but not on the next

SPECIFIC LANGUAGE DISABILITY

Specific language disability is commonly used by speech and language disorder specialists in the United States. In particular, it can be seen in the writing of Myklebust. In addition, Johnson (1967), Kirk (1962), McCarthy, J. J. and Kirk (1968), and Jeanne McCarthy (1967), authors from various fields of special education, use this term to designate learning disorders.

In order to speak intelligently of specific language disabilities, one must first consider the specifics of language development. Johnson and Myklebust (1967) indicate three kinds of language — inner, receptive, and expressive. McCarthy and Kirk (1968) use psycholinguistic terms to describe language behavior that is either representational or automatic-sequential. Strauss and Kephart (1955) follow the development of the child from a perceptually undifferentiated world to a world in which form and shape are discernible and the foundations for speech, motor skills, and cognitive functions are established.

Many neo-Myklebust students group all learning disorders under the term *language disability*. Although this is a good generic term, some differentiation may be necessary in order to see it in relation to perceptual disability and perceptual-motor disability. Perception, although related to how one interprets through the senses, covers neither conceptual thinking nor expressive language in its more specific meaning.. Neither does it include automatic-sequential response. Language, on the other hand, includes all three of them, and yet, because of them it is still dependent upon perception. Although the term language disability identifies a broad spectrum of learning methods, it does not involve motor patterns which, in addition to perception, are a significant aspect of learning. The relationship of motor, language, and perception activties to one another can be recognized from birth and has been explained by Piaget (1967), Sherrington (1951), Kephart (1960), and others. It appears then that the integration of the term *language disability* with the term *perceptual-motor disability* offers a complete approach to the malfunctioning learning process. The Roach-Kephart Theoretical Constructs (53, p. 3), reproduced in Figure A.2, show how these two are related (Kephart, 1966, p. 3).

Of all 12 categories discussed in this book, language disability and perceptual-motor disability are the two that should be most carefully considered in every case study. Even though any of the other ten categories may identify some portion of the problem, they offer little or no remedial planning. To diagnose a problem is not sufficient. One must also determine its source in order to plan remediation through the correct channels of learning. If, however, we choose to use perceptual-motor disability and/or language disability as a frame of reference, we have by our approach already established a direction for remediation. In

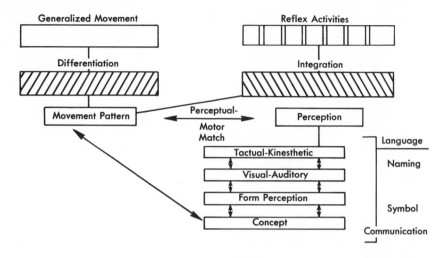

FIGURE A.2.   The Roach-Kephart Theoretical Constructs.

other words, the choice of tests for diagnosis determined by the frame of reference can subsequently aid in identifying the weakness.

Symptoms

1.   Child may be slow to express himself and may stumble over words in doing so
2.   May be a very talkative youngster yet find it difficult to express ideas about an object or situation
3.   May score below 10 on some WISC verbal subtests and yet function normally on others
4.   Instead of saying, "Both of these pianos play," child may say, "These pianos play both"
5.   Will often have difficulty in acquiring meaning and, therefore, may not follow directions adequately
6.   May find it difficult to relate experiences in normal sequence of verbal expression
7.   May have difficulty in telling time or in determining direction
8.   May read well but not grasp meaning
9.   May have difficulty in comprehending the spoken word
10.   May also have a visual problem with the written word
11.   Will likely have difficulty remembering words, spelling, and discriminating words that sound or look similar

NEUROLOGICAL IMPAIRMENT

One of the most general of all these terms is *neurological impairment* and among those who have approached learning disorders from this view are Denhoff (1968), Birch (1964), and Boshes and Myklebust (1964). Though the term *neurological dysfunction* has had fairly widespread use in the United States, its generic aspects include a myriad of characteristics that do not necessarily apply to the child with learning disabilities. By definition, neurological impairment is any malfunction that affects the nervous system in any way. It includes orthopedic impairment, cerebral palsy, and certain types of mental retardation, although the former two may or may not accompany a learning problem. The consultant has to be certain that when this kind of disorder is under consideration, the doctor or the educator identifies it specifically as neurological impairment and not as minimal brain injury or perceptual-motor impairment.

The fields of medicine, neurology, pediatric-neurology, neuropsychology, neuropsychiatry, and encephalography supply a great deal of information on this kind of malfunction. The Doman-Delacato team (1965) in Philadelphia has given special emphasis to this disorder; however, professionals in medicine, psychology, and education are not all in agreement with their theory.

WORD BLINDNESS

Word blindness has so often been used synonymously with dyslexia that it needs very little additional explanation. Kussmaul, one of the great figures in German medicine, introduced the terms *word-blindness* and *word-deafness* in 1877 as distinct from aphasia.

> In medical literature we find cases recorded as aphasia which should not properly be designated by this name, since the patients were still able to express their thoughts by speech and writing. They had not lost the power either of speaking or of writing; they were no longer able, however, although the hearing was perfect, to understand the words which they heard, or, although the sight was perfect, to read the written words which they saw. The morbid inability we will style, in order to have the shortest possible names at our disposition, *word-deafness* and *word-blindness* (caecita et surditas verbalis). [Kussmaul, 1877, p. 770]

Although the consultant will not find many sources who use the term *word blindess,* Bannatyne (1968) and Critchley (1964) are two prominent authorities who do include it in their writings.

Symptoms

The consultant should refer to the symptoms listed under dyslexia, for it is difficult to differentiate between those of dyslexia and those of word blindness.

STREPHOSYMBOLIA

In 1925 Dr. Samuel Orton (1925) from Iowa introduced the term *strephosymbolia,* which means "twisted symbols." The disorder is one of perception in which objects may appear reversed, like in a mirror. It is a reading difficulty inconsistent, however, with a child's general intelligence. Although Dr. Orton related this problem to laterality and to possible genetic factors, Victor Rosen (1955) wrote a paper which identified the term with psychological factors. For purposes of identifying and labeling this disorder, the consultant should restrict the definition to Orton's original concept.

Symptoms

    1. Confusion between similar but oppositely oriental letters (*b–d, q–p*)
    2. A tendency to reverse direction in reading

HYPERKINESIA

Specifically, *hyperkinesia* means an abnormally increased mobility, motor function, or activity. It is related somewhat to Denhoff's concept of the Hyperkinetic Impulse Syndrome and has been discussed by Strauss in relation to the Strauss Syndrome. The hyperkinetic child usually finds it difficult to remain in one position at a desk for more than a few minutes. Learning problems often accompany this disorder, however studies show that children without learning problems move around about the same amount of time. The time of day and the conditions under which the child is hyperactive can determine whether or not he is suffering from hyperkinesia. If the increased activity occurs at inappropriate times and if there is a learning disorder, the child is probably hyperkinetic, implying normal intelligence hindered by some specific learning disability.

Symptoms

1. Short attention span for age
2. Wants to move from one activity to another without due preparation time
3. Often leaves seat without permission
4. Butts into conversations and activities without being asked

The language symptoms and the perceptual-motor symptoms of a child with minimal brain injury may also be present in the hyperkinetic child.

HYPOKINESIA

Hypokinesia means abnormally decreased mobility, motor function, or activity. Often the hypokinetic child is mistakenly called lazy or disinterested because of lack of participation and inability to finish work.

The terms hyperkinetic and hypokinetic are not comprehensive enough to describe the child with a learning disability. Rather they describe characteristics that merely accompany, or in some instances cause, a learning problem. Therefore, the consultant should use them only for distinguishing behavior patterns and not for identifying a type of learning disorder. For example, "This child exhibits the traits of a specific language disability with hypokinetic or hyperkinetic tendencies."

Symptoms

1. Child may work diligently but never seems to be able to complete the work
2. Child may stop and dawdle, lose interest—this may be accompanied by other problems such as distractibility
3. Low scores may occur on tests requiring motor output
4. May be a slow reader and sometimes a poor articulator

DYSPRAXIA

The partial loss of ability to perform coordinated movements is known as *dyspraxia*. This loss of movement as it relates to the learning problem is particularly evident in the child's inability to write properly. This form of dyspraxia is known as *dysgraphia*. The prefix *dys*, meaning difficult, implies difficulty in movement (dyspraxia), difficulty in writing (dysgraphia), and difficulty in reading (dyslexia). Johnson and Myklebust

(1967) and Strong (1965) are among the writers who use the terms *dyspraxia* and *dysgraphia* in regard to children with learning disorders. *Apraxia, agraphia,* and *alexia* are also used in such literature. However, since those terms prefixed by *a* are more specifically identified with cortical lesions and since they connote an absence or an inability, educators should always use the terms prefixed by *dys* in order to avoid implications of medical diagnosis.

Symptoms

1. Child has poor eye-hand coordination
2. Has difficulty in carrying out purposeful movements
3. Unable to make proper use of objects
4. May also have difficulty expression a definite idea because other ideas are rushing into his/her consciousness

EDUCATIONAL RETARDATION

The term *educational retardation* has been used throughout the United States in the past to distinguish those children who have been held back, culturally deprived, or retarded because of unchallenging educational experiences from those who suffer from irremedial retardation. Today, although it still encompasses problems of lack of opportunity, educational retardation covers a wide range of disabilities. It has been used synonymously most often with cultural deprivation. However, the two terms are not identical, even though they overlap in meaning. Educational retardation specifically identifies a state of underachievement caused by *lack of or inadequate* opportunity, whereas cultural deprivation specifically identifies a culturally induced condition of any recognized deficiency, whether it be educational, physiological, or psychological. These deficiencies can be found at any socioeconomic level.

A glimpse into the complexity of this problem shows that educationally retarded children may be deprived because they lack: (1) gross motor development; (2) language development; (3) psychoneurological efficiency; (4) a variety of environmental experiences; (5) good teaching practices; (6) individual attention; or (7) emotional support for the sake of security and confidence in learning. Figure A.3 reveals why the terms *educational retardation* and *cultural deprivation* need to be clearly defined.

It should be emphasized that a child may be deprived in any of the above areas and still not have a learning disorder. A child may even be

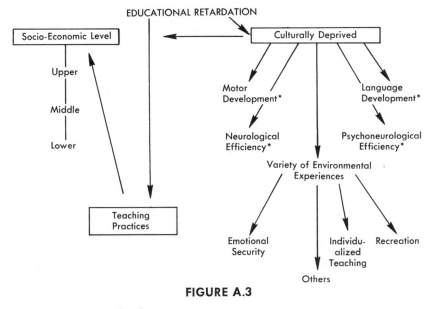

FIGURE A.3

*May result in learning disorders.

educationally retarded in that he/she is underachieving in reading, spelling, writing, or some other academic area yet still not have a learning disorder. At this point one can see the difference between a learning disorder and cultural deprivation or educational retardation, yet many culturally deprived children have learning disorders (Denhoff, 1968). The consultant should know that if a child is underachieving because of lack of educational stimulation and not because of lack of gross motor and neurological development, he/she will probably respond very readily to a program of training. If, on the other hand, the child has a lack of gross motor and neurological development in addition to the lack of educational stimulation, he/she will in all probability have a learning disorder that requires an individually structured program. In this case, remediation would be somewhat less effective. The consultant who can detect the subtle differences between these deficiencies will then be in a position to evaluate the child's need and to advise the teacher on the amount and kinds of demands made on the child.

Symptoms

Educationally retarded children may exhibit some of the same kinds of problems as those of children with physical learning disabilities. For example, they may have failed to develop the technique of moving from left to right when reading, or they may show some signs of immaturity in reversals of letters and numbers. When educational retardation is caused by lack of opportunity and is not compounded by other learning disorders, remediation can generally be achieved rather quickly.

SUMMARY

Brief coverage of the 12 most common terms used to describe learning disorders indicates the complexity of this broad area. The consultant should be willing to accept terms convenient and useful to those in other fields such as education, law, medicine, and communication media. It is imperative, however, that consultants learn the specific semantics intended so that any consultation will result in meaningful communication.

Little can be gained by insisting on the use of terminology with restricted meaning. Who can say that his is the most descriptive term when the causes for poor academic work are myriad and the manifestations are erratic, alike, and different all within the same classification?

R. CRITERION-REFERENCED TEST

NAME ▶ JEAN HARRIS STATE ▶ CALIF GRADE ▶ 3

SCHOOL ▶ MILLER TEACHER ▶ CORNING

CITY ▶ SOUTH FALLS DATE OF TESTING ▶ 09/73

PRESCRIPTIVE READING INVENTORY
INDIVIDUAL DIAGNOSTIC MAP
BLUE BOOK

+ = MASTERY OF OBJECTIVE, R = REVIEW RECOMMENDED, − = NONMASTERY OF OBJECTIVE

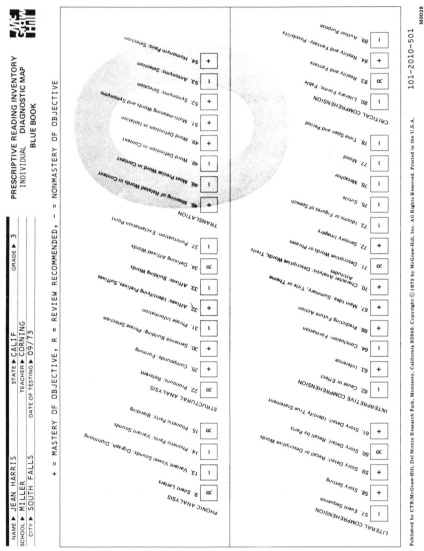

PHONIC ANALYSIS

- 9. Silent Letters — R
- 13. Variant Vowel Sounds: Digraph, Diphthong — −
- 14. Phonetic Parts: Variant Sounds — −
- 15. Phonetic Parts: Blending — R

STRUCTURAL ANALYSIS

- 22. Pronouns: Referent — R
- 25. Compounds: Forming — +
- 30. Sentence Building: Phrase Selection — +
- 31. Phrase Information — −
- 32. Affixes: Identifying Prefixes, Suffixes — +
- 33. Affixes: Building Words — −
- 34. Defining Affixed Words — R
- 37. Punctuation: Exclamation Point — −

TRANSLATION

- 45. Meaning of Related Words in Context — +
- 46. Most Precise Word in Context — −
- 48. Word Definition in Context — +
- 49. Word Definition in Isolation — +
- 51. Multi-meaning Words and Synonyms — +
- 52. Synonyms: Selection — +
- 53. Antonyms: Selection — −
- 54. Homonym Pairs: Selection — +

LITERAL COMPREHENSION

- 57. Event Sequence — −
- 58. Story Setting — +
- 59. Story Detail: Recall of Descriptive Words — +
- 60. Story Detail: Recall by Parts — R
- 61. Story Detail: Identify True Statement — +

INTERPRETIVE COMPREHENSION

- 62. Cause or Effect — −
- 63. Inference — +
- 64. Conclusion: Formation — −
- 66. Predicting Future Action — +
- 67. Main Idea: Summary, Title or Theme — +
- 70. Character Analysis: Descriptive Words, Traits — R
- 71. Descriptive Words or Phrases — +
- 72. Sensory Imagery — +
- 73. Idioms or Figures of Speech — −
- 75. Simile — −
- 76. Metaphor — −
- 77. Mood — −
- 78. Time Span and Period — −

CRITICAL COMPREHENSION

- 80. Literary Forms: Fable — −
- 83. Reality and Fantasy — R
- 84. Reality and Fantasy: Possibility — +
- 89. Author Purpose — −

Published by CTB/McGraw-Hill, Del Monte Research Park, Monterey, California 93940.

101-2010-501

M0028

321

	CONCEPT QUESTION	WHOLE NUMBERS				POSITIVE FRACTIONS				DECIMAL NUMBERS			
		+	−	X	+	+	−	X	+	+	−	X	+
PREOPERATIONAL CONCEPTS PICTORIAL FRACTIONS (1)	+												
EQUIVALENCE (3)	+												
LOWEST (SIMPLEST) TERMS (5)	−												
LOWEST COMMON DENOMINATOR (6)	−												
NUMBER LINE (MIXED NUMBER) (8)	+												

ADDITION

NO REGROUPING

LIKE (48)	+	10THS (73)	*
UNLIKE (49)	−	100THS (74)	−
MIXED (50)	+	1000THS (75)	−

REGROUPING

COLUMN (16)	+	LIKE (51)	−	10THS (76)	−
		UNLIKE (52)	−	100THS (77)	−
		MIXED (53)	−	1000THS (78)	−

SUBTRACTION

NO REGROUPING

LIKE (54)	*	10THS (79)	+
UNLIKE (55)	+	100THS (80)	−
MIXED (56)	+		

REGROUPING

3-DIGIT (20)	+	LIKE (57)	−	10THS (81)	−
4-DIGIT (21)	+	MIXED (59)	−	100THS (82)	−
5-DIGIT (22)	+			1000THS (83)	−

MULTIPLICATION

MULTIPLICATION AS REPEATED ADDITION (24)	*	PROPER X PROPER (60)	−	10THS X WHOLE (84)	−
BASIC FACTS (26)	+	WHOLE X PROPER (61)	−	100THS X WHOLE (85)	+
1-DIGIT X 2-DIGIT (27)	*			1000THS X WHOLE (86)	+
1-DIGIT X 3-DIGIT (28)	+			10THS X 10THS (87)	−
1-DIGIT X 4-DIGIT (29)	+			10THS X 100THS (88)	−
2-DIGIT X 2-DIGIT (30)	−				
2-DIGIT X 3-DIGIT (31)	−				
MULTIPLES OF 10'S AND 100'S (34)	−				

DIVISION

NO REMAINDER

BASIC FACTS (37)	+	100THS + 10THS (92)	−
3-DIGIT + 1-DIGIT (38)	+	1000THS + 100THS (93)	−

REMAINDER

2-DIGIT + 1-DIGIT (39)	+
3-DIGIT + 1-DIGIT (40)	+
2-DIGIT + 2-DIGIT (41)	−
3-DIGIT + 2-DIGIT (42)	−
4-DIGIT + 1-DIGIT (43)	−
4-DIGIT + 2-DIGIT (44)	−
5-DIGIT + 2-DIGIT (45)	−
MULTIPLES OF 10'S AND 100'S (46)	−

PROPERTIES

COMMUTATIVE (124, 125)	−	−
ASSOCIATIVE (131, 132)	−	−
DISTRIBUTIVE (138)	− ◄─►	−
IDENTITY ELEMENT (142, 143)	+	−
INVERSE RELATION (149, 150)		

IDM - 6

Published by CTB/McGraw-Hill, Del Monte Research Park, Monterey, California 93940.
Copyright © 1972 by McGraw-Hill, Inc. All Rights Reserved. Printed in the U.S.A.

	CONCEPT QUESTION	WHOLE NUMBERS			
		+	−	x	÷
ROUNDED NUMBERS (158, 159, 160, 161, 162)	−	−	−	−	−
NUMBER SEQUENCES (164, 165)	−	−	−		
INEQUALITIES (187)	−				

NUMBER THEORY		CONCEPT QUESTION
	PRIME NUMBERS (188)	−
	PRIME FACTORIZATION (189)	
	EVEN AND ODD NUMBERS (192)	+
	MULTIPLES (193)	−
	COMMON FACTORS (194)	

MEASUREMENT		CONCEPT QUESTION	WHOLE NUMBERS			
			+	−	x	÷
METRIC GEOMETRY	NONSTANDARD UNITS (201)	−				
	ANGLE (202)	−				
	PERIMETER (204)	+				
	AREA (207)	+				
	VOLUME (210)	−				
	CIRCUMFERENCE (213)					
	GRAPHS (214)	−				
DENOMINATE NUMBERS	LINEAR MEASURE (222, 223, 224)	+	−	−		
	TEMPERATURE (225)	+				
	MONEY (226, 227, 228, 229, 230)	+	+	+	−	
	LIQUID (231)					
	WEIGHT (234)	+				
	CLOCK (237)	+				
	CALENDAR (241)	−				

NON-METRIC GEOMETRY	CONCEPT QUESTION
POINTS (242)	−
LINE SEGMENT (244)	+
REGIONS (245)	+
PARALLEL LINES (247)	−
PERPENDICULAR LINES (248)	−
RAY (250)	
ACUTE ANGLE (251)	−
OBTUSE ANGLE (252)	−
RIGHT TRIANGLE (255)	−
ISOSCELES TRIANGLE (257)	
QUADRILATERAL (259)	−
PARALLELOGRAM (260)	−
INTERSECTION (264)	−
PYRAMID (266)	
POLYHEDRON: EDGES (268)	−
POLYHEDRON: FACES (269)	−
POLYHEDRON: BASES (270)	−
POLYHEDRON: VERTICES (271)	
RATIO AND PROPORTION (272)	
SYMMETRY (274)	+
MAP READING, SCALE DRAWING (281)	−
CARTESIAN COORDINATES (283)	−

PLACE VALUE	CONCEPT QUESTION
0-999 (284)	−
1,000 − 99,999 (285)	−
100,000 − 999,999,999 (286)	
EXPANDED NOTATION	
3-DIGIT (289)	−
4-DIGIT (290)	−

PROBLEM SOLVING	
ADD., DIV. WHOLE NOS. (336)	+
MULT., DIV. WHOLE NOS. (337)	−
ADD., SUBT. FRACTIONS (338)	−
ADD., SUBT. DECIMALS (341)	
MULT., DIV. DECIMALS (342)	−
CALENDAR (343)	+
PATTERN RECOGNITION (344)	−
PRIMES, FACTORS (346)	
MULTIPLES (347)	
MONEY, AREA (348)	
METRIC SYSTEM (349)	
GEOMETRY (350)	

M0017

S. GLOSSARY 1

DEFINITIONS OF CATEGORIES IN THE STRUCTURE OF INTELLECT*

OPERATIONS

Major kinds of intellectual activities or processes; things that the organism does with the raw materials of information, information being defined as "that which the organism discriminates."

C *Cognition.* Immediate discovery, awareness, rediscovery, or recognition of information in various forms; comprehension or understanding.

M *Memory.* Retention or storage, with some degree of availability, of information in the same form it was committed to storage and in response to the same cues in connection with which it was learned.

D *Divergent Production.* Generation of information from given information, where the emphasis is on variety and quantity of output from the same source. Likely to involve what has been called *transfer*. This operation is most clearly involved in aptitudes of creative potential.

N *coNvergent Production.* Generation of information from given information, where the emphasis is on achieving unique or conventionally accepted best outcomes. It is likely the given (cue) information fully determines the response.

E *Evaluation.* Reaching decisions or making judgments concerning criterion satisfaction (correctness, suitability, adequacy, desirability, etc.) of information.

CONTENTS

Broad classes or types of information discriminable by the organism.

F *Figural.* Information in concrete form, as perceived or as recalled possibly in the form of images. The term "figural" minimally implies figure-ground perceptual organization. Visual spatial information is figural. Different sense modalities may be involved; e.g., visual kinesthetic.

---

*From Mary Meeker, *The Structure of Intellect* (Columbus: Charles E. Merrill, 1969), pp. 195-96.

324

S Symbolic. Information in the form of denotative signs, having no significance in and of themselves, such as letters, numbers, musical notations, codes, and words, when meanings and form are not considered.

M seMantic. Information in the form of meanings to which words commonly become attached, hence most notable in verbal communication but not identical with words. Meaningful pictures also often convey semantic information.

B Behavioral. Information, essentially non-verbal, involved in human interactions where the attitudes, needs, desires, moods, intentions, perceptions, thoughts, etc., of other people and of ourselves are involved.

PRODUCTS

The organization that information takes in the organism's processing of it.

U Units. Relatively segregated or circumscribed items of information having "thing" character. May be close to Gestalt psychology's "figure on a ground."

C Classes. Conceptions underlying sets of items of information grouped by virtue of their common properties.

R Relations. Connections between items of information based on variables or points of contact that apply to them. Relational connections are more meaningful and definable than implications.

S Systems. Organized or structured aggregates of items of information; complexes of interrelated or interacting parts.

T Transformations. Changes of various kinds (redefinition, shifts, or modification) of existing information or in its function.

I Implications. Extrapolations of information, in the form of expectancies, predictions, known or suspected antecedents, concomitants, or consequences. The connection between the given information and that extrapolated is more general and less definable than a relational connection.

T. GLOSSARY 2*

Acalculia—The loss of ability to perform mathematical functions.

Accommodation—The ocular focusing adjustment for clear vision at varying distances.

Agnosia—The inability to identify familiar objects through a particular sense organ.

Agraphia—The inability to recall kinesthetic writing patterns; i.e., cannot relate the mental images of words to the motor movements necessary for writing them.

Alexia—The loss of ability to receive, associate, and understand visual language symbols as referents to real objects and experiences. A severe reading disability usually considered the byproduct of brain dysfunction. Not to be used synonymously with dyslexia which may have multiple causes.

Aphasia—The loss of ability to comprehend, manipulate, or express words in speech, writing, or gesture. Usually associated with injury or disease in brain centers which control these processes.

> *Auditory aphasia*—Inability to comprehend spoken words. The same as word deafness and receptive aphasia.

> *Expressive aphasia*—Inability to remember the pattern of movements required to speak even though one knows what he wants to say.

Apraxia—The loss of ability to perform purposeful motor patterns.

Astigmatism—A condition of unequal curvatures along the different meridians in one or more of the refractive surfaces (cornea, anterior or posterior surface of the lens) of the eye, in consequence of which the rays from a luminous point are not focused at a single point on the retina but are diffused or spread out.

Auding—Listening, recognizing, and interpreting spoken language. More than just hearing and responding to sounds.

Auditory association (auditory-vocal association, ITPA)—The ability to relate spoken words in a meaningful way. The ITPA uses a version of the familiar analogies tests to assess this ability. The subject must complete the test statement by supplying an analogous word. Example: Soup is hot; ice cream is _____.

Auditory closure—The act or ability to accurately conceptualize in a complete and meaningful form words and/or sounds which are perceived in incomplete form.

---

*Some terms are not explained beyond one single-concept definition. These appear to be the ones accepted and understood as having a common meaning. Other terms are elaborated upon in the hope that the coverage will more fully explain the many ideas associated with the term or concept.

Auditory discrimination—The ability to identify and accurately choose between sounds of different pitch, volume, and pattern. Includes the ability to distinguish one speech sound from another.

Auditory imperception—Failure to understand oral communication and the significance of familiar sounds.

Auditory memory (auditory-vocal sequencing, ITPA)—The ability to repeat a sequence of symbols correctly. To test this, immediate auditory recall is requested. The ITPA subtest resembles the standard digit repetition test except that (1) digits are uttered at a rate of two per second which is double the usual rate, (2) the examiner drops his voice at the end of the digit sequence, (3) sequences are repeated if the subject fails to repeat the original presentation correctly, and (4) some digit sequences contain the same digit twice.

Auditory perception—The ability to receive and understand sounds.

Auditory reception (auditory decoding, ITPA)—The ability to understand the spoken word. The ITPA subtest used to measure this function includes questions that require only "yes" and "no" responses in order to eliminate the necessity of a child's explaining what he understands. Example: Do females slumber?

Bilateral—Pertaining to the use of both sides of the body in a simultaneous and parallel fashion.

Binocular fusion—The ability to integrate simultaneously into a single percept the data received through both eyes when they are aimed at the same position in space.

Body image—Awareness of one's own body (including the precise location of its parts in time and space). It includes the impressions one receives from internal signals as well as feedback received from others.

Brain damage—Any structural injury or insult to the brain, whether by surgery, accident, or disease.

Closure—The process of achieving completion in behavior or mental act; the tendency to stabilize or to complete a situation. Closure may occur in any sensory modality.

Cognitive structure—The mental process by which an individual becomes aware of and maintains contact with his internal and external environments.

It includes the processes of discrimination, association, integration, and categorization. Since language involves a proper selection of meaningful symbols, it is representative of the processes and levels of cognition. The linguistic symbol becomes a meaningful answer when the person is able to use a word or words to name, associate, or identify specific entities of a category.

It includes such things as selectivity of attention, the deployment of attention, the categorizing of behavior, memory formation, and attitudes toward confirmable versus unconfirmable experiences.

If we locate a candy store from one starting point, we can find it from another because we "know" where it is. A smooth-running skill illustrates a learned habit; knowing alternate routes illustrates cognitive structure. It has the dimension of clarity, and its synonyms are insight and understanding.

Cognitive style—A person's characteristic approach to problem solving and cognitive tasks. For example, some persons tend to be analytical, seeing parts, while others tend to be wholistic, seeing things in their entirety with little awareness of components.

Compulsiveness—Insistence on performing or doing things in habitual ways.

Concretism—An approach to thinking and behavior in which a person tends to regard each situation as essentially new and unique. Such a person fails to see essential similarities between situations which others accept as similar or even identical.

Constancy phenomenon—The tendency for brightness, color, size, or shape to remain relatively constant despite marked changes in stimulation; a phenomenon in which the color of an ordinary object is relatively independent of changes in illumination or in other viewing conditions.

Convergence—The ocular pointing mechanism by which the eyes are "aimed" at a target. It enables one to see a single object at varying distances.

Crossing the midline—The movement of the eyes, a hand and forearm, or a foot and leg across the midsection of the body without involving any other part of the body; i.e., without turning the head, twisting or swaying the trunk, or innervating the opposite limb.

Depth perception—That aspect of visual perception which deals with the direct awareness of the distance between an object and its observer. The awareness of distance between the front and the back of an object so that it is seen as three dimensional. The ability to perceive the third dimension in a flat picture which is actually two dimensional.

Differentiation—The ability to sort out and use independent parts of the body in a specific and controlled manner. Example: the ability to innervate the muscles of one arm without innervating in a similar fashion the muscles of the other arm or any of the parts of the body not required by the task.

Directionality—The projecting of all directions from the body into space. The child must develop laterality within his own organism and be aware of the right and left sides of his own body before he is ready to or able to project these directional concepts into external space.

Discrimination—The process of detecting differences as (1) auditory discrimination or the ability to identify sounds with respect to likenesses and differences and (2) visual discrimination or the ability to discriminate between different objects, forms, and/or letter symbols.

The ability to differentiate or distinguish quality, intensity, frequency, judgments, abilities, and other characteristics. These differences may be between numbers, letters, sounds of letters, persons, objects, etc. It may refer to one's ability to differentiate essential from nonessential details.

The ability to discriminate depends in large measure upon one's relative familiarity with the object.

Discrimination learning—The process by which stimuli come to acquire selective control over behavior. Discrimination is the term used to describe the control so achieved. An organism can discriminate between two stimuli if he can be induced, under suitable circumstances, to respond differently in the presence of the two stimuli and to do so reliably.

Dissociation—The inability to see things as a whole or as a gestalt. There is a tendency to respond to a simulus in terms of parts or segments and difficulty combining the parts to form a whole.

Distractibility—The ready and rapid shifting of attention through a series of unimportant stimuli. A morbid or abnormal variation of attention; inability to fix attention on any subject. A symptom of mental functioning of a person with brain damage.

Distraction may be caused by anxiety invading the thinking process. The tendency for a person's attention to be easily drawn to extraneous stimuli or to focus on minor details with a lack of attention to major aspects.

Similar to short attention span, however the latter more appropriately suggests an inability to concentrate on one thing for very long even without distractions. The term is often used to replace "hyperactivity" in psychological literature. The child is constantly distracted from one situation to another by stimuli that may involve any sense and can be either external or internal to a child.

Dysgraphia—The inability to write or to copy letters, words, and numbers. The child can see accurately what he wants to write but cannot manage correct writing movements. Usually associated with brain dysfunction.

Dyskinesia—Partial impairment of voluntary movement abilities resulting in incomplete movements, poor coordination, and apparently clumsy behavior.

Dyslexia—Partial inability to read or to understand what one reads either silently or aloud. Condition is usually, but not always, associated with brain impairment.

Visual dyslexias rarely learn from a global word approach, but they can learn individual sounds and put them together into words. Auditory dyslexias can learn words as a whole but do not learn through phonics.

Dysnomia—The inability to recall a word at will even though one knows the word and recognizes it when said to him.

Elaboration—Embellishment by the addition of variations of associated ideas or movements.

Emotional lability—The tendency toward recurrent emotional behavior characterized by sudden unexplainable shifts from one emotion to another.

Experimentation—The ability, desire, and willingness of a child to test a newly learned movement, task, or idea to see how many different ways it can be used by itself or in correlation with other movements, tasks, or ideas. Elaboration is the result of experimentation.

Eye-hand coordination—The ability to perceptually organize by joining together in the mind's eye and to reproduce manually. Poor development of motor skills and left-right confusion could be a result of poor eye-hand coordination.

Eye-hand coordination skill—This skill consists of the eyes steering the hand(s) acurately and skillfully through the three coordinates of space— right and left, up and down, fore and aft—, which are matched with the coordinates of the body and vision, for the purpose of manipulating tools or forming the symbols of language. It enables one to make visual discriminations of size, shape, texture, and object location. It is dependent upon use, practice, and integration of the eyes and hands as paired learning tools.

Eye movement skill (ocular motilities) — This skill consists of the ability to quickly and accurately align both eyes on an object, to release and move in a controlled manner to another object, or to maintain alignment on a moving object. This skill provides a consistent visual input to be matched to other sensory inputs and the experiences of the organism.

Inadequate ability in eye movement skills is revealed in head turning instead of eye movement, short attention span, frequent loss of place on the page, omission of words and phrases, confusion of left and right directions, poor orientation, writing or drawings on the page, or stumbling and clumsiness in playground activities.

Eye teaming (binocularity) — The purpose of this skill is to provide speed and effectiveness in visual identification and interpretation of printed details. The accuracy and speed of "focusing" is dependent upon the degree of eye teaming achieved.

There are two aspects to be observed by the teacher: (1) horizontal teaming — alignment of both eyes so that they are in position to inspect the same symbol at the same instant (to provide singleness and clearness of all materials), and (2) near-to-far, far-to-near teaming — immediate clarity and accuracy of recognition of objects or symbols at all points in space.

Indications or inadequate abilities in eye teaming are complaints of seeing double, repetition of letters within words or words in the same sentence, omission of words or numbers, closing of one eye, extreme head tilt or working on one side of desk, poor orientation of writing or drawing on paper, total postural deviation that continues at all desk activities, excessive blinking, comprehension lower than apparent abilities, or extreme fatigue when working with any visual materials.

Figure-ground relationship — "Geometrical patterns are always seen against a background and thus appear object-like, with contours and boundaries. We may think of such figure-ground organization as basic to stimulus patterning. Patterns do not have to contain identifiable objects to be structured as figure and ground. Patterns of black and white and many wallpaper designs are perceived as figure-ground relationships and very often figure and ground are reversible" (Hilgard, 1962, p. 193). The part seen as *figure* tends to appear slightly in front of the background, even though you know it is printed on the surface of the page. You seem to look through the spaces in and around the figure to a uniform background behind, whether the background is white or black.

"Gestalt psychologists have been particularly interested in figure-ground relationships and other patterned aspects of stimulation and have suggested a number of principles" to explain the results of patterning and perceptual structuring (Hilgard, 1962, p. 194). There are four principles: (1) proximity; (2) similarity; (3) continuity; and (4) closure.

Proximity. Look at the dots in Figure A.5. They appear to be arranged in horizontal rows in A and in vertical columns in B. Why? Merely because in A they are closer together in rows, and in B they are closer together in columns. It takes effort to counteract proximity to see the dots in columns and rows in the other directions.

FIGURE A.5

Similarity. In Figure A.6 all the dots are equally spaced so that proximity is not an important factor in determining whether we emphasize horizontal or vertical lines. Now the influence of similarity is compelling. We see rows of dots and rows of small circles, so we group like items together.

O   O   O   O   O   O   O   O   O   O   O

●   ●   ●   ●   ●   ●   ●   ●   ●   ●   ●

O   O   O   O   O   O   O   O   O   O   O

●   ●   ●   ●   ●   ●   ●   ●   ●   ●   ●

FIGURE A.6

Continuity. In Figure A.6, what does A appear to be? It is easy to break it down into the two parts shown in B — a wavy line over a rectangular motif. Again if we expend some effort, we can break it into the two parts shown in C. But there is little doubt about the greater naturalness of B because the parts are more continuous this way. The wavy line continues as a wavy line and the right-angled figures continue at right angles.

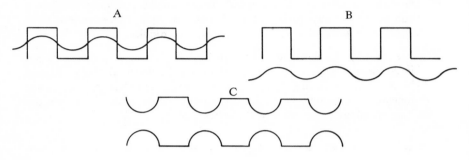

FIGURE A.7

Closure. "The tendency for incomplete figures to become complete in perception is called *closure*" (Hilgard, 1962, p. 195). The picture in Figure A.8 illustrates this tendency.

FIGURE A.8

Fine motor development — The maturation and refinement of the small muscles in the extremities of the body such as finger and wrist movements and eye-hand coordination.

Form Perception — The ability to perceive an arrangement or pattern of elements or parts constituting a unitary whole, wherein the elements are in specific relationships with one another.

Frustration level — A degree of task difficulty which a child is incapable of performing at a given time.

Generalization — The process of deriving or inducing (a general concept or principle) from particulars. For example, by recognizing many types of chairs as chairs, a child is categorizing objects that are similar and yet different.

Generalized movement — A wave of movement that sweeps through the whole body. Parts of the body such as arms and legs move, not in relation to their function, but only as adjuncts of the total movement.

Gerstmann's syndrome — A combination of disabilities including finger agnosia, right-left disorientation, acalculia, and agraphia.

Gestalt — A term used to express any unified whole whose properties cannot be derived just by adding the parts and their relationships. More than the sum of its parts.

Grammar closure (auditory-vocal automatic, ITPA) — The ability which permits one to predict future linguistic events from past experience. The ITPA asseses this ability by requiring the subject to complete a statement with an inflected word; for example: "Here is an apple. Here are two _____." The nature of the inflection supplied indicates the ability of the subject to predict what will be said. Linguistically, normal children learn these inflections in a rather systematic way. A certain number of errors are expected from children right up to the end of the test in much the same way that normal children continue to make articulation errors up to and beyond ages 7–10. Only when excessive errors are made do we infer disability.

Gross motor activity — An activity or output in which groups of large muscles are used and the factors of rhythm and balance are primary.

Hemispherical dominance — Refers to the fact that one hemisphere of the brain generally leads the other in control of body movement, resulting in the preferred use of left or right.

Hyperactivity — Excessive activity. The person seems to have a surplus of energy and is unable to control movements for even a short length of time.

Hyperkinesis — Excessive mobility or motor function or activity.

Hyperopia — Hypermetropia; a condition in which parallel rays are focused behind the retina due to an error in refraction.

Hypoactivity — Pronounced absence of physical activity.

Hypokinesis — Reduced motor function or activity often giving the appearance of listlessness.

Imperception — The inability to interpret sensory information correctly. A cognitive impairment rather than impairment of a sensory organ.

Impulsiveness — The tendency to act on impulse. Responding without thinking, which is often explosive behavior where learning disorders exist.

Inferential reasoning — The act of obtaining a judgment or logical conclusion from given data or premises. More precisely, a psychological or temporal process by which the mind passes from a proposition or propositions accepted as true to other propositions believed to be so connected to the first as to make the latter true.

Inference implies forming judgments on the basis of cognition or belief not explicitly recognized. There is transposition of previous learned knowledge to new analogous situations or cognitive restructuring and integration of prior and current experience to fit the demands of an objective.

Integration — The pulling together and organizing of all stimuli impinging on an organism at a given moment. Also involved is the tying together of the present stimulation with experience variables retained from past activities. The organizing of many individual movements into a complex response.

Kinesthetic — The sense that yields knowledge of the movements of the muscles of the body and the positions of the joints.

Kinesthetic method — A method of treating reading disability by having pupils trace the outline of words and numbers or in other ways incorporate muscle movement to supplement visual and auditory stimuli.

Laterality — Complete motor awareness of both sides of the body.

Learning disability — Children with learning disabilities are those (1) who have educationally significant discrepancies among their sensory-motor, perceptual, cognitive, academic, or related developmental levels which interfere with the performance of educational tasks; (2) who may or may not show demonstrable deviation in central nervous system functioning; and (3) whose disabilities are not secondary to general mental retardation, sensory deprivation, or serious emotional disturbance.

Learning expectancy level —

Kaluger and Kolson (1969) have suggested a formula to determine learning expectancy. It is predicated on the assumption that there is a difference of five years between grade placement and the age of an average child with no anamalies. For example, there is a difference of five years between grade one and age six and a difference of five years between grade 12 and age 17.

"When using the L.E.L. formula to find a child's potential level, use his chronological age (C.A.) in years and months (ex. 8 yrs. 3 mos.) as if it were the time that a reading achievement test was given to him. If an I.Q. is known but not the M.A., use the following procedure:

$$I.Q. \times C.A. = MA. - 5 = learning\ expectancy\ level$$

1. Multiply I.Q. (with a decimal before last two numbers) times the chronological age, also given with a decimal value (example, 8 yrs. 3 mos. = 8.25). (See table below.)
2. Then subtract 5 (always 5).
3. Answer is Learning Expecting Level, which is the grade level at which he should be accomplishing.
4. Always list reading achievement test scores with L.E.L. so they can be compared.
5. Recognize that the greater the difference between the L.E.L. and the

C.A., the more likely that extenuating circumstances could affect the reading level — for example

$$I.Q. \times C.A. \ (yrs.) = M.A. \ (yrs.) - 5 = L.E.L.$$

$$0.93 \times 8.25 = 7.7 - 5 = \text{grade } 2.7$$

Use this table to convert months into percentages of a year.

11 months	= 0.91	5 months	= 0.42
10 months	= 0.83	4 months	= 0.33
9 months	= 0.75	3 months	= 0.25
8 months	= 0.67	2 months	= 0.17
7 months	= 0.58	1 month	= 0.08
6 months	= 0.50		

Learning quotient — Myklebust and his associates have suggested a quantitative classification of learning disabilities. The extent of the learning disability is calculated as a ratio between potential and achievement.

$$\text{EA (expectancy age)} = \frac{\text{MA} + \text{CA} + \text{GA (grade age)}}{3}$$

The learning quotient is a measure of discrepancy between expected (potential) and actual achievement in various areas of learning.

$$\text{LQ (learning quotient)} = \frac{\text{AA (achievement age)}}{\text{EA (expectancy age)}}$$

A learning quotient of 89 or below determines that a child has a learning disability. (Myklebust, 1967, pp. 5-6).*

Left-to-right progression — Recognizing letter or word sequences correctly; can be disturbed if laterality has not been established.
Manual expession (motor encoding, ITPA) — The ability to express ideas in meaningful gestures. In a testing situation, the subject responds to a picture of an object by showing the examiner what should be done with the object.

---

*Helmer R. Myklebust, *Progress in Learning Disabilities*, Vol. 1 (New York: Grune & Stratton, 1967) pp. 5-6. Paraphrased by permission of the author and the publisher.

Maturational lag — The concept of differential development of areas of the brain and of personality which mature according to recognized patterns. A lag signifies a slow differentiation or irregularity in this pattern without a structural defect, deficiency, or loss.

Memory span — The number of related or unrelated items that can be recalled immediately after presentation.

Mixed cerebral dominance — The theory that hemispheric dominance has not been adequately established and that learning problems may be due wholly or partly to the fact that one cerebral hemisphere does not consistently lead the other in the control of bodily movement.

Neurological examination — An examination of sensory or motor responses, especially the reflexes, to determine whether or not there are localized impairments of the nervous system.

Nonreader — The child who is unable to profit from the best instruction in any of the skill areas; therefore, is unable to learn to read from conventional methods. Commonly referred to as dyslexia, neurological deficiency, minimum brain damage, or specific reading disability. The non-reader's disabilities are often complicated by his emotional involvement in his gross failure and physical defects.

   The nonreader is generally identified as one who has made scant progress in learning after two or more years of instruction in reading. The number of words he recognizes at sight is negligible, perhaps twenty-five or less. He confuses words and has difficulty in spelling.

Organicity — Refers to central nervous system impairment.

Perception — A cognitive process which involves understanding, comprehension, and organization. The interpretation of sensory influences. The mechanism by which intellect recognizes and makes sense out of sensory stimulation. The accurate mental association of present stimuli with memories of past experiences.

Perception of self — Perceptions of the self may have varying degrees of agreement with reality. What apparently occurs, as a result of emotional blocking, is deficiency of perception of self, a deficiency which is not understood by the person involved and which he cannot prevent or overcome without help. Therefore, when a person is said to be suffering from a deficiency of perception, either his insights are inconsistent with one another or the deductions made from them do not concur with the data of observation.

Perceptual-motor — The perceptual-motor process includes input (sensory or perceptual activities) and output (motor or muscular activities). A division of the two is impossible, for anything that happens to one area automatically affects the other. Any total activity includes input, integration, output, and feedback.

Perceptual organization — A more or less systematic arrangement of relatively separate parts into a whole in order to fulfill a function. It involves voluntary attention and the ability to organize and join together in the mind's eye. Perceptual organization includes spatial orientation.

Perseveration — The inability to develop a new response to a new or altered stimulus. Continuing to behave or respond in a certain way when it is no longer appropriate.

Psychoneurology — The area of study concerned with the behavioral disorders associated with brain dysfunctions in human beings.

Redundancy — The art of presenting the same information to as many of the senses as simultaneously as possible in a given task. For example, when tracing a square on sandpaper with the finger, a child sees the square, hears the movement of the finger across the rough surface, feels the tactual contact of the finger with the paper, and also feels the kinesthetic or muscular movements in the hand and arm.

Remediation — That function which redirects or circumvents an impaired procedure in learning. It implies compensatory methods that facilitate learning rather than cure learning disorders.

Rigidity — Resistance to undertaking a new kind of response.

Rotation of design — The revolving of a visual pattern on its axis, clockwise or counterclockwise. In the *Bender Visual-Motor Gestalt Test,* if the rotation of a design is spontaneous, it may be indicative of an emotional disturbance and/or neurological disorder.

Sensorimotor skill — A skill in which muscular movement is prominent but under sensory control. For example, riding a bicycle is not simply a pattern of skilled movements. The bicycle rider has to watch the traffic and the bumps in the road and guide by them. These considerations in calling attention to the sensory control of skill explain the somewhat awkward term *sensorimotor skill.*

Sensory-motor ability — The ability to act and perform as directed by the senses; the ability to hear and do things in response to a given stimulus. It is associated with how well a person is coordinated when dealing with the senses of hearing, seeing, tasting, smelling, feeling, and motor ability.

A person becomes aware of the external world by applying all sense modalities and movements simultaneously. He becomes aware of himself as being separate from the outside world. He learns to control the skeletal movements, to control the movement of specific parts of the body, and to manipulate objects.

Size constancy — The tendency for the perceived size of an object to remain constant irrespective of the size of the retinal image caused by that object.

Sociopath — A person characterized by a social or antisocial behavior. One who cannot adjust to the culture. A personality disorder in which behavior expresses rebellion against, or at least an unwillingness, to conform to the demands of society. Individuals classified as such are not neurotic, psychotic, or mentally defective but manifest a marked lack of ethical or moral development and an inability to follow the socially approved codes of behavior. Sociopaths often accompany their acts with regrets and expressions of proposed future behavior that is socially acceptable. They are quite vain and lack guilt feelings, and they seem unable to form lasting relationships or to reform even under threat of punishment.

Space perception — The direct awarness of the spatial properties of an object, especially in relation to the observer. The perception of position, direction, size, form, and/or distance by any of the senses.

Spatial relationship — The ability to perceive the position of two or more objects in relation to one's self and in relationship to one another. The ability to see similarities in shape, size, etc., of two or more objects.

Children's perception of spatial relationships has a direct bearing on their performance in reading and computations. They must be able to perceive positional relationships between various objects or points of reference. Spatially, a person is the center of his/her own world and perceives objects in relation to self. Body image acts as a zero focus or point of reference in terms of the knowledge of the person's space world. Any fault in body image will be reflected in the perception of outside objects.

Piaget and Inhelder state that there are five basic steps in the process of the perception of space. They are not necessarily unique or distinct but may very well overlap (Piaget & Inhelder, 1967, pp. 5–8).

1. The most elementary spatial relationship that can be perceived is that of "proximity" or "nearby-ness".
2. The second spatial relationship is that of separation; that is, the blending of two nearby elements may be segregated as analytic perception develops.
3. The third relationship is order or succession — the positioning of one element before the other. One fundamental part of order is symmetry, represented by double-order or reverse-order perception.
4. The fourth relationship is that of enclosure or surrounding, which develops as a concept of "betweenness" and undergoes a complex evolution as the first three steps develop. This evolution brings about three-dimensional perception.
5. The last relationship is that of continuity. This is the development of continuous perception in relation to lines, surfaces, etc.

Spatial-temporal translation — The ability to translate a simultaneous relationship in space into a serial relationship in time, or vice versa. For example, the child must recognize the square as a whole when seen in space and reproduce it in time as an organized series of lines and angles. To achieve in many of the tasks we set before him, the child must be able to organize impressions in both of these areas and to shift fluently from one to the other as the situation demands.

Specific language disability — Usually the term is applied to those who find learning to read and spell very difficult but who are otherwise intelligent. More recently any language deficiency — oral, visual, or auditory — is identified by this term.

Splinter skill — A restricted approach to a specific problem that exists in isolation, "splintered off" from the remainder of the child's activity. Its usefulness is limited, adequate for only one type of activity. This isolated response also confuses the child, since he/she is required to live with two basic learning sets between which there is little or no connection and with educational skills that have been memorized because they were learned out of context, that is, outside and above the child's performance level. They, too, are isolated facts that the child can neither elaborate nor integrate.

Stimulation level — The level of activity that demands just enough effort on the child's part to keep interest and to encourage further experimentation.

Strabismus — That condition wherein the extraocular muscles are not in a state of balance and a dysfunction of fusion is present. As a result, the eyes are out of alignment. Lack of coordination of the eye muscles so that the two eyes do not focus on the same point.

Strephosymbolia — Twisted symbols. A reversal of symbols observed in the reading and writing performance of children with learning disabilities (e.g., *was* for *saw*).

Structuring — The act of arranging an activity in a way that is understandable to children and conducive to performance, or in other words, arranging the task so that children are aware of what is expected of them. Once the task is structured, the children should be left to perform without additional cueing.

Tactile or tactual — Refers to the sense of touch. The term expresses both the child's sense of touch as applied to a given object or task and the instructor's tactual clues that the child receives.

Tactual-kinesthetic — A combination of the sense of touch and the sense of muscle movement.

Temporal — Pertaining to time or time relationships. The ability to recognize the limits of time with understanding. In early childhood time is not "an ever-rolling stream" but simply concrete events embedded in activity. Time and space are not differentiated from each other. Movement must occur in time, and the child must project awareness of time into object relationships.

Tolerance level — The level at which the child can perform without any effort and at which he/she will soon become bored or uninterested.

Unilateral — One-sided; the child who is unilateral uses one side of the body and ignores the other.

Verbal expression — The ability to express ideas in spoken words. The ITPA tests this ability by asking the subject to describe a simple object such as a block or ball. The score depends on the number of unique and meaningful ways in which he/she characterizes a given test object.

Visual association (visual-motor association, ITPA) — The ability to relate visual symbols in a meaningful way. To measure this, the ITPA requires the subject to select from among four pictures the one which "goes with" a given stimulus picture.

Visual classification and grouping — A cognitive process which gives meaning, organization, and structure to the visual field or a subdivision of it, depending upon the concentration of the viewers' gaze. It is related to the physiological and psychological maturation of the viewer. The identification of objects or elements within the visual field or subdivision thereof and the establishment of a pattern of relationships dependent upon the identification.

Visual closure — Measures the perceptual interpretation of any visual object or thing when only a part of it is shown.

Visual memory (visual-motor sequencing, ITPA) — The ability to reproduce a sequence of visual stimuli from memory. The IPTA uses chips, each having a picture of a geometric form. The examiner arranges the chips in a certain order, allows the subject to observe this order for five seconds, mixes the chips, and requires the subject to reproduce the sequence.

Visual-motor ability — The ability to visualize and to assemble material from life into meaningful wholes; the ability to see and to perform with dexterity and coordination; the ability to recognize part-whole relationships in working toward a goal which may be unknown at first. The ability to control body or hand movements in coordination with visual perception.

Visual reception (visual decoding, ITPA) — The ability to comprehend pictures and written words. The ITPA uses a picture test, and the child responds by pointing to pictures indicating that he/she comprehends them.

REFERENCES

Abeson, A. Movement and momentum: government and education of handi-capped children. *Exceptional Children,* Sept., 1972, 63–66.

Ayers, J. *Sensory integration and learning disorders.* Los Angeles: Western Psychological Services, 1972.

Ball, R. Comparison of thinking abilities of five-year-old white and black children in relation to certain environmental factors. Final report, Project No. 9-70-0067, Grant No. OEG 9-9-120070-0018(057), U.S. Dept. of Health, Education, and Welfare.

Bannatyne, A. Diagnosing learning disabilities and writing remedial pre-scriptions. Reprinted from the *Journal of Learning Disabilities,* 1968, 1, (4), 242–49.

Barnes, B. Specific dyslexia and legislation. *Journal of Learning Disabilities,* 1968, 1 (1), 58–64.

Barsch, R. H. *Achieving perceptual motor efficiency.* Seattle, Wa.: Special Child Publications, 1967.

Bateman, B. *Temporal learning.* San Raphael, Ca.: Dimension Publishing, 1968.

Bender, L. Communication in children with developmental alexia. Hoch, P.H., Zubin, J. (Ed.), *Psychopathology of Communication.* New York: Grune & Stratton, 1958.

Bender, L. *A visual-motor gestalt test and its clinical use.* Research Mono-graph, No. 3. New York: American Orthopsychiatric Association, 1938.

Bender, L. Presentation at Conference on Learning Disabilities, Napa County Office of Education, Napa, Ca., Nov. 1969.

Bigge, M. L., & Hunt, M. P. *Psychological foundations of education.* New York: Harper & Row, 1962.

Birch, H. G. *Brain damage in children: the biological and social aspects.* Baltimore: Williams & Wilkins, 1964.

Boder, E. Developmental dyslexia: a diagnostic screening procedure based on reading and spelling patterns. *Academic Therapy,* 1969, IV (4), 285–87.

Bonder, J.B., & Wilson, J.A.R. Should you be told your child's I.Q.? NEA Publication, #38–232, National Education Association, Washington, D.C.

Bormuth, J.R. The cloze readability procedure. *Elementary English,* 1968, XLV, 429–36.

Boshes, B., & Myklebust, H. R. A neurological and behavioral study of children with learning disorders. *Neurology,* 1964, 14 (1), 7–12.

Beatty, J.R. The analysis of an instrument for screening learning disabilities, *Journal of Learning Disabilities,* 1975, 8 (3), 180–185.

Bush, W.J., & Giles, M. T. *Aids to psycholinguistic teaching.* Columbus: Charles E. Merrill, 1969.

Bush, W.J., & Mattson, B. D. WISC test patterns and underachievers. *Journal of Learning Disabilities,* 1973, 6 (4), 251–56.

Bush, W.J., & Waugh, K. W. Psycholinguistic and interaction techniques: a wholistic approach to remediation. Paper presented to Danish Congress of Speech and Voice Therapists, Nyborg, Denmark, Apr. 11–12, 1975.

Cannon, T. M. Change and the school psychologist. *The School Psychologist,* 1973, XXVII (4), 10.

Chalfont, J. & Scheffelin, M.A. Central processing dysfunctions in children, NINDS Monograph No. 9, U.S. Department of Health Education and Welfare, 1969.

Chaney, C. C., & Kephart, N. C. *Motoric aids to learning.* Columbus: Charles E. Merrill, 1968.

Clements, S. D. Minimal brain dysfunction in children. U.S. Department of Health, Education and Welfare, 1966.

Clements, S. D., Lehtinen, L. E., & Lukens, J. E. *Children with minimal brain injury.* (May 1964.) National Society for Crippled Children and Adults, 2023 West Ogden Avenue, Chicago, 60612.

Clements, S. D., & Peters, J. E. Minimal brain dysfunction in the school-age child. *Archives for General Psychiatry,* 1962, 6, 185—197.

Cratty, B. J. *Developmental sequences of perceptual-motor tasks.* Freeport, L. I., N. Y.: Educational Activities, 1967.

Cratty, B. J. *Perceptual motor behavior and educational processes.* Springfield, IL.: Charles C. Thomas, 1969.

Cratty, B. J. *Psychology and physical activity.* Englewood Cliffs, NJ: Prentice-Hall, 1968.

Critchley, M. *Developmental dyslexia.* London: Heinemann, 1964.

Cruickshank, W. M., & Johnson, G. O., eds. *Education of exceptional children and youth.* Englewood Cliffs, NJ: Prentice-Hall, 1958.

———— et al., eds. *The teacher of brain-injured children.* Syracuse: Syracuse University Press, 1966.

de Hirsch, K., Jansky, J.J., & Langford, W.S. *Predicting reading failure: a preliminary study of reading, writing, and spelling disabilities in pre-school children.* New York, Harper & Row, 1966.

Delacato, C. H. *The diagnosis and treatment of speech and reading problems.* Springfield, IL.: Charles C. Thomas, 1965.

Denhoff, E. The measurement of psychoneurological factors contributing to learning efficiency. *Journal of Learning Disabilities,* 1968, 1 (11), 636–44.

Denhoff, E., Hainsworth, P.K., & Siqueland, Marian L. "Development and predictive characteristics of items from the meeting street school screening test. *Journal of Developmental Medicine and Child Neurology,* 1968, 10, 220–32.

Dorland's Medical Dictionary, 24th ed. Philadelphia: W.B. Saunders Co., 1965.

Durrell, D.D., & Sullivan, H.B. *Durrell-Sullivan reading capacity and achievement tests.* New York: Harcourt Brace Jovanovich, 1965.

Erwin, W.M., & Cannon, T.M. Ethical consideration in the role of the school counselor. *TPGA Journal,* 1974, 3 (1), 12.

Gates, A.I. *The improvement of reading.* (rev. ed.) New York: Macmillan, 1935.

Gearheart, B.R., & Willenberg, E.P. *Application of pupil assessment information: for the special education teacher.* Denver, CO.: Love Publishing, 1970.

Gesell, A. *The first five years of life.* New York: Harper & Bros., 1940.

Glass, G.G. Perceptual conditioning for decoding: rationale and method, in Bateman, Barbara, *Learning Disorders.* (Vol. 4) Special Child Publications, 1971.

Glasser, A.J., & Zimmerman, I.L. *Clinical interpretation of the Wechsler Intelligence Scale for Children.* New York: Grune & Stratton, 1967.

Goodenough, F.L. *The measurement of intelligence by drawings.* World Book Co., 1954.   ,

Grady, R. "Medication and the child with learning disability." Presentation at the Virginia Association on Children with Learning Disabilities, Roanoke, VA., Apr. 1974.

Graham, E.E. Wechsler-Bellevue and WISC scattergrams of unsuccessful readers. *Journal of Consulting Psychology,* 1952, 16 (4), 268–71.

Guilford, J.P. *The nature of intelligence.* New York: McGraw-Hill, 1967.

Guilford, J.P. Three faces of intellect. *The American Psychologist,* 1958, 8, 469–79.

Jones, C. A view of problems in early childhood. Presentation for Region XVI, Education Service Center, Amarillo, TX., 1974.

Hakin, C.S. Task analysis: one alternative. *Academic Therapy,* 1974–75, X(2).

Haring, N.G. *Behavior of exceptional children.* Columbus: Charles E. Merrill, 1974.

Hegge, T.G.; Kirk, S.A.; and Kirk W. *Remedial reading drills.* Ann Arbor, MI.: Wahr, 1965.

Hilgard, E.R. *Introduction to psychology.* (3rd ed.) New York: Harcourt Brace Jovanovich, 1962.

Hiskey, M. *Hiskey-Nebraska Test of Learning Aptitudes* (manual). Lincoln, NE.: Union College Press, 1966.

Huber, J.T. *Report writing in psychology and psychiatry.* New York: Harper & Row, 1961.

Hyman, I. Editorial in *The School Psychologist,* 1942, XXVI (4).

Jastak, J.F., & Jastak, S.R. *Manual of instruction: the Wide Range Achievement Test.* (rev. ed.) Wilmington, DE.: Guidance Associates, 1965.

Johnson, D.J., & Myklebust, Helmer R. *Learning disabilities: educational principles and practices.* New York: Grune & Stratton, 1967.

Johnson, D., Educational Principle for Children with Learning Disabilities. *Minimal Brain Dysfunction,* 1968, Society for Crippled Children and Adults, 2023 West Ogden Avenue, Chicago, IL. 60612.

Johnson, K. Personal letter, 1974.

Kalugar, G., & Kolson, C. *Reading and learning disabilities.* Columbus: Charles E. Merrill, 1969.

Kephart, N.C. *Learning disability; an educational adventure.* West Lafayette, IN.: Kappa Delta Pi Press, 1967.

Kephart, N.C. *The slow learner in the classroom.* Columbus: Charles E. Merrill, 1960.

Kirk, S.A. *Educating exceptional children.* Boston: Houghton Mifflin, 1962.

Kirk, S.A. *Educating exceptional children.* (2nd ed.) Boston: Houghton Mifflin (1972).

Kirk, S.A., McCarthy, James J., & Kirk, Winifred D. *Examiner's manual, Illinois Test of Psycholinguistic Abilities.* Urbana, Il.: University Press, 1968.

Koppitz, E.M. *The Bender-Gestalt Test for Young Children.* New York: Grune & Stratton, 1964.

Koppitz, E.M. *Psychological evaluation of children's human figure drawings.* New York: Grune & Stratton, 1968.

Krantz, L.L. (ed) *The author's word list for the primary grades.* Minneapolis: Curriculum Research Co., 1945.

Kraus, H. & Hirschland, R.P. Minimum muscular fitness test in school children. *Research Quarterly of the American Association for Health, Physical Education, and Recreation,* 1954, 25, 178–88.

Kussmaul, A. Disturbances of speech. In von Ziemssen, H. (Ed), *Cyclopaedia of the Practice of Medicine.* (vol. 15) New York: William Wood, 1877.

Lagemann, J.K. Let's abolish I.Q. tests. *The P.T.A. Magazine,* 1966, 56 (4), 7–11.

Langford, W.S. Developmental dyspraxia — abnormal clumsiness. *Bulletin of the Orton Society,* 1955, 5, 3–9.

Lutey, C. *Individual intelligence testing,* 1967, Colorado State College Bookstore, Greeley, Co.   ,

McCarthy, J.J., & Kirk, Samuel. *The Illinois Test of Psycholinguistic Abilities.* (rev. ed.) Urbana, Il.: University of Illinois Press, 1968.

McCarthy, J.M. How to teach the hard to reach. *Grade Teacher,* May–June 1967, pp. 97–101.

McCarthy, J.M. & Elkins, J. Psychometric characteristics of children enrolled in the child service demonstration centers: the search for homogenous clusters. (unpublished paper) Leadership Training Institute in Learning, Department of Special Education, University of Arizona, Project # 6-2003, Tucson, Az.

McCarthy, J.M. Personal letter, October, 1974.

McGlannan, F.K. Familial characteristics of genetic dyslexia: preliminary report from a pilot study. Reprinted from the *Journal of Learning Disabilities,* 1968, 1 (3), 185–191.

Machowsky, H. The school psychologist and the parent's right to know. *The School Psychologist,* 1973, XXVII (4).

Martin, W.T. *Writing psychological reports.* Jacksonville, Il.: Psychologist and Educators, Inc., 1971.

Meeker, M.N. *The structure of intellect.* Columbus: Charles E. Merrill, 1969.

Meeker, M.N. Unpublished research. Institute for Applied S.O.I. Studies, El Segundo, Ca. 90266. 1973, 1974.

Money, J. ed. *Reading disability: progress and research needs in dyslexia.* Baltimore: Johns Hopkins Press, 1962.

Money, J., & Bobrow, N.A. Birth defect of the skull and face without brain or learning disorder: a psychological and pedagogical report. Reprinted from *Journal of Learning Disabilities,* 1968, (5), 289–98.

Murdock, J.B. Who is the client? *The School Psychologist,* 1971, XXVI (2).

Myklebust, H.R. *Progress in learning disabilities.* (Vol. 1) New York: Grune & Stratton, 1967.

Myklebust, H.R., & Boshes, B. *Minimal brain dysfunction in children: final report contract 108-05-142 neurological and disease control program.* Washington, D.C.: Department of Health, Education, and Welfare, 1969.

Myklebust, H.R. *The development of disorders of written language.* New York: Grune & Stratton, 1965.

North Carolina Department of Education, *Exceptional children: rules and regulations,* 1973–74.

Ohio Department of Education, *Ohio's comprehension plan for the education of the handicapped,* July 1, 1973.

Orton, S.T. Word blindness in school children. *Archives of Neurology and Psychiatry,* 1925, 14, 581–615.

Osgood, C.E., Suci, G.J., & Tannenbaum, P.H. *The measurement of meaning.* Urbana, IL.: University of Illinois Press, 1957.

Osgood, C.E. Psycholinguistics: a survey of theory and research problems. *Journal of Abnormal Social Psychology,* 1954, 49:4, part 2, Supplement.

Penfield, W. *Speech and brain mechanisms.* Princeton, NJ.: Princeton University Press, 1959.

Pennsylvania Department of Education, *Special education standards of the Pennsylvania Department of Education,* 10–2–72.

Piaget, J. & Inhelder, B. *The child's conception of space.* New York: W. W. Norton and Co., 1967. Permission to reprint was granted by Humanities Press Inc., New York, holder of U.S. rights, and Koutledge & Kegan Paul Ltd., holder of world rights.

Prescott, D.A. *The child in the educative process.* New York: McGraw-Hill, 1957.

Reitan, M.R. & Boll, T.J. "Neuro-psychological Correlate of Minimal Brain Dysfunction." *Annals of the New York Academy of Sciences,* 1972, 65–88, 205.

Roach, E.C., & Kephart, N.C. *The purdue perceptual-motor survey.* Columbus: Charles E. Merrill, 1966.

Robbins, M.J., & Carrigan, W.C. "Professional Liability and School Psychology." *The School Psychologist,* Vol. XXV No. 2, 1971.

Rosen, V.H. "Streposymbolia: An Intrasystemic Disturbance of the Synthetic Function of the Ego." In *The Psychoanalytic Study of the Child,* Vol. 10. New York: International Universities Press, 1955, 83–99.

Ross, S.L., DeYoung, H.G. & Cohen, J.S. "Confrontation: special education placement and the law. *Exceptional Children,* Sept. 1971, 5–12.

Sattler, J.M. Analysis of functions of the 1960 Stanford-Binet Intelligence Scale, Form L-M. *Journal of Clinical Psychology,* 1965, 21 (2), 173–79.

Sherrington, C. *Man on his nature.* Cambridge: Cambridge University Press, 1951.

Serio, M. Know the Child to Teach the Child. *Academic Theory,* 1970, (3), 222–27.

Skinner, B.F. *The behavior of organisms.* New York: Appleton-Century-Crofts, 1938.

Strauss, A.A., & Kephart, N.C. *Psychopathology and education of the brain-injured child.* (Vol. 2) New York: Grune & Stratton, 1955.

Strauss, A.A., & Lehtinen, L.E. *Psychopathology and education of the brain-injured child.* (Vol. 1) New York: Grune & Stratton, 1947.

Strong, R. Identification of primary school age children with learning handicaps associated with minimal brain disorder. Doctoral dissertation, University of Utah, 1965.

Texas Education Agency, *Administrative guide and handbook for special education,* Austin, Texas, Bulletin 711, March, 1973.

Thompson, L.J. *Reading disability: developmental dyslexia.* Springfield, Il.: Charles C. Thomas, 1966.

Tiegs, E.W., & Clark, W.W. *California Achievement Tests.* Monterey, California: California Test Bureau, 1957.

Tveresni, M. The internal consistency of the WISC scores for ages 5–16. *Journal of Consulting and Clinical Psychology,* 1968, 29 (2), 192—95.

Valett, E. *The remediation of learning disabilities.* Palo Alto, Ca.: Fearon Publishers, 1968.

Waugh, K.W. Unlocking the gifted underachiever: intellectual reservoir of the 70s. Presentation to the American Personnel and Guidance Association, Apr., 1971.

Wechsler, D. *The measurement and appraisal of adult intelligence.* (4th ed.) Baltimore: Williams & Wilkins, 1958.

Weed, L.L. *Medical records, medical education and patient care.* Cleveland, Ohio: The Press of Case Western University, 1969.

Wilbur, H. Finding the appropriate level of reading material for each student. Presentation at 3rd annual Texas State Council of the International Reading Association, El Paso, Tx., Apr., 1975.

Wissink, J.E., Kass, C.E., & Ferrell, W.R. A bayesian approach to the identification of children with learning disabilities. *Journal of Learning Disabilities,* 1975 (3).

Zedler, E.Y. Public opinion and public education for the exceptional child— court decisions 1873–1950. *Exceptional Children,* 1953, 187–98.

Zimmerman, I.L., & Woo-Sam, J.M. *Clinical interpretation of the Wechsler Adult Intelligence Scale.* New York: Grune & Stratton, 1973.

Subject Index

Author Index